The
Bakairí Indians
of Brazil

The Bakairí Indians of Brazil

Politics, Ecology, and Change

Debra Picchi

Franklin Pierce College

WAVELAND

PRESS, INC.

Prospect Heights, Illinois

For information about this book, write or call:
Waveland Press, Inc.
P.O. Box 400
Prospect Heights, Illinois 60070
(847) 634-0081
www.waveland.com

For
the Bakairí Indians of Brazil
who let me share their world for a little while
and
the students of Franklin Pierce College
who helped me tell this story.

CONTENTS

Preface and Acknowledgments xi

1 Beginning Fieldwork 1
Arriving at Pakuera 1
Preparations for Fieldwork 5
Negotiating a Role 15
Techniques for Learning about Indians 19
Summary 24

2 The Changing World of the Bakairí Indians 25
Before We Begin . . . 25
Serendipity and Making Time for History 27
The Ancestors Arrive in the New World 28
In Search of Slaves and Gold: The Colonial
   Period and the Bakairí (1500–1822) 30
The Bakairí Divide:
   The Postcolonial Period (1822–1920) 32
At Home on the Paranatinga: The Bakairí on
   Their New Reservation (1920–1958) 36
Teachers and Indian Agents: The Bakairí and
   Government Development
   Policies (1958–1980) 38
The Bakairí Divide Again: Pakuera Fissions
   in the 1980s (1980–1990) 42
Summary 44

3   **Bakairí Households, Fertility, and Mortality**   **47**
Some Methodological Points   48
Village and Household Composition   49
Sex, Menstruation, and Marriage   55
Fertility   60
Nursing, Abortion, and Infanticide   63
Causes of Deaths   65
Population Trends   67
Summary   71

4   **Making a Living, Bakairí Style**   **73**
An Ecological Question   73
The Ecology of the Region   76
Slash-and-Burn Horticulture and
    Mechanized Agriculture   82
Fishing, Herding, and Hunting   89
The Bakairí and Sources of Cash   95
Summary   97

5   **Living and Working in Groups**   **99**
Daily Social Life   99
Marriage and Families   106
Gender-Based Groups   115
Summary   119

6   **The Bakairí and Their Dancing Masks**   **121**
Excerpts from My Field Diary   121
A "Ritually Powerful Event"   123
The History of the Masks   124
Kwamba, the Playful, and
    Yakwigado, the Dignified   124
The Masks Organize the Bakairí Economy   128
The Masks Bind Bakairí Society Together   130
The Masks Reflect a Living Belief System   133
A Final Word about the Masks   136

7   **Leading the Bakairí into
    the Twenty-first Century**   **137**
Leadership and Ecology   138
Leadership and Socioeconomics   143
What Bakairí Headmen Say   149
Summary   154

**8   The Bakairí: Indians, Ethnic Minority,
      or Both?**   **157**
The Bakairí in a Global Context   157
Peasants, Small Farmers, and Indians   167
The Bakairí as an Ethnic Minority   174
Dissonance and Identity   181

Appendix: Learning Guide   185

References   203

Index   213

PREFACE AND ACKNOWLEDGMENTS

My interest in Brazilian Indians began in the late 1960s and early 1970s when the press circulated reports about the appalling conditions under which these people lived. One such account is found in Adrian Cowell's poignant film, *The Tribe That Hides from Man*. Cowell documented the contacting and pacification of the Kréen Akaróre Indians, who numbered about three hundred when they first responded to the efforts of Indian agents. But within just a few years, their numbers dropped to about eighty-five. Ravaged by disease and confused by exposure to Western culture, Kréen Akaróre women began to kill their infants systematically rather than allow them to face what they had experienced.

If the plight of the Kréen Akaróre was the only example of such a terrible fate, it would be bad enough. But it was not. As the international community digested this information, a chorus of protests grew. It was clear that Brazil needed to reexamine how it related to the Indians who lived within its borders.

Soon after I began to study Brazilian Indians seriously, and I found myself impressed not only by their resiliency, but by the variety and complexity of their cultures. Europeans colonized Brazil nearly five hundred years ago, and their occupation of the region was as brutal as it had been in North America. And yet, the more I read, the clearer it became that despite what happened to the Kréen Akaróre, some

Indians survived contact with non-Indians. They survived and even managed to multiply.

The Book

This book is about an indigenous group called the Bakairí who live in central Brazil. I have placed them squarely in the middle of an exciting dynamic context. All around them changes are occurring, and these are the backdrop against which I describe their culture. Many ethnographers tend to address culture change in only the last chapter of their works. I do not. Rather I build each part of this study on the premise of change and show ways in which it has altered various aspects of Bakairí culture.

When I first arrived in the Bakairí reservation, initial culture shock and ensuing confusion prevented me from seeing how embedded in Brazilian society the Indians were, and I focused on only the microcosm of the village of Pakuera where most of them lived. However, within a few months I realized that they were engaged in a constant pas de deux with those outside their reservation. They moved back and forth between the borders of their territory, visiting farmers and managers of agribusinesses. And they traveled regularly to nearby towns to buy goods and to more distant cities to visit government offices.

The links between the Bakairí and outsiders are not new. There is historical evidence that they were established centuries ago when the region was explored and then colonized by Europeans seeking gold and slaves. Long-standing networks of trade and labor exchange have characterized relations between the two groups. Yet the Bakairí have neither been assimilated nor destroyed.

It is true that at first glance they do not epitomize Indians in the same way that other people do. For example, I previously worked with a more isolated group called the Nafuquá. It took two days by canoe to reach their village from a government post that was itself restricted to authorized personnel. The Bakairí are more accessible, and I flew directly into their reservation in a six-seat Cessna plane rented in a nearby city.

The Nafuquá did not possess a lot of European artifacts. They wore no Western-style clothing in their village and continued to fish in the traditional manner with bows and arrows. The Bakairí wear the same clothes that local Brazilians do, and they depend on some of the same technology non-Indians use, such as guns and knives. Yet the Bakairí and the Nafuquá are similar in that distinct languages, rituals, social systems, and other customs occupy central roles in their lives. And these lifeways offset the Indians from rural Brazilians who live nearby.

Although relations with non-Indians have surely shaped the institutions and practices we find today in such villages, some indigenous cultures remain largely intact. How have groups like the Bakairí managed this? In this book I argue that adequate group size and access to land for food production have enabled them to survive with cultural integrity.

Over the past one hundred to one hundred fifty years, their numbers have varied from about three hundred in the late nineteenth century to about five hundred today. Sometimes their population decreased to dangerously low levels, such as in the 1930s when they struggled with European epidemic diseases. But they overcame this setback. The size of their group has allowed for the successful transmission of their traditions from generation to generation, and thus ensured the continuation of their culture.

At the same time, the Bakairí have had constant access to land for gardening, hunting, and fishing both in the Paranatinga River area where they now live and in the headwaters of the Xingú River where they resided for a while in the nineteenth to early twentieth centuries. The retention and social reproduction of their way of life are inextricably bound up in their ability to provide a living for themselves as a group. Without such opportunities, they would have been forced to forfeit their distinctive culture as they dispersed in search of means for survival.

They could have shared the fate of the Kréen Akaróre or the Indians I saw begging on the side of the roads in southern Brazil. Like millions of Brazilian poor, they might have been relegated to living on the streets with little hope of escape except through premature death. But that has not happened. The Bakairí villages are peopled with generally healthy individuals who organize the months of each year around activities, many of which their forefathers practiced for centuries before them.

This book could be considered a celebration of a people's continuation against incredible odds because it is essentially a success story. And without denying the important role that Brazil has played in threatening their survival, it attempts to portray the actions of such government agencies as the Brazilian Indian Foundation in a balanced manner. For example, in the 1970s in response to international criticisms, it significantly improved the medical programs made available to indigenous peoples. These efforts undeniably saved many Bakairí lives, and in the 1990s, we saw the fruits of the "Bakairí Baby Boom" that subsequently took place. In a world that sometimes seems to want to stifle diversity and flush minorities from their lands, the Bakairí story is even more precious because it suggests what is possible for other nation-states.

Audience

This book has been written for the typical undergraduate student who may have an interest in anthropology, ecology, environmental studies, Latin American studies, and/or Native Americans. For over fifteen years I have taught anthropology and general education courses, at first naively, then stubbornly, and finally despairingly, assigning ethnographies that frustrated and angered students. With some notable exceptions these case studies were written at levels most undergraduate students could not understand. I believe this book is different. Although I discuss some complex topics such as demography, ecology, and ethnicity, I do so in ways that most students can understand. My classroom has been my laboratory, and I have worked through most of what is written in these chapters with students' feedback.

To increase the chances of students understanding what I have written, I have provided study guide materials in an appendix. For each chapter, there are lists of concepts and terms that are italicized when introduced in the text. I have also included sets of discussion questions that students can use in collaborative-learning groups, or in essay writing if small-group discussions are not an option. Lists of recommended readings provide suggestions for students who may want to pursue a given topic. In several chapters there are boxes that summarize discussions that some students might find overly complicated. Summaries recap the main points presented in the text.

Throughout the book, readers will find short personal vignettes that, I hope, liven up the material. During my years of teaching, students have said, and written in teaching evaluations, that hearing about what it is like in the field helps anchor information in their minds. Thus, river ecology itself may not interest every student. However, my stories about cayman-tail-slapping by the Indians help such students remember at least something about riverine flora and fauna.

Anthropology faculty searching for supplemental readings or for texts for appropriate courses may want to assign this book for reasons other than its readability. Our discipline is broad, encompassing many different approaches. Those of us who like to expose students to the full range of current research try to include examples of various kinds of ethnography. This one investigates the political and ecological parameters within which a people live their lives.

Another reason for assigning this book concerns its very ordinariness. A colleague once said to me that the Bakairí are (unfortunately, he implied) neither "sexy" nor violent like other groups about whom anthropologists have already written. They are not exotic cannibals, hallucinogenic drug ingestors, or gang rapists. He said that when you read about them, they seem just like us. My friend concluded by saying that he realized that I am fond of these Indians, but frankly they are not very exciting.

I would argue that part of this is true and part of this is how I have chosen to write about the Bakairí. I have purposefully tried to downplay the differences between "us" and "them" as representatives of what is now called "the Other" in the anthropological literature. This theme is further developed in my treatment of the problems confronted by the Bakairí. Students immediately see that they are the same ones shared by peoples all over the world, including many Americans. They identify with these Indians who struggle with questions about how to control family size, how to make a living, how to live in communities when there is tension and hatred, how to work through being a man or a woman when gender roles seem to change every day, and how to express a spiritual dimension.

By emphasizing our common humanity, I may have deglamorized the Bakairí. But at the same time, I know from my own classroom experiences that by doing so I have managed to convince many students that these Indians are indeed people, like them, who deserve respect and admiration. I cannot help but hope that this will increase the chances of the survival of such indigenous peoples.

Theoretical Notes

Although this book is an ethnography that I hope will stand the test of time, it also makes a theoretical point. In it, I use the political ecology model to account for the survival strategies of the Bakairí Indians by triangulating three sets of factors. These include (1) the policies and actions of the Brazilian state, (2) the way in which the Indians use their environment and how this has changed over the years, and (3) the demographic characteristics of the group that inhabits the reservation.

The interconnections between these three variables lie at the heart of our understanding the recent past, and the possible configuration of the future, of these Indians. For example, the decision to demarcate specific lands as a Bakairí reservation was political in nature. Among other things, competition between local power brokers and interest groups influenced government decisions, affecting the size and the composition of the reservation, and subsequently impacting on the economic activities of the Bakairí today. As we will see, the reservation is small in size, and the lands are poor in quality from the point of view of agricultural potential.

Government-sponsored development projects widely implemented on indigenous reservations in the 1970s also affected how resources are used as well as the general ecology of Indian lands. In many cases such as the Bakairí's, these projects shifted the entire focus of the indigenous economy from one part of the ecosystem to another. As the attempt was made to create an indigenous export crop that would lead to self-sufficient Indian reservations, government officials also encouraged dependence upon industrial pesticides and fossil fuels. We are still evaluating the effects these programs have had on reservation environments.

The political decision made on international and national levels to accelerate the development of western Brazil exacerbated pressures placed on regional land use. Landless farmers and other rural workers frequently moved onto Indians' lands in search of opportunities to make a living. This, of course, impinged upon indigenous resource utilization.

More recently, in the late 1990s, political support for government agencies responsible for the protection of Brazil's Indians has waned in certain quarters, and as I write this, it looks likely that key medical and educational programs that successfully brought many Indian groups back from the brink of extinction may go unfunded. A similar fate may be in store for technical programs being implemented on Indian lands. It seems that indigenous peoples will have to fend for themselves, or compete with other interest groups to link up with nonprofit organizations.

These are only some of the political processes that are influencing Bakairí choices about resource use and distribution. But these Indians are not passive victims. In the chapter on making a living, I show how they are aggressively pursuing a strategy that allows them to piece together an eclectic production system. And in the final chapter of this book, I show how they parley their ethnic identity into a politico-economic commodity that they "trade" in the international market and how they plan to generate cash through the establishment of ecotourism and museums, both of which are predicated upon their "Indian-ness."

The documentation of the complex relationship between Bakairí politics, ecology, and demography allows us to take a closer look at the political ecology paradigm itself. Certainly one of its strengths is that it has a broader perspective than did ecological anthropology or human ecology as it was practiced in the 1960s and the 1970s. By building in political dimensions that affect ecosystems used by local communities, researchers explore the implications of national and international policy decisions within an inclusive and integrated theoretical framework. The theoretical mandate that we situate reservations such as the Bakairí's in the middle of a fairly complex mix of competing, and sometimes contradictory, forces, helps researchers avoid the pitfall of studying indigenous communities as if they were autonomous units relating to the environment in a vacuum.

However, I suggest in this book that by focusing on wider political–economic influences such as development models and class conflict, there is the risk of losing sight of the people who live in local communities and use specific resources. Descriptions and analysis of macrolevel policies may curtail the study of human actors and the choices they make about political and economic power. I argue for balancing this theoretical approach so that it fully accommodates individual and community variation.

Chapter Organization

This book is organized into eight chapters. The first chapter explains how I first arrived in the Bakairí reservation and began to do research. In it I also provide advice on preparing for fieldwork, because many of my students ask how anthropologists get to the point of doing such research. Special attention is given to the problem of role definition, which is problematic for many anthropologists but which is glossed over in final write-ups. A discussion of methodological considerations concludes the chapter.

In the second chapter I present the history of the Bakairí. I begin by explaining how the New World was settled by humans who eventually moved south to occupy the Amazon. I present these archaeological findings to help students understand where the Bakairí came from and why they are so different from the Europeans who arrived on the scene thousands of years later. I then proceed to lay out the colonial history of the Indians as well as nineteenth- and twentieth-century events that affected them. I give special attention to recent economic development programs initiated by the Brazilian government and to the division of the Bakairí village in the 1980s.

In chapter 3, I discuss issues concerning fertility, mortality, and population trends among the Indians. I show that the Bakairí are clearly increasing in number, and then go on to probe the implications of this for their future. Because demographic concepts may be foreign to some undergraduates, I spend a considerable amount of time setting up the questions that organize this chapter and providing comparative information so that readers can appreciate the implications of the information I present.

In chapter 4, I explain how the Indians make a living. They depend on a combination of slash-and-burn horticulture, farming with modern technology, working for wages, and receiving government stipends. I refer to an ongoing, and provocative, argument in the literature that asks whether traditional peoples such as the Bakairí should adopt Western production technology. Should these Indians reject it on the basis of the damage it does to the environment? Some believe that indigenous peoples have used their resources on a sustained basis without ecological degradation, and they question the wisdom of making any fundamental changes. Another option is that the Bakairí and others like them depend on a mixture of ways to produce food and access cash so that they can maintain their physical and cultural identity. The rationale is that if they are left to depend on only traditional ways to produce food, there may be unpleasant consequences. They may have to go hungry, adjust their population size, or leave their reservation to work in the city.

Chapter 5 examines social organization and gender definition. In it I describe the rhythm of daily social life for children, adolescents, and adults as well as for men and women. I present time-allocation data that show how the Indians organize their days and how they get work done. I go on to look at marriage, the family, and the kinship-terminology system used by the Bakairí and to relate these topics to economic and political aspects of their culture. I also look at gender-based groups. Men are organized into two non-kin groups, which I describe and attempt to account for.

Chapter 6 presents materials about the Bakairí mask dance. I try to communicate the power of this ritual before going on to discuss its history and the various ways it contributes to the workings of the indigenous society. Although the masks are undeniably things of beauty, they also serve important economic, social, and ideological functions.

Chapter 7 reviews how contact with non-Indians has transformed traditional modes of leadership. While I note that demographic trends have affected the pool from which leaders are drawn, I also show how political and economic changes have altered the way leaders come to power and express their authority.

Chapter 8 concludes by asking who the Bakairí are today and how they will manage in the twenty-first century. I open the chapter by describing how I revisit the reservation twenty years after I first began working there. The region and the Indians themselves are undergoing many exciting changes, and it is quite clear that the Bakairí are going to play a key role in determining how they will fare in the future.

I describe how they intend to parley their ethnic identity into something of value through activities that will preserve and promote their Indian heritage. The downside of these efforts is that they somewhat trivialize Bakairí culture because they require the Indians to self-consciously, almost cynically, peddle their traditions. However, success under these circumstances will be measured in terms of the long-term cultural and physical survival of these people.

In the final analysis, it is the Indians who are the proper authorities for determining the price they will pay for what they want. Long gone are the days when FUNAI officials, missionaries, and anthropologists played the paternalistic role of decreeing what is appropriate for Indians. In the same way that Indians today have the power to reject social scientists' requests to enter their lands to do research projects, and to deny the authority of government officials, so too can they disagree with our research conclusions and policy recommendations.

Acknowledgments

One person can rarely lay claim to such a project. In the 1970s I traveled to the University of Florida in Gainesville to study Brazilian Indians with Charles Wagley. Since his seminal work on the Tapirapé Indians in the 1930s, he was considered one of the leaders in the field. Although my conversations with him proved extremely helpful, in the end it was a new generation of anthropologists and other social scientists at the University's Latin American Center who profoundly influenced me.

Maxine Margolis guided my original work with the Bakairí and helped me formulate my theoretical approach to this project. John Alexander, Leslie Lieberman, Tony Oliver-Smith, and Russ Bernard provided me with the methodological tools and concepts that facilitated fieldwork and analysis of my findings. Daniel Gross and Robert Carneiro, affiliated with other institutions at that time, also advised me. Dennis Werner, who had just completed his doctoral research in Brazil, was also helpful.

George Zarur, a Brazilian anthropologist in Brasilia, introduced me to the idea of working with the Bakairí. Following his strong urging, I abandoned another research project I had planned to do and traveled to the Paranatinga River area to begin work with them. Elizabeth Gameiro, the Brazilian Indian Foundation librarian in Brasilia, generously helped me find many of the historical sources I needed. Idevar José Sardinha, who has spent a lifetime working with Indians, has most kindly helped me enter the Bakairí reservation several times, first as an Indian agent based in the reservation and later as the chief administrator of the entire region.

More recently, the South American Indian Meetings organized each August by Ken Kensinger at Bennington College in Vermont constituted a place where my fledgling ideas were critiqued and grown. Conversations with Kathleen Adams, Raphael Bastos, Janet Chernela, Bill Crocker, Warren DeBoer, Jeffrey Ehrenreich, Bill Fisher, Nancy Flowers, Jonathan Hill, Emi Ireland, Ken Kensinger, Don Pollack, and David Price were particularly helpful.

Field research has been funded by grants from the Fulbright-Hays Organization, the Inter-American Foundation, and the Whiting Foundation. Franklin Pierce College has supported the final research and the writing of this manuscript while I was on sabbatical. Dr. Richard Weeks, who was Academic Vice President and Dean of the Faculty at Franklin Pierce College between 1990 and 1998, deserves recognition and thanks for creating an academic environment where faculty members like myself were encouraged to experiment and to take chances in their disciplines. I benefited greatly from the process he initiated, and this book is in part a result of the work I did under his encouragement.

Finally, I am grateful to Tom Curtin at Waveland Press, who guided me in the production of this manuscript over the past year. Adam Witham and Brian Witham capably handled the production of the maps. I am also indebted to the following individuals, who read and made comments on earlier drafts of this manuscript. Anne Burke Lannin, Kelli Costa, Bill Fisher, Judith Lisansky, Patricia Lyon, and Steve Picchi provided me with thoughtful and thought-provoking criticisms. I am especially indebted to my husband, Tom Desrosiers, who patiently spent many hours reading sections of my work out loud to me and who never failed to give me his honest opinion.

Of course, ultimately, I am indebted to the Bakairí Indians of Mato Grosso to whom this book is dedicated. They were extremely kind to me while I stayed with them, and although I am solely responsible for what this research says about them and any mistakes made, I hope that they approve of my conclusions and that they find them useful.

Chapter 1
BEGINNING FIELDWORK

"Over the years . . . the Tapirape have never been for me only objects of research, or abstractions; instead, they have been my
friends."

(Wagley 1977:25)

Arriving at Pakuera

The first thing that struck me when I arrived in the Bakairí reservation was the heat. Flying in a small plane from Cuiabá, the capital
of Mato Grosso, a western Brazilian state, we landed in the reservation on a dirt airstrip near the village. Cuiabá was hot, but the
reservation felt a lot hotter to me. Maybe it was because the landing
strip lay some distance from the cool forests and high banks of the
Paranatinga River that I could see in the distance. I climbed down
from the plane onto bleached soil that felt harder than concrete. Heat
radiated back up into my face from the ground while the sun beat
down from above. I felt like I was being roasted.

The region's climate is classified as hot and semihumid. As is typical of places close to the equator, there are only two different sea-
sons: rainy and dry. The rains occur between the months of Novem-

1

ber and March, and the dry season takes place between the months of May and September. Faced with the blinding, enervating heat of the dry season, I thought I would prefer the rains. My opinion changed, of course, when I experienced the red mud and copious mildew that they brought with them.

The landing strip is close to Pakuera, the largest village in the reservation. Of the 500 or so people who inhabit the Bakairí territory, about 170 live in this village. Another 90 Indians occupy Aturua, the second largest village, and the rest of the Indians divide themselves between five other hamlets in the reservation. I later discovered that there were also a number of non-Indians living illegally in the reservation. Agents from Fundação Nacional do Índio (*FUNAI*), the Brazilian National Indian Foundation that administers indigenous areas, clearly wanted to evict them because such landless, hungry people had invaded and taken over Indians' lands in other parts of Brazil. However, FUNAI lacked the muscle to force these people to move on.

Yuka, a middle-aged Indian with a grown son standing by his side, approached me. He spoke gruffly without smiling, and I found him to be somewhat intimidating. Later I discovered that Yuka was, in fact, tough and aggressive. He had the courage to visit the capital of Brazil, where he lobbied for his people in the offices of FUNAI, and he had served as headman, or political leader, of the Bakairí who lived in Pakuera. I also found out that he could be kind, such as the time he helped me when I became sick.

Yuka invited me to live with him and his family, and I quickly and gratefully accepted. It is always difficult to choose where to live when one does *fieldwork*, which for anthropologists is the firsthand study of a society. By living with a family, one runs the risk of inadvertently getting in the middle of warring political factions, but by living alone, one misses opportunities to practice speaking the language and to join in family activities. I always prefer to live with families although I know other anthropologists who feel strongly about remaining independent.

I followed Yuka down a lane lined with houses and tall, fragrant mango trees. I asked him who planted the trees. He said that when he was a child, Indian agents reorganized the Bakairí village, arranging the houses in rows, rather than in traditional circles. At that time, they also planted trees and bushes. Although contemporary FUNAI personnel tried to be more sensitive about such Indian traditions as settlement formation, Pakuera's houses still formed neat lines that ran on an east-west axis, intersecting at a point where the Bakairí built a men's house, the site of important ritual and political activities.

We arrived at Yuka's home, which was a square house with clay walls and a palm roof. Yuka explained that men and their male kinsmen constructed a house by erecting a wooden frame that they then covered with wet clay. Women gathered and dried palm, which the

A lane in Pakuera lined with mango trees.

men then arranged in thick layers on top. Later, when I observed a young man named Jere building a home for himself and his new wife, I noticed the festive atmosphere that pervaded the scene. They appeared to be enjoying themselves, laughing and joking with people who passed by, seemingly oblivious to the hard work they were doing.

Yuka's house was several years old, and he said that sometimes the roof leaked when it rained. The house felt cool and restful inside after the hot landing strip, and the scent of palm pervaded the room. Yuka told me to sit down, directing me to a chair of which he was clearly proud. A chair was a status symbol, brought from outside of the reservation. Most Bakairí homes were furnished only with hammocks and an occasional stool or cured animal skin. Women made the hammocks of cotton from the gardens or of palm from the forests, while men carved the stools from hardwood, often making them in the shape of an animal such as an armadillo or a turtle. I glanced around the room and saw no such stool, but draped over an interior wall, I spotted several hammocks obviously pulled out of the way of daily traffic. I suspected people would sleep in them that night.

Beri, Yuka's wife, shyly entered the room. Her mother Alia followed her more slowly. Over the years I became fond of Beri. I liked Alia, too, but she did not possess Beri's mildness. The first day I met these two women, I immediately saw a family resemblance. Both left their dark hair long and unbound, unlike some of the younger Bakairí women who cut their hair short, imitating Brazilian women they saw in Paranatinga, a nearby town. Beri and Alia wore shiftlike dresses similar to those used by other Indian women in the reservation. These dresses were simple to cut out and sew on a manual sewing machine or by hand. Women such as Beri owned two or three such shifts so they always had a clean one to put on after doing chores or working in the garden.

Beri asked if I would "accept a *cafezinho*," a tiny cup of strong, sweet coffee that is popular in Brazil. The Bakairí acquired this custom from their non-Indian neighbors. Brazilians drink many such cups in the course of a day, and the custom of asking you to "accept" coffee is their way of offering it. I drank the beverage, which I found refreshing even in the midday heat.

An uncomfortable silence fell upon the group. I tried to put them, and myself, at ease by asking some general questions about the people who lived in the house. Yuka began by listing himself and his wife, Beri. He went on to talk about Beri's parents, who lived with them, and a young daughter, who was visiting family in Cuiabá. Nai, their grown son, and his new wife, Rea, also belonged to the household. Rea had recently found out she was pregnant, and the family looked forward to the arrival of the new member.

After some casual conversation about my home and family in the United States, Rea, Beri, Alia, and I went down to the river. Several rivers flowed through the reservation, but the Paranatinga River was the closest to the village, and it provided water for drinking, bathing, and washing clothes. The Indians also fished and canoed in the rivers.

Alia and Beri chattered and laughed as they led me down the trail to the section of the river where the women bathed and filled huge cans with water. The men used a separate section; a patch of trees divided the two areas. To actually get to the water, I clambered down a well-worn rocky path that was slippery and steep to me the first time I managed it. As I carefully picked my way through the rocks, women with bundles of wet clothes and huge cans of water balanced on their heads barreled past me as if I were standing still. With some relief I made it to the rocky beach, where I admired the green water and the huge trees that lined the river. It was peaceful. I sat on a rock and absorbed the sounds of the women talking as they worked and the children shouting as they played in the water.

When Alia and Beri were ready, they filled some cans with water to take back to the house. I offered to help, but they laughed and said I had to practice negotiating the path before I could carry things. So I helped Rea raise a heavy can to her shoulder, and then to her head. Later, when I learned to carry water this way, I discovered that getting the can up to the shoulder is the hardest part of the task. Once on the shoulder or head, the weight is not difficult to manage because it distributes itself evenly.

We climbed up the path and walked the kilometer or so back to the house. It was already getting dark even though it was only 5:30. Being from a temperate climate, the early sunsets close to the equator always surprised me. My mental clock equated hot weather with long days, so that the nearly twelve hours of darkness in the tropics were unexpected.

Back at the house Beri helped me set up the hammock I brought from Cuiabá in the small area the family had generously vacated for me. Nai and Rea set up their hammocks close by, while the others shared a space in another part of the house. It seemed we all had a modicum of privacy. However, sounds and light carry easily. Walls reached only three-fourths of the way to the ceiling, allowing air to circulate. As I swung back and forth in my hammock congratulating myself on a relatively painless beginning to a fieldwork session, I heard the murmur of Nai and Rea's voices. Then silence fell. Not wanting to keep the family awake, I blew out the candle I had placed on the ground next to my hammock and went to sleep.

Preparations for Fieldwork

Beginning fieldwork is difficult, and it has not gotten easier for me with each new project I start. However, I suspect the nervousness is normal since many other anthropologists report experiencing similar kinds of misgivings. Napoleon Chagnon wrote a now famous account of how he began field research in 1964 with the Yanomamö Indians of Venezuela. He described how his clothes were soaked with perspiration and his hands swollen from gnat bites as he approached the entrance of a Yanomamö village. When he, with pounding heart, stooped to go through the entry, and then straightened up, he was face-to-face with men who had been snorting a hallucinogenic drug. Strands of dark-green slime dripped from their noses and ran down onto their chests (1992:11–12).

Much earlier, Hortense Powdermaker explained how she felt when she started fieldwork in 1929 on an island in the southwest Pacific. Although not as dramatic a beginning as Chagnon experienced, her sense of alienation was similar.

> This was my first night in Lesu alone. As I sat on the veranda of my thatched-roofed, two-room house in the early evening, I felt uncertain and scared, not of anything in particular, but just of being alone in a native village. I asked myself, "What on earth am I doing here, all alone and at the edge of the world?" (1966:51)

Several anthologies exist for those interested in understanding better the range of experiences anthropologists confront, and the coping mechanisms they rely on to weather them (Spindler 1970; Golde 1986; DeVita 1992). Some of the stories are poignant, such as Paul Winther's (1992) account of how he had to cope with the shock of discovering the fate of a young woman he knew. She lived in a village in India where he was doing a field project, and he found that her throat had been cut and her body thrown in a well, presumably by her father, who was shamed by her untimely pregnancy. Other stories are less appalling and involve sensible advice for the reader, such as one should avoid loaning money while in the field (Hull 1992). All are worthwhile reading, even for the veteran.

Establishing an Anthropological Context

When students ask my advice on how to prepare for fieldwork or how to choose a field site, I always begin by talking to them about anthropology. If they are taking, or have completed, an introductory anthropology course, it is easier because they possess basic working knowledge

---

Box 1-1: Checklist for Fieldwork Preparations

- ❏ Establishing an anthropological context.
- ❏ Determining personal predilecctions and motives.
- ❏ Making preparations.
    Choosing a culture area, or place to study.
    Learning a language.
    Designing a project.
    Developing a budget.
    Applying for funding.
    Securing a passport, visa, and permit, if needed.
- ❏ Figuring out logistics.
    Arranging for transportation.
    Getting supplies.
    Foreseeing medical needs.
    Choosing "mental health" articles.
- ❏ Establishing routines.
    Arranging for the basics, i.e., eating, sleeping, etc.
    Living with pests.
    Getting and processing data.
    Avoiding conflict.
    Controlling ethnocentric reactions.
    Finding a role.
- ❏ Leaving the field.

about the discipline. They understand that four fields make up anthropology—archaeology, cultural anthropology, linguistics, and physical anthropology—and that each has a specific focus although the four share a conceptual basis. Choosing which of these they find the most interesting is an important first step.

I am a cultural anthropologist, and as one, I attempt to study and to describe the cultures of people in other societies. The concept of *culture* is fundamental to the field, and a definition of it that is frequently offered to students was first developed in the 1870s by a man some call "the father of anthropology." Edward Tylor defined culture as "that complex whole which includes knowledge, belief, art, law, morals, custom, and any other capabilities acquired (learned) by man as a member of society" (1920:1).

Cultural anthropologists make certain assumptions about culture. For example, they believe that it organizes human behavior and that it is adaptive. There are people who believe that other people's cultural traditions are silly or irrational, but anthropologists believe you can make sense out of most customs and understand them. Culture is also made up of parts that are interrelated and that function together to make up the whole. Anthropologists frequently talk about the holistic perspective, which is our way of trying to understand these cultural aspects and how they fit together (Nanda 1994:xvi).

When I find students who are interested in this kind of work, I encourage them to read up on anthropological theories that account for the nature of culture, how it changes, and how it relates to human adaptation. There are, of course, entire undergraduate- and graduate-level courses on this subject, but for those who are just getting their feet wet, reviewing some of the main theories is sufficient. Most introductory textbooks include chapters outlining major theories and appendices providing greater detail. And there are a variety of texts that explain any one theory, its history, and its implications in greater detail. I currently assign R. Jon McGee and Richard Warms's (2000) *Anthropological Theory: An Introductory History* in the theory course I teach. The editors of this volume not only present a selection of essays written by a variety of seminal thinkers in the field, but they provide supportive materials in the form of informative introductory essays and footnotes.

What is all the fuss about theory? A theory is a systematic explanation for observed data. It accounts for the empirical observations that we make while doing fieldwork, and it guides our study of the culture in question. The role theory plays in any anthropologist's work can be controversial. Some believe that the more rigorously theoretical our research, the greater its value. Others caution that it guides us too closely. They argue that it can lead to a priori judgments about what is important and what is not. They urge anthropologists to make their observations in the field, and then to work backward in time and outward in space to account for them (Vayda and Walters 1999:168–169). The theory I used to organize my research is called political ecology. This model focuses on the political influences that affect how humans interact with their environment. The political factors usually belong to a wider system and may, as in the case of the Bakairí, include national and international organizations. For example, international financial organizations at least partially paid for many of the development projects that impacted the Bakairí reservation.

The study of the relationship between humans and their environment typically begins with the researcher identifying a specific problem. Examples include the growing shortage of gardening lands, the discovery of river pollution, and a dwindling supply of fish. This type of research may also concern a political event that will obviously affect the environment, such as a government agency introducing an industrial production system to traditional people.

My project included several such interrelated variables, and I considered it part of my research to tease them apart, document them, and try to account for them. Accounting for them involved identifying those political structures and events that triggered the processes that led to the changes. For example, why were the Indians running out of lands on which to garden? What historical and political circumstances led to the Bakairí being relegated to an impoverished reservation? What regional political constraints prevented them from expanding its size? What other political trends affected how the Indians used their environment?

A subsection of political ecology researches the ways in which groups from different economic classes interact with their environments (Smith and Young 1998:493; Stonich 1995:145). This type of research tries to understand how access to power influences the distribution of such key resources as land and capital, and then goes on to examine the implications of this to such processes as pollution, deforestation, and other kinds of ecological damage.

This school of political ecology would be particularly useful to me if I were to return to study rural workers in the impoverished municipal center of Paranatinga. The relationship between them, as a class, and the power brokers in the region would make a fascinating project. I could study what kinds of resources each group used and what the environmental consequences of their behaviors were. Documenting the implications of the power differences between the two groups would be a key part of the study.

The Bakairí's case required a different emphasis. Although I do not doubt that the Indians are part of a disenfranchised subordinate class that is in opposition to a wealthy and privileged dominant one, Brazil's reservation system, along with the role FUNAI plays in representing indigenous interests, complicates the situation. I felt the need to narrow down the problem I intended to study, and so I focused on the resources the Bakairí actually used in their production activities and those precise political decisions that affected these resources.

Determining Predilections

As students consider the four fields of anthropology and sort through theories, I usually continue to meet with them and in time ask them if they know what the word *predilection* means. The dictionary says that a *predilection* is a "preconceived liking or a preference." In working with advisees, I interpret this idea in a very literal manner. I really do want to know their likes and dislikes. This is because I believe they affect our ability to successfully do research on a given problem at any given field site.

For example, if someone does not like the cold, then it would be crazy to attempt field research with the Inuit in the ice and snow of Greenland. Or if one was born and raised in an urban center, and needs city air to breathe and feel alive, then a project with a group of Bedouin in the empty deserts of eastern Egypt would not be the best choice. It is my opinion that fieldwork should be enjoyed as much as possible, rather than endured or suffered through. Very simply, if you are doing what you like, you do a better job.

I tell students that the same is true for the kind of project they choose. Margaret Mead and her husband Gregory Bateson, two notable anthropologists, completed a sophisticated study of Balinese theatre, dance, and ceremony with the use of photography. Their book *Balinese Character: A Photographic Analysis* (1962) is an extraordinary work. However, not everyone has the interest, or talent, in art or photography to do such research.

Laura Graham's (1995) study of the Xavante Indians of Brazil consists of an in-depth analysis of the performance of an indigenous leader's dream. Her book includes descriptions of the preparations, rehearsals, and public performance of the dream. Although fascinating to read about, it is clear that Graham's research involved a knowledge of music and its transcription that not everyone shares.

Making Preparations

Once personal preferences are factored into the fieldwork experience, preparations can begin. These consist of choosing a specific culture area, researching it, learning any language that might be helpful, designing a project, developing a budget and applying for funding, and securing any visas, licenses, or permits that might be needed.

In my case, I decided to study Brazilian Indians as a senior in college and chose a graduate program that specialized in such research. Once I began course work, I took classes not only about indigenous peoples but about Brazil, too. I also enrolled in Portuguese language classes since Portuguese is Brazil's national language. As the weeks passed, I found myself reading anything and everything I could on Brazil and Indians. I found that novels that took place in Brazil, especially ones written by Brazilian authors, were particularly helpful. These gave me impressions about the culture and its people that I did not find in other books.

Conversations with people who were from Brazil or who had visited the country were also useful. For example, international students were invaluable. They were generous with their time and advice, as were senior graduate students and professors who had already traveled to South America. One Brazilian graduate student, to whom I will be forever grateful, gave me a number of suggestions for inexpensive hotels in Brasilia. When I arrived there for the first time, at five in the morning, I was able to steer clear of the expensive places Americans normally frequented, thus preserving my modest living allowance.

As I was learning about this exciting culture area, I worked on developing a research project. By this time, I knew enough about Brazilian Indians to understand that they tended to live in small communities of between fifty and three hundred individuals. The mechanisms for holding such societies together are generally kin based. However, other cultural traditions also contribute to social cohesion. For my first project, I decided that I would look at how economic exchange helped integrate a number of small indigenous communities.

The process outlined above took about a year, at the end of which I felt confident enough to apply for a small grant that would enable me to do a summer field project in Brazil. With the help of travel agents and others who were informed about the cost of traveling and living in Brazil, I developed a budget. Then I wrote a proposal describing what I hoped to accomplish, appended the budget to it, and submitted the document to a tropical research foundation. They agreed to award me a modest grant.

Once I had these funds, I found out that I would need a permit to enter an Indian reservation from FUNAI. The first time I did research in Brazil, it took me two weeks to get a license. The second time, it took a month; and the third time, almost five months went by before I was authorized to do my research. Most recently, my permit did not arrive until almost a year after I applied. Fisher writes that "FUNAI has been quite efficient, at times even draconian, in limiting access by anthropologists" to Indians (n.d.:4). Graham accuses specific FUNAI agents of sabotaging her work and unjustly expelling her from an Indian reservation (1995:ix). My own experiences have been more positive on the whole than the ones they describe, but I still have not enjoyed them.

Figuring Out Logistics

Logistics is a term frequently associated with military operations. It refers to how to move troops and how to keep them supplied. I was surprised one day to hear one of my advisors asking me about logistics. How did I intend to get to the Bakairí village? How would I eat? What if I got sick? When would I write up my field notes? Asking me about these practicalities was helpful because, up to that point, I had focused on culture area, science, and grants. These questions thrust me into the commonsense world of how to survive in the field.

I recalled a book written by an anthropologist who had studied in a village near the Bakairí reservation. I found out that he worked at a college in a nearby state. After setting up an appointment, I took a train to the city where he lived, and he kindly spent hours giving me advice. He explained that he used Cuiabá, the capital of Mato Grosso, as a "jump off" town for fieldwork. It was large enough to have stores and hotels but close enough to the Indian reservation to allow me to minimize travel costs. He also told me that he rented small Cessna planes from private airlines or from missionaries to get to the reservation. And he cautioned me that I could take only 400 kilograms, or under 900 pounds, on the plane. Finally, he helped me to make a preliminary list of things to take with me, such as a hammock to sleep in and red beads for presents.

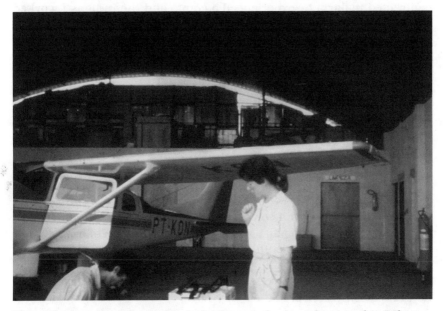

The author, on the right, in front of a Cessna plane used to travel to Pakuera. The pilot, on the left, weighs gear that is to go into the plane.

My list of "400 kilograms of supplies" grew over the months as I talked obsessively with everyone I knew about what to take to the field. I noticed that most people had clever ideas for solving complex problems. For example, if you needed two months' worth of a high-quality protein source, and you knew you would not have refrigeration, and there were weight constraints on what you could carry, what would you take? Based on the advice I received, I ended up taking a case of fifty cans of sardines packed in oil—sardines for the protein and oil for the fat.

Health in the field is always a concern. Not only is it unpleasant to be sick when one is far from home's creature comforts, but hospitals and doctors are unavailable. In Brazil, there were concerns at that time about malaria, hepatitis, typhoid, and yellow fever, and I took them seriously. I arranged for vaccinations and other inoculations through my doctor, who also made sure that I had antibiotics and other medical supplies.

One anthropologist nearly scared me out of my wits by telling me about his fear of getting malaria and going into a coma while in the field. He said he was afraid the group with whom he worked would think he was dead. Then, as was their custom, they would burn his body and eat his ashes in a soup. He said that at the beginning of field-work, he always made a specific Indian promise that his body would be sent to a FUNAI post when they thought he was dead. It turned out that this anthropologist's concern did not really apply to me. I never contracted malaria or experienced a coma, and the Indians I worked with did not practice cannibalistic rituals.

Another anthropologist I spoke with said he never traveled without morphine when in the field. He reasoned that if he broke a leg or something, he would at least have a painkiller. I was never worried about that, but I was concerned about snakebites. Today I am even more fearful than before because I have seen too many of them. None of the Indians I knew who were bitten ever died, but the pain and trauma they suffered were terrible. Needless to say, I always carry antivenom serum.

When I advise students, I always add a final word on supplies. I caution them not to forget to bring "mental health" articles. These are special treats to use as rewards at the end of a long day, or motivators when fatigue sets in. At a conference, I joined a group of anthropologists informally exchanging stories about fieldwork. When we shared with each other our "mental health" items, the list was incredibly diverse. It included such things as jelly beans, a Walkman and favorite music, special coffee, cigarettes, canned fruit, chocolate, a favorite pillow, murder mysteries, and so on.

Establishing Routines

Once in the field, setting up some kind of routine that allows for survival and the regular collection, and processing, of data is imperative. Eating, sleeping, bathing, and washing clothes need to be built into one's life in one way or another. Some researchers arrange to have their cooking and cleaning done for them, while others do these tasks themselves.

Survival also implies coping with unusual kinds of pests. Tarantulas and bats were two such animals that really bothered me. During one piece of fieldwork, I stayed temporarily in the FUNAI infirmary, which lay on the outskirts of the village. Since the building was not inhabited, all sorts of creatures had moved into it. A couple of times a month, pairs of six-inch tarantulas showed up in my room. I killed them with a broom.

Anthropologists who work in the tropics frequently complain about bats. My field journals indicate that, while I stayed in the infirmary, I had an on-going war with them. The small ones would settle above my desk or hammock and urinate on me. At times I had to string up a plastic parka over my sleeping area for protection. However, my special fear was of the huge ugly fruit bats that appeared only once in a while, hanging from the rafters in my room. Dennis Werner (1990), who also despised these animals, wrote:

> I could hear the lip-smacking sound of their nibbling away at the bananas that hung next to the oven. Turning on the flashlight, I saw them hanging upside down, completely covering the banana bunch as they ate their meal. It was a grossly ugly sight, but at least I felt a little better knowing they were mostly fruit bats and would not be looking for blood. (p. 153)

With regard to data collection, I discuss this in more detail in the last part of this chapter. However, it is important for researchers to build time into their schedules on a weekly, if not daily, basis for processing information. This procedure is vital, not only for organizational purposes, but because it allows for the generation of new questions while still at the field site.

Keeping a low profile and avoiding conflict are other good pieces of advice while in the field. Discord sometimes disrupts small-scale societies, but since they are organized along kin lines, differences are frequently resolved without serious repercussions. Anthropologists, on the other hand, have no kin group to support them. If they are unwise enough to take sides in a dispute, they may find themselves on the outside when the village returns to normal.

Attempting to control *ethnocentric* reactions also contributes to surviving fieldwork. *Ethnocentrism* is judging another society by one's own standards. Anthropologists are trained to try to control such impulses because their goal is to study, not change, other cultures.

I was fortunate in that my ability to separate my ethnocentric reactions from my anthropological perspective was not seriously tested in the field. The Indians I worked with were not headhunters, as were the Achuar (Descola 1993). Nor did they practice gang rape, as did the Yanomamö (Chagnon 1992). They were not cannibals, as were the Warí (Conklin 1993), and they did not have their children ingest hallucinogenic drugs, as did the Jívaro (Harner 1972).

It is true that some Bakairí behaviors would have been unpleasant for me to witness, but it is equally true that I find some U.S. practices, such as the death penalty, to be shocking and offensive. The Bakairí selectively practice *infanticide*, the killing of infants, usually newborns. Most of such cases occur when the mother is still nursing an older infant and cannot properly care for another baby.

Another behavior that made me feel uncomfortable to imagine witnessing involved witch killing. Until recently the Bakairí killed people whom they suspected of witchcraft. I remember an incident when an elderly Indian was accused of witchcraft by a faction in the village. This is a very serious charge indeed, because people are so terrified of witches that, even today, if they do not kill them, they ostracize them or harm them in some way. When the Bakairí man was implicated in a sorcery case, I was extremely upset because I liked him as a person, and I feared for his life. Luckily, the conflict resolved itself. But even now, I do not know how I would have handled it if the villagers had tried to kill him.

Leaving the Field

By the time I completed my first field project at Pakuera, I had been in Brazil for two years, and I had logged fourteen months in the Bakairí reservation. I liked the people I had been working with very much and was deeply upset when I had to return to the United States. As I read through my field journal today, the level of emotion I see reflects a degree of involvement on my part for which I was unprepared.

Under such pressure, it is sometimes difficult to say good-bye properly to people you care about. And yet it is necessary to do so. The termination process is important not only for the anthropologist, but it may also be critical for key informants who have become attached to the fieldworker on some level.

The process of disengagement may take a long time. Looking back on it, I do not think it was completed for me until I returned to Pakuera almost ten years later and did another stint in the field. Somehow, by returning and making sure everybody was all right, I was finally able to close out that chapter of my life. And I believe my return was a positive experience for many of the Indians I had known during my initial field research. I hope that I was able to signal to them that they were much more to me than subjects of scientific articles.

However, as an anthropologist, I did, in fact, have publishing responsibilities that I could not ignore. I was required to send my conclusions to the people who had funded my research, as well as to the Brazilian government. And I wanted to publish the information about the Bakairí for anthropologists who were interested in such groups. Margaret Mead (1972) once wrote that she promised herself that she would not begin another field project until she had reported the results of her last trip. I believe that this is a good example to follow.

Negotiating a Role

Students frequently ask why people such as the Bakairí Indians let me come and live with them. Certainly this is an excellent question that could be asked of any anthropologist. To tolerate strangers who pester them with boring questions must be difficult. Simultaneously, these people must figure out who we are and what we are doing in ways that are meaningful to them. All too often, anthropologists' superficial explanations about "learning about your life ways so we can tell other people about you" do not satisfy even the youngest informant (Kurin 1980).

Working through the process of role definition is sometimes time-consuming and emotionally charged (Wagner 1975; Kracke 1987). In my case, it went through several phases, some of which were amusing and some alarming.

Anthropologist as *Karaiwa* or Non-Indian

I distinguished three separate phases through which the Bakairí and I passed. Phase one consisted of my arrival and our initial perceptions of each other. They immediately, and understandably, classified me as a *karaiwa* or non-Indian and imposed on me a number of expectations about how I should behave, developed presumably from their past interactions with wives of Brazilian ranchers and government officials. I was not supposed to cook or clean for myself. I could not carry my own water from the river, nor could I wash my own clothes. Furthermore, I was expected to retain an Indian servant and remain in my house as much as possible, crocheting or receiving visitors. I was not to visit the Indians in their homes, and I certainly was not expected to go to their gardens or into the forest.

I was a stranger, and I wanted to please them in order to be accepted. However, my research project dealt with resource utilization, so it was necessary for me to travel to the gardens to measure such things as area under cultivation, harvests, and time spent in subsistence-related activities. Furthermore, the hallmark of anthropological methodology is *participant observation*, which requires the researcher to make systematic observations while approximating the people's lifestyle as much as possible. With this in mind, I attempted to compromise by living in Yuka's house where much was taken care of for me. However, I washed my own clothes in the river and walked around the village freely, visiting people at will. After a few weeks, I gradually began to visit the forests and the gardens, which were my primary objective.

Anthropologist as Missionary

Phase two took place about two months into my initial period of fieldwork. The Indians, perhaps impressed by the consistency with which I failed to meet their expectations, reevaluated my identity. They concluded that if I was not a typical Brazilian karaiwa, then perhaps I was a second type of non-Indian they knew: a missionary. As a result, a whole other set of behaviors was generated, and the Indians began to apply a new kind of subtle pressure on me. I was not supposed to smoke cigarettes, dance in the village in the evenings, or bathe nude in the river. There was tremendous pressure on me to spend additional time studying the Bakairí language, and they asked me many questions about Bible translations and church building, which they experienced in the 1950s and 1960s when American missionaries worked in their reservation.

I was irritated a great deal during this phase of fieldwork. The situation was ludicrous, but all the more serious because of the element of the absurd. Our dissimilar expectations about how I was to behave created a strain and threatened to affect the outcome of my work. At that time, I smoked cigarettes, danced, and took baths in the river. I spent a certain amount of time studying the Bakairí language, but I expressed no interest in the Bible or church. Although the tension between us relaxed over time, and they seemed to forget about my missionary identity, I can still recall how trapped I felt during that period.

Anthropologist as Bakairí Woman

As the months passed, the Bakairí and I gradually engaged in Phase three, during which time they decided that if I was neither a karaiwa nor a missionary, then I could safely be treated like a Bakairí woman. When I realized what was happening, I felt relieved and even excited. I expected to learn about what it was like to be a woman in this society. However, several drawbacks immediately presented themselves. One of the most serious ones concerned my relationship with an important field informant named Yare. This young man lived with his crippled aunt and his grandmother. He was a hardworking and helpful person who volunteered to show me gardens I needed to measure and to explain certain aspects of ritual mask dancing that intrigued me.

After some time, gossips in the village speculated that Yare and I had more than a professional relationship. A small amount of investigation into the question by any one individual would have demonstrated that we were not romantically involved. However, I let people think what they liked, assuming that if I earnestly explained the facts every time someone made a joke, I would just exacerbate the situation.

This innocuous relationship, combined with expectations that I behave like a Bakairí woman, soon became problematic because many villagers wanted me to take responsibility for chores the typical Indian woman did each day. I was expected to wash Yare's clothes and to harvest manioc, their staple crop, from the garden. The women tried to show me how to clean the tubers so as to remove bitter poison from them, an arduous process that took all afternoon. They also helped me learn how to prepare manioc pancakes over the fire on a clay griddle. And I was supposed to chop and carry wood for the fire in Yare's house.

At the same time, some people exerted pressure on me to behave with the modest decorum that married or betrothed women exercised. I was supposed to avoid going to the gardens alone because illicit sexual relations normally take place there. Nor could I talk to the other young men in the village, even if it were about gardening or fishing. And I was discouraged from participating in village dances.

I believed that some compromise was desirable, as it had been in the other phases of my relationship with the Bakairí community. I learned to perform many of the household chores and came to share them with the other women in Yare's house. I reduced interactions with the other men in the village, and tried to go to the gardens only when other women were present. I stopped attending the dances in the village or I sat with the matrons.

My efforts were appreciated but residual problems remained, mainly because of my own shortcomings. Either I am unusually clumsy or one simply has to learn some of these things when one is young. For example, I never did learn how to turn cotton balls into thread with a spindle. Nor were my manioc pancakes very good. And washing clothes became a special source of frustration. Bakairí women use a technique that consisted of rubbing soap on the clothes, slapping them several times on the wet stones, letting the soapy clothes bleach in the sun, and finally rinsing them. This process is not only time-consuming, but it requires a great deal of upper-body strength. So I abbreviated it. The women at first patiently explained to me that I was not getting my clothes clean, but later they became so insistent that I adopt their technique, that I started washing my clothes when no one was around.

Despite these minor problems, the adjustments I made in my behavior alleviated some of the pressure on me during this period, although a few of the older women continued to accuse me of spending too much time performing esoteric tasks related to my study and too little time "working."

Anthropologist and "the Other"

The problem of how people like the Bakairí regard anthropologists may seem like an insignificant point. In my experience, however, the role of a researcher is a serious issue that needs to be confronted every day in the field. If this question is ignored, then confusion, anger, and resentment will poison the field episode.

Groups like the Bakairí can appear at first to be exotic and unfamiliar, and some of us from Western society may make the mistake of assuming we are observing them from superior positions. Others may make the equally unwise error of supposing that no significant differences exist and that we are from the same "place." The reality is that profound cultural differences divide us and make it hard for us to work together. How can anthropologists circumvent disaster? Supposing we will not be readily, if ever, accepted on our own terms is a good starting place. And going to work at the time-consuming process of negotiating a satisfactory role to play while in the field is a next step.

Negotiating a role while doing fieldwork touches on a larger dispute in anthropology, which includes the differences between what are called modernism and postmodernism. Modernism is a term drawn from the study of literature and art. In anthropology it refers to those writings characterized by detachment and the assumption of scientific neutrality and rationalism. Manganaro (1990) assigns modernism in anthropology to the years between 1920 and the mid-1970s.

Postmodernism emerged partially in reaction to modernism, taking issue with the premise that objective knowledge of another culture is possible. Followers of this school argue that all knowledge is a product of interpretation, colored by such factors as personal experience, culture, and political orientation (McGee and Warms 2000: 518–520). Although a full discussion of postmodernism is outside the scope of this work, one of its more powerful critiques is that researchers set up an artificial dichotomy between themselves, as "scientists," and those whom they study, as "subjects." Through this process, they turn their "subjects" into what postmodernists call "the Other." Scientists, in their role of omniscient observers, go on to interpret the reality of the Other, and since they are considered authorities in their fields, reports of their findings on the Other are considered authoritative accounts. The Other's voice, whether it agrees with the scientist's or not, is silenced. Postmodernists conclude that which interpretation of reality is accepted is ultimately a matter of who has power, rather than which one most closely resembles what is.

Although many anthropologists disagree with some of what postmodernism espouses, I suspect that the movement has forced fieldworkers, such as myself, to examine carefully how we treat people while we do research and how we write about them when we return home. I know I am very concerned about the way I describe who the Bakairí are. I do not want to make them seem like exotic primitives, or make myself, as a Western scientist, seem superior to them, or even to exaggerate the differences between our cultures. On the other hand, I need to give the reader a sense of how their culture differs from ours. Although it is true we share a common humanity, it is also true we come from radically different worlds.

This balancing act is hard to manage, sometimes because of who we are, but sometimes because of what we find in the field. Bridging the chasm between ourselves and what postmodernists call the Other can pose special challenges under certain circumstances. Colin Turnbull's *The Forest People* (1961) was widely acclaimed by anthropologists and students alike as a sensitive and sympathetic study of the Pygmies. But when he returned to Africa to study another group called the Ik, he had a very different field experience. Turnbull wrote that he actually had to learn not to hate these people. He described how they were under such stress from regional political upheaval that they had "lost their humanity" (1972:11–13).

Techniques for Learning about Indians

Most anthropologists use a wide range of data-gathering techniques while they are doing fieldwork because they are trying to learn as much as possible about the people with whom they are living. However, at the same time, individual anthropologists tend to favor a particular type of methodology since they are usually researching a specific problem. They anticipate finding answers to questions they formulated before beginning fieldwork, answers which they hope to eventually share with other scientists, and perhaps even with the public, when they publish articles and books.

Additionally, most anthropologists receive grants to do their research, and the organizations that fund them hold them accountable. When their field projects are completed, anthropologists must file reports with their sponsors. Even when they are beginning projects without official proposals and grants, as sometimes happens when they are moving into new research areas, they still write up their results to share their findings with others.

Quantitative versus Qualitative Methodologies

The particular problem anthropologists choose to study in part determines which type of methodology to use. I have already mentioned that the first time I worked with the Bakairí I studied how macrolevel political variables impacted on indigenous food production systems and on the environment. I focused on examining how a government-sponsored industrial agriculture project affected the Indians' culture and their reservation's ecosystem. I planned to go on to examine the dietary and health-related implications of what I discovered.

This is quite different, and indeed even humdrum, when compared to Gerald Herdt's (1981) research on the implications of homosexual behaviors upon child development among the Sambians of New Guinea. Herdt discovered that the Sambians require that their male children spend a requisite amount of time living away from their families in groupings where they are expected to perform oral sex on teenage boys who live with them. When these younger children reach their teens, boys newly introduced into the groups, in turn, perform fellatio on them. All men are expected eventually to give up, or drastically reduce, participation in homosexual behaviors. They then go on to marry and have children when they are in their twenties. The underlying symbolic rationale for this child-rearing tradition that is so different from our own American way is that semen is seen by the Sambians as a sacred growth-inducing agent. The male child must consume it in order to mature (1981:1–4).

The methodologies that Herdt used to document child-rearing practices among the Sambians are distinctly different from the ones that I employed to understand the effects of political processes on the Bakairí's environment, food-producing traditions, and overall health. For our purposes here we can differentiate them by referring to the two types as *quantitative* and *qualitative methods*. Quantitative methodologies generate information that can be described in numerical or statistical terms, while qualitative methodologies produce systematic descriptions of phenomena. Clifford Geertz (1973) refers to one kind of qualitative method as "*thick description*," which is a richly detailed explanatory account of what the anthropologist has observed. This method takes into account the fact that human behavior has various levels of meaning that the anthropologist must interpret.

An example of how I used a quantitative methodology is when I did an infant weight-gain project during my stay with the Bakairí. Every three months, I asked mothers with children of two years or younger to let me weigh and measure their infants. I also used a plastic caliper to determine how much body fat they had. After a year, I had four sets of data for each child who began the project with me, and between one to three sets for those who were born during the time I was doing the study. From this information, I was able to make some general statements about how rapidly Indian children gained weight when compared to American children, and whether or not periods of high stress in the village dangerously affected their size and health.

Herdt's study did not rely on the generation of numerical data or statistical analysis. Rather, he employed qualitative methodologies such as unstructured and open-ended interviews with men who had experienced Sambian child-rearing practices firsthand. He did life histories, questioning these individuals in detail about how they grew up. Also, he recorded and analyzed myths and stories that provided the cultural foundation for the homosexual development phase through which each male child was required to pass (Herdt 1981:255–294).

While I produced charts and graphs showing average weight gain and how epidemics in the Bakairí village affected it, Herdt translated and contextualized myths that explained why semen was sacred. My field notes were full of discussions about how long babies breast-fed and when infants started eating semisolid foods such as mashed bananas. Herdt, on the other hand, provided detailed descriptions of men remembering that their initial homosexual experiences had not always been pleasant and had sometimes been frightening (Herdt 1981:3).

Meaningful Accounts

Clearly, both qualitative and quantitative methodologies are capable of producing useful information as well as valuable insights into other people's cultures. Although there is some conflict in anthropology at the present time about the role of science in the discipline, I would argue that both methods are, or can be, scientific in the sense that each is able to provide a meaningful account of a cultural reality that is verifiable by others.

What do we mean by a *meaningful account*? Michael Agar discusses the importance of "paraphrasing" or "decoding" sense perceptions by assigning culturally appropriate meaning to them (1980:78). He states that we will know if we are right about our interpretations only if we open them up to review by key informants and/or other members of the communities where we study. If the way we have decoded what we have observed resonates with their understanding of their world, then we know we are on the right track.

Of course producing something people recognize can be quite different from producing something they endorse, depending on how sensitive, complex, or controversial the information one is gathering. For example, when I first began to work with the Bakairí, I mapped the village and then did a household census. As I interviewed each household head, I asked whether he had a garden, and, if so, what crops he grew.

After a few weeks of drinking innumerable demitasses of coffee, I felt I could say with some certainty that there were about forty-four gardens made the previous year, and forty-eight made in the current year. When I had visited a prescribed percentage of these gardens and measured their size, I found that, on average, each was about 4,100 squared meters, or a little less than one half of a hectare. I went on and added to this subtotal several large communal gardens. In the end, I could report with some assurance that a total of about 44.5 hectares of land were under cultivation by the Bakairí of Pakuera using traditional subsistence methods.

This was important because of two factors. First, the Bakairí Indians had been given a relatively small reservation of about 60,000 hectares in the 1920s. Over 80 percent of their land was not arable using the traditional methods. This, combined with the fact that the number of Bakairí in the reservation was growing, concerned me. How would they survive in the twenty-first century? Would they suffer from famine? Would young adults begin to migrate to nearby towns where they might lose their cultural identity or suffer from high rates of alcoholism as Native Americans in North America had? Or would they turn to industrial agricultural technology and confront the negative consequences of pollution and erosion?

When I discussed my findings with Bakairí informants, they both recognized and agreed with my conclusions and questions. Garden size and makeup were not controversial to them. Yet, other kinds of information are much more difficult to collect because people may not want to discuss certain topics, or because there are culturally prescribed prohibitions against them doing so. And once the information is gathered, informants may not agree with the way anthropologists interpret it.

Herdt only stumbled upon ritualized homosexuality some time after beginning fieldwork because it was kept secret by the Sambians. And Chagnon's initial problems with collecting genealogies from the Yanomamö are now quite well known. When he first tried to get people to describe their family histories to him so he could chart them, he was unaware that the Yanomamö were forbidden to say the name of a dead person out loud. When Chagnon pressed them for people's names, his informants took advantage of the fact that he did not yet speak their language well. They gave him obscene names such as "Eagle Shit" and "Fart Breath," which he dutifully wrote down and later repeated in subsequent genealogy interviews, much to everyone's amusement (Chagnon 1992:20).

Nancy Scheper-Hughes (1992) confronted another kind of problem. Her complex and ambitious study of high rates of infant mortality in the northeastern region of Brazil documented how people living in poverty responded to their difficult situations in ways that contributed to the premature deaths of their infants. She showed that when children got sick with hunger-related illnesses, the mothers bought expensive medicines instead of wholesome food to cure them. At the same time, these women rejected the tradition of breast-feeding, which produces free and nutritious milk, opting instead for the use of powdered infant formulas, which they inadvertently contaminated with polluted water.

Yet, the women and families with whom she worked could not endorse her conclusions because they were convinced that medicine would cure their hungry children. And they spurned breast-feeding because the media and other cultural trendsetters had taught them that it was old fashioned, while the use of infant formula was part of the modern world to which they wanted to belong.

My most significant data-gathering roadblocks did not have to do with the ritual secrecy that confronted Herdt, or the humorous incidents Chagnon experienced, or the impasse between Scheper-Hughes and her informants. Rather, they evolved from two distinct problems. The first was trying to get the Indians to talk about certain things they simply did not want to discuss. Sex and sex taboos, spontaneous abortion, and infanticide were conversationally off-limits.

During the first couple of months I lived in Pakuera I tried to interview mothers about these topics and found them far too sensitive. I retreated to safer subjects and hoped that the Indians would become used to me. In time that happened to a certain extent. But far more important for the success of that part of my project were relationships I developed with older women who knew everything about the other women in the village. Once they felt it was safe to share some of this information with me, my research forged ahead.

The second, and certainly more mundane problem had to do with the limitations of my own physical abilities. For example, some of the gardens I needed to measure were over seven kilometers, or four miles, away—adding up to a round-trip distance I could not easily walk. Other gardens were over a year old, and the weeds were chest-high, making it difficult to rope off the borders of the cultivated area so that I could measure it accurately. And a couple of times I ran into animals such as otters and anteaters that I was unprepared to confront. None of the animals I met were dangerous, though both jaguars and wild pigs inhabited the area and were hunted by the men.

Whether one depends on qualitative or quantitative methods to get information while doing fieldwork, almost all anthropologists agree that sometimes it is easy to get informants to cooperate in providing us with assistance and sometimes it is not. Additionally, it is important for us to get feedback to verify whether or not our accounts of their reality are accurate. Because my study of politics, resource utilization, and the environment ended up being uncontroversial, I was able to involve many informants who helped me evaluate the accuracy of my findings. Those anthropologists who work in more sensitive areas do not have this advantage.

Summary

In this chapter I introduced the Bakairí Indians who live in central Brazil, and I described what my first day with them was like. I then outlined the process whereby many anthropologists prepare for, and successfully complete, fieldwork. I included a section on role negotiation because I do not think anthropologists have given this problem enough attention.

I would like to recap, and add to, my observations about methodology. Research was carried out in Mato Grosso, Brazil, between 1979 and 1981, followed by additional visits in 1989 and 1999. During the collection of baseline data, I logged fourteen months in the actual village of Pakuera. My schedule was comprised of spending three months in the village and a week or two outside, usually in Cuiabá, where I bought supplies. Research was carried out in Portuguese and in Bakairí. Although I studied the Indian's language intensively, I never learned to speak it as fluently as I wanted.

In addition to time spent in the Indian reservation, I also spent seven months in Cuiabá and in Brasilia, going on a daily basis to FUNAI offices where I worked in the library, sifted through government reports, interviewed officials, and, in general, talked to anyone I could. During those months, I gathered a substantial amount of information on what FUNAI was attempting to do in indigenous reservations, why it was doing so, and what problems it anticipated in operationalizing its plans.

In 1989 I returned to Brazil and spent a month in Pakuera and a month in Brasilia and Cuiabá. At that point my goal was to focus on the political processes at work both outside and inside the reservation. In 1999 I traveled to Cuiabá and to the reservation briefly for an update while I finished this book.

Chapter 2

THE CHANGING WORLD
OF THE BAKAIRÍ INDIANS

"The Bakairí have been dying fast. Fevers seem to decimate them rapidly, though all efforts are made to keep medical supplies on hand and to supply medical attention. Contact with white people, such as is had when a small group of natives go to Cuyabá, has brought syphilis to them, and it may be their mortality is due to this."

(Petrullo 1932: 128-9)

Before We Begin . . .

The myths of "the ecologically noble savage," "*the untouched primitive,*" and "the pristine wilderness" are just that. They are myths. And although newspapers such as the *New York Times* might inadvertently promote such misconceptions when they write about Papua New Guinea as "having the last extensive stretches of pristine tropical forest [in the world] . . . a land that time forgot . . . untouched by the outside world" (Shenon 1994), anthropologists know that such places no longer exist.

The extent to which anthropologists have contributed to the myth of "the primitive isolate" is debatable. It is true that some of us may not

25

have adequately described the history of our research subjects. Early editions of Chagnon's popular *Yanomamö: The Fierce People* (1968, 1977, 1983) are examples of how anthropologists can focus on the here and now to the detriment of our work. This case study chronicles the behavior of a people Chagnon described as being aggressive. Accounts of what he called their "individual vindictiveness" and "collective bellicosity" make up a good part of his monograph (Chagnon 1977:7). By giving little attention to these Indians' past, Chagnon seems to assume that violence and aggression have always been an integral part of their culture.

Chagnon's most recent edition of the book (1992) and Ferguson and Whitehead's work (1992) remedy this situation by discussing in some detail how contact with non-Indians modified the world of the Yanomamö and led to the amplification of patterns of violence in their culture. The intrusion of gold miners into Yanomamö territory during the late 1980s illustrates how this could have happened. Chagnon reports that these miners at one point numbered forty thousand. They used hydraulic pumps to suck gold-bearing ore from the river bottoms, passed the ore through troughs into which they added toxic mercury compounds to extract the gold, and then let the mercury-poisoned residue flow back into the rivers, along which the Indians lived.

In addition to polluting the environment of the Yanomamö in ways that have surely affected their health, these men raped indigenous women, killed men and children, and desecrated their bodies. When the Indians tried to fight back, they discovered they lacked the arms to make any kind of an impact on these non-Indians (Chagnon 1992:212–213). Such chapters in the history of any Indian group in North or South America are not uncommon, and awareness of them helps us to understand cultural traditions and their evolution.

American anthropology has always valued the historical perspective. However, sometimes the desire to get into the field and begin research becomes a priority for individuals. Also, solid historical data about indigenous societies are hard to find. There are cases where only meticulous archival research turns up relevant information, and frequently, ethnographers do not have the time, inclination, or funding to take on such work (Stearman 1997:622). I would hate to concede that anthropologists might choose to ignore pertinent data in any study they are doing. Yet when resources are limited, we make choices about what to study first, and what to put off until later.

Another related question that has recently surfaced concerns how indigenous peoples manage their environments (Headland 1997). If these people have indeed been using resources such as the Amazon rainforest for thousands of years, then we can make some generalizations about their impact on such ecosystems. They offer us help in understanding how to live within our ecological constraints and in warning us against some of the effects of technological innovation.

Reports about indigenous uses of their resources both dovetail and conflict with the efforts of a wider international conservation movement. Ecotourists, rock stars like Sting, environmentalists, and politicians who advocate such causes regard Indians as intuitive conservationists who are the symbolic guardians of the natural world. Some research supports such a view, while other findings do not. Would the latter disillusion the general public about indigenous peoples, and thus undercut attempts to protect their rights and lands? Beth Conklin and Laura Graham (1995) speculate that if indigenous peoples lose their status as "guardians of the natural world," then a backlash could occur, providing a rationale for taking their lands and turning them over to private or government developers.

Whether anthropologists can layer historical and ecological insights into our studies without damaging the future of indigenous peoples may depend on how effectively we speak to the media. It is somewhat ironic that South American Indians such as Raoni, a Kayapó tribal leader, mastered the art of talking to journalists despite the vast cultural differences between them, while we anthropologists often find our observations relegated to obscure academic journals.

In this chapter, I present historical information about the Bakairí in an attempt to firmly situate them in a complex, changing world. It should be clear at this point that I am convinced that they are living as they do because of, not in spite of, the world around them. Cultures are dynamic, and the Bakairí culture is no exception. What these people are experiencing today is not an anomaly, nor are they or their culture being tainted in some way by their interactions with other Indians or with non-Indians. We would do them a disservice if we did not fully appreciate their intricate history and culture and the resiliency with which they, as a people, have confronted the many challenges they have faced over the years.

Serendipity and Making Time for History

I once had a professor who told our class that good anthropology was all a matter of *serendipity*. I looked up *serendipity* in the dictionary, which said, "the gift of being able to make delightful discoveries by pure accident." A group of us puzzled over this statement after class, trying to figure out what this faculty member was telling us. Was he saying that you had to be lucky to be a good anthropologist? If so, that did not sound hopeful to me. I have always put my stock in preparation and planning rather than in chance. When we finally asked the professor to expand on his comment, it turned out that he meant you have to be prepared for setbacks when you do research. And not only do you have to expect them, you have to be ready to turn them to your advantage.

I have had many occasions to remember this. One of them was when I flew to Brasilia to pick up my authorization papers so I could begin my research. I checked into my hotel and went over to FUNAI's headquarters to introduce myself and pick up my license to enter an Indian reservation. But there was a problem. To make a long story short, over the next several weeks, I discovered that FUNAI preferred that I work on another project. Since I could not do research without their permission, I felt compelled to accept their proposal. The officials I spoke with casually added that getting my papers in order would take months. In fact, it took exactly four months and ten days. I had plenty of time to think about the meaning of *serendipity*.

As I look back over my field diaries, I find a lot of emotional ventilating and four-letter words. But I also notice that I took my professor's advice about turning obstacles into opportunities. I set two practical goals for myself during that period—improving my Portuguese and doing archival work on the history of the Bakairí Indians. FUNAI headquarters housed a small, but highly specialized and excellent, library on indigenous peoples, and the librarian was a friendly woman who was willing to provide anthropologists with no end of assistance.

As the days and weeks ticked by, my pile of notes on the Indians' history grew. Later I supplemented these when I traveled to Rio de Janeiro, another Brazilian city. While there, I visited a library that had many government records from the 1940s and 1950s on microfiche. All of these resources proved invaluable when I began to reconstruct the Bakairí's past.

The Ancestors Arrive in the New World

When I first read about indigenous peoples such as the Bakairí, the story always started with the arrival of the Europeans in the *New World*, or North and South America. Those days are behind us now, and as archaeological information accumulates, we better understand how people migrated to this part of the world thousands of years before the Europeans began their explorations.

There have been heated arguments about how early humans reached the New World. At one time it was thought that the first migrations occurred prior to thirty thousand years ago. However, these claims have now been refuted. Another hypothesis was that humans had arrived in North America before fifteen thousand years ago. This conjecture was based on artifacts that archaeologists excavated in both North and South America. But scientists have expressed concerns about how old these materials are as well as whether or not humans actually made them. As a result, most anthropologists have not accepted the fifteen-thousand-year date either.

It is human remains that allow for clear and certain dating of the occupation of the New World, and at this time we have such remains dating back to twelve thousand years ago. It is also widely accepted that the ancestors of contemporary indigenous peoples reached the Western Hemisphere through, not one, but a series of migrations over the Bering Land Bridge that connected Asia and North America. These took place over many millennia.

The early explorers were members of the modern human species, *Homo sapiens sapiens*, and they most closely resembled the Mongoloid population groups of northeastern Asia. The earliest widespread culture associated with these people is called Paleo-Indian, which means that they probably lived in small bands of about thirty to forty individuals and that they mainly hunted using lithic, that is stone, technology. They also gathered wild foods.

There is evidence of the presence of Paleo-Indians in the Amazon area dating back to between 11,400 and 10,000 years ago. In the past, anthropologists believed that the Amazon environment was a "counterfeit paradise" that actually hindered human occupation (Meggers 1971). The prevailing view was that civilizations evolved in the Andes and in Mesoamerica, but that the Tropical Rain Forest ecosystems could support only small-village societies relying on slash-and-burn gardening. However, recent archaeological evidence suggests that the rainforests supported a great variety of people and cultures. In fact, a long and complex history characterizes this immense region (Roosevelt 1994).

Between about 4,500 and 2,000 years ago, people with a lifeway similar to that of indigenous peoples such as the Bakairí Indians set up villages along the banks of the Amazon. And between 2,000 and 1,000 years ago, new cultural centers appeared. They had large populations, public works, elaborate ceremonial art, pottery, and long-distance trade. Based on these characteristics, many anthropologists have judged them to be complex chiefdoms in which there was ranking. Anthropologists use the term *rank* to suggest there are formal differences in prestige in a given society but no important restrictions on access to resources (Roosevelt 1994; Carneiro 1995).

These powerful chiefdoms coexisted with small-village societies that more closely resemble today's indigenous cultures. It is possible that the latter were displaced from the fertile banks of the Amazon by the culturally complex groups that evolved there. This periodic relocation of villages could have been the result of warfare that was connected to competition for resources (Carneiro 1995).

Both the chiefdoms and the small-village societies were traumatized by the arrival of the Europeans. Through a process of military defeat, decimation, forced migration, enslavement, and culture change, these newcomers transformed Amazonia (Arvelo-Jimenez and Biord 1994). Depopulation of the region as well as extensive dislocations of villages provide us with evidence of the turmoil these people experienced. Also, skeletal remains from that period suggest a rapid deterioration of their health as they attempted to cope with new diseases and chaos.

However, some indigenous peoples managed to adapt to conquest in a wide variety of ways. A few actually flourished as they took advantage of military and trading opportunities (Whitehead 1994). Others de-emphasized agriculture and became nomadic hunters and gatherers, similar in some ways to their Paleo-Indian ancestors. And still others retreated into marginal areas, deep in the Tropical Rain Forest, where they escaped notice for a time.

Many case studies about Indians neglect to explain that their lifeways reflect changes caused by conquest as well as adaptations to a tropical environment. What we see today, or even what we would have seen a hundred years ago, is not a replica of what their cultures were like before contact. With that in mind, let's proceed to look at some of the earliest records of contact with the Bakairí.

In Search of Slaves and Gold: The Colonial Period and the Bakairí (1500–1822)

The Colonial Period spans from the time Spanish and Portuguese explorers first visited the New World to when Dom Pedro, the son of King João VI of Portugal declared Brazil's independence in 1822. Portuguese explorers began to settle along the eastern coast of South America after Pedro Cabral claimed the land for Portugal. The earliest permanent Portuguese settlement was organized in 1532 in what is now the state of São Paulo. From this site and others like it, *bandeirantes paulistas*, who were Portuguese explorers, traveled into the interior of South America in search of slaves, gold, and precious stones.

The Spanish, with whom the Portuguese were competing for control of South America, were actually the first to move into what is now Mato Grosso, the western state in which the Bakairí live today. Jesuit priests, journeying north and west from Paraguay, created some of the original European centers in that region. However, the Portuguese quickly followed, and in 1718, such intrepid adventurers as Antonio Pires de Campos and Pascoal Moreira Cabral made the five-month, 1,865-mile trip from São Paulo to Mato Grosso, through the heat and insects, in search of slaves and gold. Pascoal Moreira Cabral is credited with starting the village of Cuiabá in 1719. Today it is the booming capital of Mato Grosso, with a population of over 330,000.

Around the same time, another explorer, Miguel Sutil, discovered gold in the vicinity of Cuiabá. This news stimulated a gold rush of such magnitude that people poured into the area. Their journey was facili-

A square in Cuiabá. The colonial architecture in the background is a legacy of the 1700s, when the city was founded.

tated by the discovery that Mato Grosso could be reached from the Amazon River through the interior river systems, eliminating the arduous overland journey. By 1748, only thirty years after the discovery of gold, the population reached forty thousand. The first Portuguese governor, Antonio Rolim de Moura, arrived and established an administrative center, from which he attempted to stabilize the region and to prevent the Spanish from invading and taking over the gold mines.

During the next seventy years, early settlers saw demographic fluctuations, mineral exploitation, and open armed conflict between the Portuguese and the Spanish, who persisted in trying to invade and take over this region. Then, between 1815 and 1820, Mato Grosso entered into a period of decline. A mineral company created by the governor to develop the best possible mining techniques did not have the desired effect. At the same time, military, civil, and ecclesiastic expenses rose. As a result of these setbacks, the government went into debt, and the population ceased to grow. By 1819 there were about 29,800 people in the area, with an additional 10,948 slaves.

What were the Bakairí doing during this time? When Europeans first occupied the Mato Grosso region, historic sources such as letters from Manoel Rodrigues Torres to King João V, then king of Portugal, suggest that the Indians inhabited the general area between the Arinos River on the west, the Kuliseu River on the east, the Paranatinga on the south, and the elevated areas of the headwaters of the Verde River in the north (see figure 2-1). Torres's report (1738) mentions the Bakairí, along with other Indian groups such as the Kayabí and Parecis, as being a possible threat to the governor's power. Apparently, at that time, the Indians in that part of South America were still numerous enough to pose a danger to the fledgling Portuguese colony.

In addition, it is clear that the treatment they had received at the hands of the Europeans discouraged them from establishing an alliance with the Portuguese. Antonio Pires de Campos, in the first recorded meeting with the Bakairí in 1723, visited the Indians on his way to the gold mines located in the general vicinity (Campos 1862). In his report to the governor, he described how they lived in the headwaters of the Amazon River and were abused by marauding bandeirantes in search of slaves.

By the mid-1700s scholars believe that a gold miner named Correia either forced or persuaded the Bakairí to build a village on the banks of the Paranatinga River. He planned to have the Indians ferry travelers and businessmen from the mines across the river in their canoes (von den Steinen 1940:497). We are provided with few ethnographic details about the Indians at this time, and can only draw one or two general conclusions. Certainly they were more numerous then than they are now, and they were located in the same region that we find them today.

The Bakairí Divide:
The Postcolonial Period (1822–1920)

During the nineteenth century, the economic base of Mato Grosso underwent a transformation. Gold mining declined in importance until, in 1844, even the famous mines of Diamantina were exhausted. A new enterprise, cattle raising, replaced mining, and ranchers took huge tracts of land from which they created pastures that reached all the way to the headwaters of the Paranatinga River. But like mining, this industry had its ups and downs, and toward the end of the nineteenth century, it was in decline. When Karl von den Steinen (1940), a famous German explorer, passed through the area around 1885, he commented on the number of abandoned ranches there.

News about the Bakairí in the early part of the 1800s is scarce, but an 1848 government report sketches for us the horrible conditions

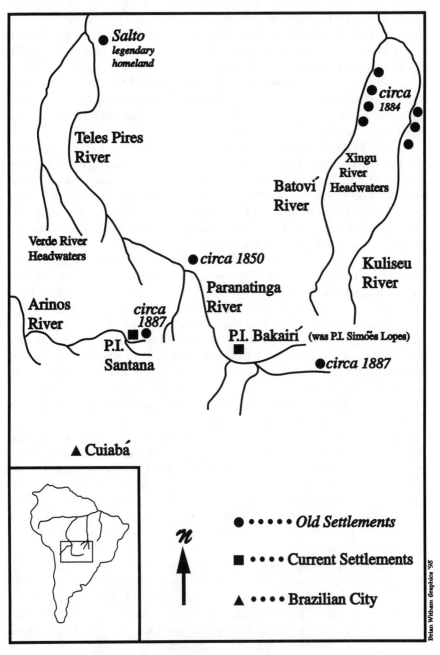

Figure 2-1: Old and Current Bakairí Settlements.

under which the Indians lived at that time. It says that the Bakairí lived in two impoverished villages on the banks of the Paranatinga River and the headwaters of the Arinos River. They were visited once in a while by expeditions of adventurers who were looking for gold. These men introduced syphilis and measles into the population. Measles, even today a serious killer of Indians in South America, caused the deaths of many Bakairí who, lacking medicines to treat the fever and rash, could only run into the river and take cold baths to find relief (von den Steinen 1940:496–497).

An 1872 report states that about two hundred Bakairí continued to live in the headwaters of the Paranatinga and the Arinos Rivers where they had fled the attacks of other indigenous peoples such as the Nambiquara and Kayabí. They were described as a peaceful people who lived by hunting, fishing, and gardening. They raised corn, manioc, sweet potatoes, beans, and sugar cane and made hammocks, baskets, and sieves. Few spoke Portuguese (von den Steinen 1940:appendix 2).

The writings of Curt Nimuendajú, a great Brazilian Indianist, provide us with some insight into the tension between the Bakairí and such indigenous enemies as the Kayabí. He explains that raiding between the two groups was common during that time because the Kayabí controlled the stone ax trade, vital artifacts for making a living when metal tools were still scarce. Nimuendajú describes two Kayabí women who were found in a Bakairí village. They had been captured during their childhood by a Bakairí raiding party and brought back to a village on the Paranatinga River where they were raised. There is evidence of skirmishes between the Kayabí and the Bakairí as late as 1901 (Nimuendajú 1963:307–320).

Up to this point in our discussion, we have been able to lump the Bakairí into one group; however, their histories diverged in the nineteenth century. The western Bakairí on the Arinos River were absorbed into the ranching economy. They worked on ranches, spoke some Portuguese, and sold artifacts they made in the towns. Von den Steinen met some of them in 1887 in Cuiabá during his travels. Today, they live at Posto Indígena (P.I.), Indian Post, Santana, a reservation that lies to the west of P.I. Bakairí.

The eastern Bakairí lived near the Paranatinga River. At a certain point in time, probably in the late eighteenth or early nineteenth century, a group of them traveled northeast into the headwaters of the Xingú River, one of the major tributaries of the Amazon, where they settled on the banks of the Batoví and Kuliseu Rivers. There is no clear record of the reasons for this migration or the way it took place. The legend they now tell begins with them living at the Salto, a waterfall near the Paranatinga River, which lies north of where they are located today. Political infighting riddled their village, and one group decided secretly to form a new settlement. They took a trip to the

Xingú River headwaters, where they made a large garden. Over the next few months, they cultivated this garden in secret until the crops were ready to harvest. Then they stealthily gathered up all of their belongings and left without saying goodbye. The story concludes with the observation that several years passed before the Bakairí who remained at the Salto realized how they had been tricked (Pina 1977).

Whatever the reasons for the relocation of part of the eastern contingent of Bakairí, by 1884, when von den Steinen arrived, three separate groups of these Indians lived in a west–east arc across Mato Grosso. They spoke the same language with little dialectical variation, suggesting that their separation had been quite recent. There was some infrequent contact between them, as there continues to be today. And yet the three groups were culturally distinct. The western Bakairí participated in the local economy, spoke Portuguese, and traveled regularly to nearby towns to buy and sell goods, while the eastern Bakairí raised most of their food in small gardens and worked on cattle ranches to earn some cash.

The Xinguano Bakairí were quite different from the other two groups. There were seven Bakairí villages in the Xingú area, with over 300 Indians at the end of the nineteenth century. They used only stone tools for gardening, which suggested that there had been little or no recent contact between them and non-Indians, since metal tools had already rapidly spread through the region. In their gardens they cultivated manioc, maize, yams, squash, peanuts, peppers, and sweet potatoes.

A Nafuquá Indian village in the Xingú area where the Bakairí lived in the nineteenth century and early part of the twentieth century. Note the large elliptical houses.

Although they did not make pottery themselves, they obtained clay pots and griddles, used in cooking and storage, from another group who also lived in the Xingú area. They fished and hunted, using bows and arrows, and they preferred fish to game. The Bakairí lived in elliptical houses made from palm. These houses were large, about 10 meters by 20 meters in size, and several families shared each house. There was also a men's house for rituals in the center of the plaza, around which the longhouses lay (von den Steinen 1940:87–98; Levi-Strauss 1948:327).

Between 1890 and 1920 the Xinguano Bakairí left their villages in the Xingú area for the Paranatinga River, where the eastern Bakairí were living. They departed gradually, after a number of serious epidemics decimated the population in the Xingú. By 1900 when Max Schmidt, another German explorer-scientist, visited the area, 34 Bakairí had moved to the Paranatinga, and when he returned in 1927, over 180 had resettled there (Schmidt 1947). A few remained in the Xingú area and were absorbed by other tribes.

The eastern Bakairí numbered about 22 individuals when the Xinguano Bakairí began their migration. They were inundated and finally absorbed by the large number of Xinguanos who came to live with them (Pina 1977). Initially they all lived together peacefully, but when infighting began, they established different villages in the same vicinity. In 1918, the SPI (Indian Protection Service) demarcated their territory as a reservation of about 58,000 hectares, and in 1920, they created an Indian Post named Simões Lopes, where a government representative soon came to live.

At Home on the Paranatinga:
The Bakairí on Their New Reservation (1920–1958)

The new 1920s world of the Bakairí was a sparsely populated Mato Grosso with few roads or communication networks. The large number of Indians and the lack of infrastructure discouraged businessmen from entering the region. The underdeveloped cattle-raising industry from the nineteenth century was still in place, and remained so until about 1958 when dramatic changes started to occur in the region.

The Xinguano Bakairí quietly settled down on their reservation, living much as they had in their previous home territory. However, beginning in the 1930s, the SPI made a concerted effort to change their culture. One of the first things they did was to draw the Bakairí out of the four small villages they had made and to organize them in one large settlement near the Indian post. The Indian agent forbade them to make their traditional elliptical longhouses and insisted they make smaller clay houses with palm roofs, similar to the ones constructed by the Brazilian farmers in the area. SPI purchased a small cattle herd in the 1920s, and by the 1930s the herd had increased in size to five thousand head. The cattle grazed in the reservation. The Bakairí were unfamiliar with such large domesticated animals, but the Indian agent taught some of the men how to catch and brand them and how to put out salt licks so that the animals would not wander too far away from the SPI post (Pina 1977).

The Bakairí were required to wear European clothes, which they did although they continued to wear their traditional G-strings underneath their clothes and to file their upper front teeth to a point. Vincent Petrullo, an explorer who visited their reservation in the early 1930s, noted that they spoke little Portuguese, and he needed an interpreter to talk to them (Petrullo 1932).

By the 1940s the Indian agents required the Bakairí to work in SPI fields. The men were organized into groups and sent to the fields at the beginning of the week and brought back to their families at the end of the week. The Indian agent in charge kept a list of the work done by each individual, and payment was made with cloth, tools, and other items not produced on the reservation. The Indians also maintained their own garden plots because they could not consume the crops produced in the SPI fields. These were harvested and sold in nearby towns. Money from the sale of the harvests supported the administrative costs of the Indian Post and the salary of the Indian agent. Bakairí women also worked for SPI. They processed rice and manioc for the agent's use, made hammocks for him to sell, and worked as domestic servants in his house (Petrullo 1932; Schmidt 1947).

In a relatively short time, the Xinguano Bakairí passed from a relatively isolated state into permanent contact. They were forced to adjust to the innumerable changes that were foisted upon them in the new reservation. The culture shock they experienced, along with effects of new diseases, resulted in a significant decline in population. Alarmed, SPI officials acted to turn the situation around. In 1943 they began donating a heifer to every family that gave birth to a child. This policy worked. As we will see in greater detail in chapter 3, depopulation among the Bakairí was halted in the 1940s, and their numbers steadily increased after that.

This phase of history is remembered by many of the Indians with whom I spoke. Their impressions differ. Some are bitter because they remember with shame and anger how they worked "like slaves" for the Indian agents. One man told me that their history is the history of robbery by the karaiwa. He said he would never trust the karaiwa again. Yet, others remember the 1940s and 1950s with pride. They describe how all the administrative buildings at the Indian Post were filled with rice and corn that they had produced, and they say that the

Bakairí who now live on the reservation are "lazy" and "weak." For them, the mid-1900s was a kind of golden age when an abundance of food and goods was available to them. Life today seems much more impoverished.

Teachers and Indian Agents: The Bakairí and Government Development Policies (1958–1980)

By the mid-1950s two important events changed the world of the Bakairí. More Brazilians began to migrate to the area, establishing ranches and small farms, and the SPI abolished the use of organized indigenous labor in reservation lands. Not having to work the Indian agent's land meant the Indians had more time to work in their own gardens, and the proliferation of ranches meant opportunities to earn cash. Many Bakairí sought employment on nearby ranches so that they could earn money to buy goods such as kerosene, sugar, and cloth. Around this time, there is also evidence that the Bakairí were consuming alcoholic beverages, which rapidly became a problem in the reservation.

With the abolition of forced indigenous labor in the late 1950s, SPI replaced its Indian agent with a female schoolteacher who remained in the Bakairí reservation until 1968. Violeta acted as unofficial agent as well as teacher. Much respected by the Indians, she taught the Indians to speak, read, and write Portuguese as well as to do arithmetic. She also outlawed the consumption of alcoholic beverages in the reservation and was strict about the Indians adhering to this rule. Records of letters of complaint about various "troublemakers" are still on file at the Indian Post.

Today people are discouraged from selling alcohol to Indians in Mato Grosso. Around the reservation where Indian agents monitor behaviors, non-Indians who sell or give the Indians alcohol are immediately contacted by government officials. In 1981 the son of a nearby rancher sold liquor to some young Bakairí men. The Indian agent spoke to the young man and to his father, but when this did not have the desired effect, the agent contacted his superiors in Cuiabá. They wrote a letter to the rancher threatening him with two years in prison and a fine.

In the late 1960s, the SPI was dissolved because of allegations of corruption. It was replaced by the National Indian Foundation (FUNAI). FUNAI sent an Indian agent named Brauvin to the Bakairí reservation, and he worked for a while with Violeta before their views about policy conflicted, and she was asked to leave the reservation.

Violeta was in favor of rapidly integrating the Indians into national

Brazilian society. She encouraged them to work outside the reservation, to speak Portuguese, and to discontinue their rituals. Brauvin supported teaching Indians Portuguese but attempted to prevent the Bakairí from leaving the reservation to work on ranches. He also blocked non-Indians from entering the reservation and trading with the Indians. FUNAI was concerned, not only with the overt exploitation of peoples such as the Bakairí, but also by the growing number of indigenous men and women who were ending up in towns and cities in Mato Grosso, either ill, drunk, or as prostitutes.

Brauvin's actions confused and displeased the Indians. They perceived him as trying to frustrate their attempts to earn money, which they needed to purchase necessary goods. In 1975 a group of men attacked and ransacked the Post, burning some of the buildings. Brauvin fled in the dark. He was unharmed but did not return to the Post. In his place, FUNAI sent Idevar José Sardinha. Sardinha had two goals: one was to instill in the Indians pride for their culture, and the other was to determine a way they could earn cash without leaving the reservation. These goals must be understood within the context of wider Brazilian national economic policy as well as FUNAI's plans for indigenous lands.

In the early 1970s the economic profile of Mato Grosso shifted as Brazil adopted a *regional development* plan. In order to develop more rapidly into an economic world power, government officials divided the country into regions and identified a town or city in the center of each area in which to invest large amounts of capital made available by international banks and development agencies. Their plan was to improve infrastructural features such as roads, power, and communication lines, thus creating an environment more conducive for business and for the creation of jobs for skilled labor. The effects of these changes would ripple out from the towns into the regions around them, thus stimulating economic development.

The *Polonoroeste Project*, or the Northwestern Regional Project, was considered a priority by the Brazilian government (*Cultural Survival* 1981:11–13). It planned to spend about $1.1 billion between 1981 and 1985 mainly on the small frontier state of Rondonia, which lies directly west of Mato Grosso (see figure 2-2). Over half of the money would be spent building roads to connect Cuiabá with Porto Velho, the capital of Rondonia, as well as access roads from farms in the region to this highway. Additional funds would also be spent improving the administrative agencies that were overseeing the colonization of the area by small farmers. *Cultural Survival* adds that one of the unstated purposes of the project appeared to be ". . . to bring a chaotic, often violent, frontier situation under the control of the government" (1981:12).

The regional development model worked in that although Rondonia

Figure 2-2: Rondonia and Mato Grosso in Relation to Other Brazilian States.

was the target, the project affected Mato Grosso. The government's plans for road building, large-scale cattle ranching, and rice production indirectly supported economic growth in the entire region. Businessmen, attracted by low-cost loans from government-supported banks, created agricorporations, which bought up tracts of land. Their employment of modern agricultural techniques contrasted with the small-scale production methods used, up to that point, by the smaller establishments in the region.

FUNAI was expected to help realize the objectives of national development, and in the 1970s, it promoted the use of *industrial agriculture* (large-scale, mechanized farming) on many indigenous reservations. For example, Ricardo Santos and his colleagues (1997) describe the twenty-year history of what FUNAI called "the Integrated Development Plan for the Xavante Nation." The Xavante are an indigenous group who live on several reservations in Mato Grosso. Beginning as early as 1974, FUNAI initiated a series of rice-production projects on their lands.

Government agencies supported such initiatives because they wanted indigenous reservations to be self-sufficient, and they wanted the Indians to make—what officials considered to be—modern and efficient use of their resources. Consistent with the model that was being implemented all over the country, FUNAI planned for large capital investments in technology to produce crops targeted for sale in urban markets. The cash proceeds from these sales would allow Indians to purchase consumer goods.

In 1977 Sardinha and a number of Bakairí leaders developed a proposal for a modest low-technology project that would result in the production of *rapadura*, which are hard squares of raw brown sugar made from sugar cane, and of rice, raised by traditional slash-and-burn methods in about 10 hectares of gallery forests along the rivers. The stated objectives in the proposal included improving the food supply for the reservation and minimizing the Indians' dependency on "society" (FUNAI 1977:1). Sardinha estimated the cost of the project to be 98,000 cruzeiros or about $33,000.

However, this proposal was not accepted by FUNAI, and in early 1980, after Sardinha was replaced by another Indian agent named Lirvasir, a second, more ambitious, proposal was formulated and approved. This project cost five times as much as the original one, and involved the production of rice, corn, and beans. Rice production alone would involve 50 hectares of land, and it would occur in the *cerrado* (prairie) part of the reservation, rather than in the more limited gallery-forest lands. In addition to crops, the project involved increasing the community's herd of cattle and learning how to manage it better.

FUNAI released funds for the purchase of agricultural equipment and supplies, and in 1980 the first tractor arrived in the reservation. The transition between Sardinha and Lirvasir did not prevent the project from going forward on schedule. Bakairí men who had experience running tractors on nearby ranches took responsibility for getting things underway, and in late 1980 they cleared and planted rice in 50 hectares of cerrado. The rice project alone is a fascinating phase in the history of these Indians. We will return to it in chapter 4 so that we can discuss in more detail how it worked out.

The Bakairí Divide Again:
Pakuera Fissions in the 1980s (1980–1990)

By the late 1970s and early 1980s, the Bakairí Indians found themselves in the middle of a rapidly growing region in the interior of
Brazil. Significant numbers of people moved to Mato Grosso
attracted by the opportunities provided either directly or indirectly by
the regional development process. Simultaneously other people were
pushed west from areas of Brazil that similar government development efforts affected in unexpected ways.

For example, government-supported projects in the state of Amazo-
nas initially made funds available for small-farm colonization. However, at the end of the 1970s, the government switched its policy to
favor corporations involved in such activities as large-scale cattle
ranching. Because of this change, many small-scale farmers were
forced off their lands either because they lacked clear legal title or
because they could not compete with larger enterprises. Wage-earning
workers were also deprived of their jobs during this period. They were
displaced by more skilled workers who moved from southern Brazil
in hopes of taking advantage of some of the development-related
opportunities in the northeast (Schmink, 1986; Lisansky, 1990).

Many of these disenfranchised people made their way to Mato
Grosso. The need to designate new administrative units provides evidence of this massive population shift. In 1978 the state of Mato
Grosso divided into Mato Grosso and Mato Grosso do Sul, and in
1979 the municipality of Chapadas dos Guimarães, where the Bakairí
reservation was located, partitioned. The Indians found themselves in
the new district of Paranatinga. By 1999 yet another administrative
unit was formed because of population growth in the region, and the
Bakairí reservation ended up straddling two municipalities.

By 1979, the reservation was surrounded by ranches, agribusinesses, and *posseiros*, which are landless farmers. The Indians became
concerned about the distant borders of their lands, having heard that
posseiros invaded other indigenous territories in search of land to
farm. In the 1980s, Pakuera, which the Bakairí had inhabited since the
1930s, broke apart. The Indians formed seven small villages that were
scattered all over the reservation (see table 2-1 and figure 2-3.)

A set of complex demographic, political, and ecological factors
account for this (Picchi 1995). However, one obvious outcome was
that the Bakairí gained tighter control over their lands. Looking at figure 2-3, the distance between the two villages located farthest from
each other—the village of Paixola in the west and Kaiahoualo in the
east—is estimated to be about 35 kilometers, nearly the width of the
entire reservation. These "outposts" were responsible for securing

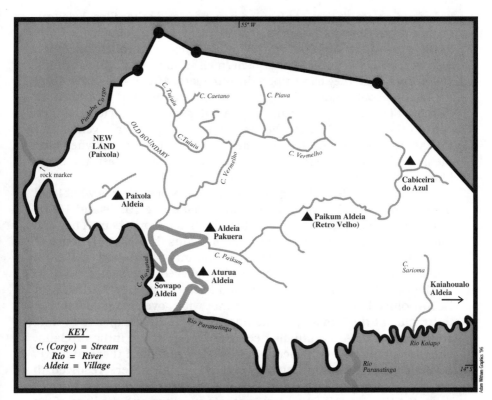

Figure 2-3: Bakairí Villages in Reservation.

borders that are distant from the heart of the reservation where
Pakuera, Aturua, and Sowapo are located.

The relocation of Bakairí villages at strategic points throughout the
reservation facilitated the Indians'
defense of their lands and resources.
However, in spite of this defensive
move, an alarming thirty-seven non-
Indians lived illegally in the reservation by 1990. The Bakairí leaders I
interviewed about the situation were
convinced the non-Indians posed no
real danger since watchful villagers
lived nearby, but I thought there was
cause for concern.

The growing awareness of the tension between themselves and non-
Indians in the region led to a more
aggressive posture on the part of the

Table 2-1: 1989 Bakairí Villages and Their Inhabitants	
VILLAGE	**INHABITANTS**
Pakuera	171
Aturua	87
Sowapo	54
Kaiahoualo	39
Paixola	37
Paikum	28
Cabiceira do Azul	15
Total	**431***

*394 Indians and 37 non-Indians.

Indians. As a result they confronted poachers and other illegal visitors several times during the 1980s. One incident was ongoing while I was in the reservation in 1989. In July of that year, several Bakairí men discovered nets of professional fishermen in the Paranatinga waters. Following a trail, they came upon the intruders. After some discussion, the Indians confiscated their two boats and motors and took them to Pakuera. The fishermen went to Paranatinga and re-ported the incident to the police. IBAMA, the Brazilian environmental agency, and FUNAI attempted to resolve the conflict, but, up to the point when I left the field, the Bakairí remained firm in their resolve to keep the boats hidden in the reservation as a "lesson" to the fishermen.

Another example of their growing awareness of danger is what I call the Paixola case. The Bakairí contended that in the 1950s and 1960s a section of their reservation was illegally taken from them. They call this area Paixola after a small stream that runs through it. It consists of about 9,000 hectares, a significant amount of land, and in 1980 it was occupied by Brazilian farmers who believed they owned it.

The Bakairí resolved to get the land back. First, they worked with FUNAI officials in Cuiabá, but later met with government personnel in Brasilia at the Ministry of the Interior, at no little expense in time and money. FUNAI eventually decided to support the Indians' claim, but they still had to convince the Brazilians who lived there to move. Some went peacefully when asked to leave, but others resolved to remain. One night a group of Bakairí went to Paixola and burned down the Brazilians' farms, risking their own lives and the lives of the Brazilians. After Paixola was made secure, about forty Bakairí moved there and founded a village.

Summary

Clearly the Bakairí Indians are not an example of "the untouched primitive." In fact one would be hard-pressed to find such an individual in Brazil today. Rather they are a people with a documented history that reaches back at least into the 1700s.

Today they share a kind of cultural adaptation with many other Indian groups such as those indigenous peoples who continue to live in the headwaters of the Xingú River and on other designated reservations throughout Brazil. There are similarities between how they and other Indians in Brazil make a living, organize their social relations, and view the supernatural.

But there are significant differences too. Although the Bakairí resemble other Indian groups found in the lowlands of South America, they are unique in many ways. That is, in part, because of their particular history, which is made up of events and processes that distinctively mark these Indians. Many of these are political in nature. For example, the Northwestern Regional Project, which was part of a larger, macrolevel development scheme, invested huge amounts of money at the western part of Brazil. The economic, political, and ecological vibrations of these funds are still being felt both in the Indians' reservation and the surrounding region.

The way in which the Bakairí managed such situations affects their identity and their future. Their efforts to manipulate situations, to claim them for themselves as opportunities, and even to go beyond original plans for change are notable. The way in which they took over the mechanized agriculture project during a transition period between two FUNAI agents' administrations and their struggles to get back the Paixola part of their reservation are just two examples of such behaviors.

Chapter 3

BAKAIRÍ HOUSEHOLDS, FERTILITY, AND MORTALITY

"Regardless of one's view about the culture-biology connection, all anthropologists must recognize that a society's demographic parameters have important implications. Even the most symbolically oriented of anthropologists, should have some interest in demographic information."

(Hill and Hurtado 1996:7)

Anthropological demography is the science of vital statistics of a population's births, deaths, marriages, and so forth. It includes using these data to address problems such as reproductive and health issues and their implications on population growth rates. Anthropologists frequently avoid gathering such information on indigenous tribal peoples because their numbers are small. Conclusions drawn from these data are limited when compared with those from studies done on larger national societies. Yet identifying demographic characteristics of smaller groups uncovers trends affecting how they live and die as well as their long-term prospects for survival.

Indigenous South American people pose a special challenge for those interested in demographic research. Following contact with Europeans in the sixteenth century, some groups were decimated and became extinct. Others now teeter on the brink of extinction as their numbers plummet below what is necessary for cultural transmission.

Still others survived enslavement and epidemics and are rapidly increasing. They confront new obstacles to their survival in the form of economic and political pressures, many of which are associated with modernization and development.

Although it is difficult to specify a single, typical level of fertility for small societies that are in contact situations, cross-cultural studies suggest that women have between four to eight children with an average of six (Campbell and Wood 1988:45). Societies with fertility rates higher than eight tend to be those that are rapidly expanding into new territories. It is believed that such groups abandon or alter *fertility inhibiting practices* that, up to a point, have kept their population growth rates at low or moderate levels.

Fertility-inhibiting practices are among those factors responsible for limiting the size of a group. Some examples of these practices include the age at which people marry, the existence of taboos on sex after the birth of a child, and the preference for breast-feeding over bottle feeding (Romaniuk 1981). Recently researchers have taken a fresh look at the impact on fertility of sexually transmitted diseases (STDs) (Harpending 1994; Hill and Hurtado 1996). Certainly Brazilian Indians were exposed to syphilis and gonorrhea early in their contact history. Chlamydia now poses a new threat to them.

The Bakairí endured a grueling period of contact with non-Indians that reduced their population to dangerously low levels. But they did not become extinct. Rather, their numbers are increasing, and the rate at which this is occurring within the small reservation on which they live was a key part of my project. Thus I needed to give careful attention to questions about children and reproduction in general. In the course of my research I worked with concepts demographers frequently use, such as fertility rates, family size, and population increase rates.

In the pages that follow I set the stage for this discussion by briefly describing settlement and household composition. I then go on to examine fertility and reproduction patterns, mortality and causes of death, and population levels. I also make some observations about the presence or absence of specific fertility-inhibiting practices.

Some Methodological Points

One of the first tasks I set myself after arriving at Pakuera was doing a census in which I determined the sex and age of the people who lived in each house. I ascertained the ages of the Bakairí in several ways. I asked how old they were, and although many claimed to know their birthdays, some did not. In either case, I verified the information by checking with another adult or with the elderly Bakairí medic, who knew a great deal about the people in the reservation. I also examined the official records kept by the FUNAI agents, and although they provided some leads, I found them to be incomplete.

Each time I returned to the field I talked to my key informants about how everyone was. Births, deaths, and illnesses are natural topics of conversation in any community, and I suspect they would have thought I was strange if I had not been interested in such questions. I had little trouble getting people to talk about what they knew.

However, as I mentioned in chapter 1, some kinds of fertility data are notoriously difficult to collect. With Brazilian Indians, problems are compounded by fears that FUNAI will punish them for behaviors field agents officially discourage. For these reasons, the fertility data presented in this chapter were collected in three ways, which, when used together, allowed for self-correction and verification.

First, I interviewed the individual women in the village alone. In order to help them pinpoint time of pregnancies and deaths of children, I asked them how old the child would be if it had lived. For example, would the child be as old as Maisa, who was three, or as old as Maiare, who was twenty. This method had good results because women apparently lumped the children in the village into groups based on proximity of age.

The second method of data collection was to interview the old women in the village in order to verify the results of the individual interviews. They reviewed the materials, making corrections and offering suggestions. These older women often remembered pregnancies and deaths that the younger women did not mention. I questioned the young women again, and they sometimes remembered, but if they did not, I threw the case out. The third method used was to consult FUNAI death-birth records. As already mentioned, these records were incomplete, but often included entries that I discussed with members of the community.

Although I constantly had the feeling that I was pursuing one last elusive birth or death that had happened years ago, the data accumulated month by month until they began to point to some interesting demographic trends in the reservation.

Village and Household Composition

In 1980 approximately 288 Indians inhabited the Bakairí reservation, where they lived in the village of Pakuera. By 1989 this community had divided and there were six additional villages in the reservation. Although the general Bakairí population numbered about 395, only 170 Indians inhabited the original settlement. But by 1999, its size had increased once again, and nearly 300 Indians lived in Pakuera alone. About 500 lived in the reservation.

Village Composition

Pakuera's general layout is clear from figure 3-1. Two main sections make up the village. The FUNAI administrative center lies in the southeastern corner. A school, storage building, house for the Indian agent, and infirmary are located there. Over the years, this area has been referred to as the P.I. Simões Lopes, P.I. Bakairí, and most recently P.I. Pakuera.

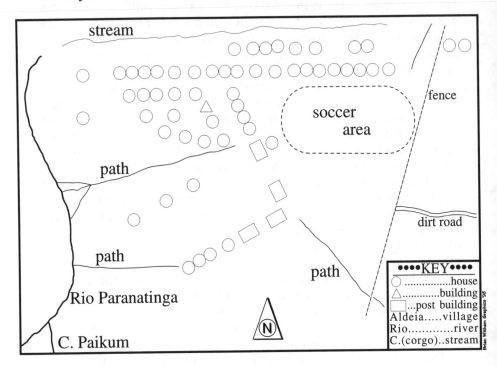

Figure 3-1: Aldeia Pakuera

The Bakairí Indians, supervised by SPI officials, constructed the administrative buildings between 1940 and 1947. The structures have cement walls with tile or tin roofs. A large elevated water tank stands outside of the infirmary. It is no longer used, but in the 1950s when measles and tuberculosis epidemics took place, and the infirmary was full of sick people, the tank was an important source of clean water.

Today the infirmary is underutilized. The Bakairí medic uses one room for a clinic, which is opened for two hours each morning and evening, and the FUNAI agent has turned another room into an office. The rest of the building is empty except for bats and other pests.

The schoolhouse is large, with a room for students and living quar-

Bakairí medic in the foreground with his medical supplies arranged behind him.

ters for a schoolteacher and his or her family. Since the 1980s, Bakairí Indians, who live in the village, have been hired as teachers. The schoolhouse living quarters are now used for storage. The FUNAI agent's house has suffered a similar fate in that when Bakairí individuals began to assume leadership roles in FUNAI, they opted to live in the village, leaving the FUNAI building empty.

The administrative area tends to be empty and quiet, and the rest of the village is lively and busy compared to it. During the dry season, people participate in many activities, such as ritual dancing, visiting, and going to the gardens or river. Even during the rainy season when people stay indoors more often, groups congregate to talk or to work on projects such as hammock weaving.

Housing

There are about sixty households in the main village, and the number is steadily increasing. Most of the Bakairí construct their houses by spreading clay over interwoven sticks. Roofs are made of buriti palm. Over the past twenty years, more people are making houses from cement with tin roofs. One reason for this is that materials such as buriti palm are becoming scarce in the reservation. Another reason is

Bakairí school teacher with Bakairí children clustered around him.

that the Bakairí are under pressure to assume the technology and traditions of the Brazilians who surround their reservation. Some submit to this pressure in spite of the fact that materials like tin are not improvements over what they used before. Tin roofs are extremely noisy when it rains, and they make it very hot in the house when the sun shines. Palm roofs, on the other hand, are quiet in the rain, cool in the heat, and fragrant all the time.

Bakairí houses have a minimum of two internal divisions, two windows that can be shuttered, and two doors. Larger houses have three internal areas. Kitchens are located inside the house or in a separate structure that is constructed at the back of the house. The Bakairí cook over the fire or on a cooking platform made from rocks. They prefer to either roast food directly on the fire, as in the case of fish, or cook it in pots, as in the case of rice or soup. Food is prepared on the dirt floors or on makeshift tables.

The Bakairí use little furniture. They sleep in hammocks woven from cotton they cultivate in their fields. During the day they throw these hammocks above the rafters to make more room. Some families have makeshift shelves leaning against a wall. However, most people just tie a string from one wall to another and hang their belongings on it. In front of each house there is a bench where people sit during the hottest part of the day or during the evening hours when visiting occurs. Some of these wooden benches are beautifully carved in the shape of a turtle or armadillo. Others are planks nailed or tied together. Many couples who have children throw pieces of dried animal hide on the ground on which the youngsters play.

The women clean the houses every morning after the men have eaten and gone to the men's house to plan their day's activities. They use palm brushes to sweep out the trash that has accumulated in the house and to uncover a fresh layer of dirt. After sweeping, they sprinkled water on the ground to settle the dust. Rubbish is burned in back of the house or simply swept into the brush that borders the back area.

Household Composition

Bakairí households are small. The majority of them consist of between three and six individuals, with a *median* of four. The median is computed by arranging all the household sizes in order from smallest to largest. The size that lies at the midpoint of the ordered list, with the same number of larger sizes above and smaller below, is the median (see table 3-1). The *mean*, which is the arithmetic average, is five people. A married couple constitutes the core of each household. The couple's children, grandchildren if they have any, and parents make up the rest of the group.

Of the total fifty-nine Bakairí households, forty-seven (80 percent) are made up of a single married core couple, six (10 percent) consist of two married couples living on the premises, and six (10 percent) are composed of a widow or widower. In the six cases where two married couples live together in one house, two of them considered the situation to be temporary. In both instances, the daughters of the core couple recently married and were waiting to give birth to their first children before moving into their own homes. In the other four cases, aging parental couples lived with middle-aged daughters and their husbands.

Table 3-1: Bakairí Household Composition by Number of People			
NUMBER OF PEOPLE IN HOUSEHOLD	**NUMBER OF HOUSEHOLDS**	**HOUSEHOLD %**	**HOUSEHOLD CUMULATIVE %**
1	1	1.7	(1.7)
2	1	1.7	(3.4)
3	12	20.3	(23.7)
4	15	25.4	(49.1)
5	9	15.3	(64.4)
6	14	23.7	(88.1)
7	2	3.4	(91.5)
8	2	3.4	(94.9)
9	1	1.7	(96.6)
10	1	1.7	(98.3)
11	1	1.7	(100.0)
Total	59	100.0	(100.0)

Power and Water

In late 1998 and early 1999, workers from a Mato Grosso electric company began to set up generators in Pakuera and to run lines in the houses. The governor of the state had committed himself to providing electricity to the more remote ranches and villages in the region. Sockets for lightbulbs dangled from the rafters below the palm roofs in many homes, and satellite dishes loomed outside a couple of houses. The possibility of having electricity was very exciting to the Bakairí.

At this point, many questions remain unanswered. For example, who will pay for the electricity? Will the electric company wire only Pakuera for power? What kinds of appliances will the Indians choose to purchase? How many will they use, and how many will gather dust on shelves? The satellite dishes mean that at least some Indians will purchase televisions. They plan at this point to watch soccer games, but what else will they view? How will television programs impact on their culture? The documentation of the effects of electricity on their

One of the main water sources of Pakuera is a well built in the 1940s by government officials.

way of life promises to be an interesting project.

In 1976 FUNAI encouraged the Indians to build some latrines around their houses. Some Bakairí use them, but many do not, preferring to go into the woods around their homes. They complain that the latrines have attracted large numbers of mosquitoes to the village, and they are afraid that these insects will bring malaria to the region.

The Bakairí have three main water supplies. Of the three, the Paranatinga River, located 800 meters from the village, is the most popular. Although it lies a distance from the village, most people prefer to use it, probably because they socialize when they go there. The Indians descend to the banks of the Paranatinga at least three times a day in order to bathe, wash clothes, and collect water, which they carry back up the riverbanks in large kerosene tins.

A second source of water is the two wells that were dug by the SPI in the 1940s. One of these does not produce water during the dry season, but the other can be used throughout the year, although it gets muddy. A third and new source is the plastic pipes that carry water from the wells to community spigots along the village lanes. It remains to be seen in what ways the Indians will incorporate this new technology into their routines.

Sex, Menstruation, and Marriage

Sexual relations in South American indigenous communities tend to be casual and open. Thomas Gregor (1985) discovered the Mehinaku Indians to be frank about their relations, and children even ticked off the names of their parents' extramarital lovers for him. He once calculated that in a group of thirty-seven adults, eighty-eight extramarital affairs were being conducted at one time (1985:15, 35).

William and Jean Crocker (1994) discovered in their work with the Canela Indians that one's body should be shared with others. Girls begin having sexual relations between the ages of ten and thirteen before they start having their periods. Even after girls marry, they are expected to be generous with their sexual favors, sometimes with sequential partners. And if not, they can be "taught to be generous" by punitive methods. Men are also expected not to be "stingy" with their bodies unless they are sick, and if desirous women ask them for sex and they refuse, they must do so with appropriate apologies (Crocker and Crocker 1994:33–34, 156–157).

Typically the Bakairí are quite active sexually. They become sexual early in life and remain active as long as possible. Adolescence is a period of experimentation, and both males and females are allowed to have a number of different sexual partners. Intercourse takes place in the gardens or the forest, or in the girl's hammock. If it occurs in the girl's house, it takes place secretly and rapidly so that no one will discover the couple.

Sometimes relationships take place between unmarried adolescents and older married individuals. These tend to be temporary situations, but from time to time a married person divorces his or her spouse and marries the younger person. This is extremely disruptive to village life and does not take place frequently. For example, in the case of Odi, an older married man, and Innoc, a young single woman, they eloped to his garden after an affair and waited until family members signaled them it was all right to return to Pakuera. However, the situation between Odi and his ex-wife's family remained tense, and the couple eventually moved to a different village.

Affairs can last for a week or several months, and they can end in marriage or termination. Reasons for ending a relationship include parental objection, jealousy on the part of the male or female, and incompatibility.

After marriage, individuals are expected to be more discreet about their activities, but they continue to have sexual relations with people other than their spouses. Although mates will react jealously if infidelity is made obvious to them, they turn a blind eye to it if a modicum of tact is observed.

Menstruation

The average age at which menstruation begins is about twelve years of age, and a mother announces this event to the village by running from house to house calling out the news. She and other older women then rub a bitter herbal solution on the girl's body and pass a scraper made of fish teeth over her skin until it draws blood, after which they apply fragrant oil from the piquí plant. The girl remains secluded at home, lying in her hammock for between a week and a month. Afterward she takes a ritual bath and resumes her normal routine.

During both her first period and subsequent ones, a woman must observe certain food taboos. She and her husband, if she has one, are forbidden from eating fish. It is believed that if she breaks this taboo, her body will swell up and look ugly. She is allowed to eat only rice and manioc, and perhaps a little chicken if it is available. Sex is also forbidden. If a couple have intercourse during menstruation, the man's health and ability to fish will suffer.

The average age of first menstruation varies widely from society to society. For example, the women of the Gainj tribe in New Guinea begin to menstruate at the mean age of 20.9 years (Johnson 1990), while Western girls commence at the average age of 13 years (Diggory et al. 1988). If we compare the Bakairí to such groups, we must conclude that menstruation begins at a relatively early age for them. How do we account for this?

Nutrition plays a key role in determining the age at which menstruation begins. Evidence suggests that body weight and fat depositions are important factors in causing its onset. It is thought that the greater the proportion of fat relative to muscle in the body, the earlier menstruation begins. This is because the availability of energy, in the form of fat in this case, affects reproductive hormone levels, in particular those that initiate puberty (Frisch 1984; Hopwood et al. 1990; Hill and Hurtado 1996).

This hypothesis has been supported by data from studies on hunter-gatherers who give up their traditional way of life and join sedentary communities (Bari-Kolata 1974; Hill and Hurtado 1996). One of the effects of this transition is that girls begin to menstruate earlier. Two key changes in their lifestyles are responsible for this change. The first is exercise. Hunter-gatherers are nomadic, and they normally walk and carry more weight than most sedentary agricultural peoples. This contributes to the formation of muscle in women's bodies and reduces fat levels.

Another factor concerns their high protein–low carbohydrate/fat diet. Hunter-gatherers consume a lot of meat and vegetable protein such as nuts. This also mitigates against the accumulation of fat in their bodies. When these people move into sedentary communities, their diets change to include greater percentages of carbohydrates such as rice, potatoes, and manioc. Consequently, fat ratios increase while muscle ratios drop. Together, the exercise and dietary alterations lead to menstruation beginning at an earlier age.

This line of reasoning suggests that the relatively early average age at which Bakairí girls begin to menstruate may be connected to diet and weight, and my research findings support this supposition. The Bakairí consume a high-carbohydrate diet. About 87 percent of their diet consists of carbohydrates (Picchi 1982:307). A study of their heights and weights showed that adolescents are generally robust and healthy. About 10 percent of adolescent females between the age of twelve and nineteen weighed at least the standard weight-for-height, while 90 percent weighed above the standard weight-for-height, and none weighed less than the standard (Picchi 1982:157).

Although Bakairí women get some exercise on a daily basis when they go to the river and gardens, a time-allocation study I did indicated that they are not a physically stressed people. Over 50 percent of their time was spent in "nonwork" activities that included eating, hygiene, conversation, idleness, visiting, recreation, and ritual activities (Picchi 1982:231).

Marriage as It Affects Demography

Although having a series of affairs appears to be a natural part of a young person's development, the Bakairí believe that getting married and having children are very important. I will discuss marriage traditions in greater detail in chapter 5, but it is important to provide at this point some salient facts about the age of marriage and number of marriage partners.

Marriage takes place in mid- to late teens. Forty years ago it was not unusual for a thirteen-year-old girl to be married, but now women wait until later. The average age of marriage for a female is about sixteen years. Men are encouraged to wait until they are fifteen years old, the age at which it is believed they can care for their own gardens and support a family in a responsible manner.

How does the average age of marriage among the Bakairí compare to other, similar, cultures? In a study of preindustrial societies, the mean age of first marriage was determined to be between sixteen and eighteen years of age (Coale 1986:8). The Bakairí fall into this range.

Families play a critical role in the choice of marriage partner. In fact sometimes the parents of a couple meet and decide on the future of the two without them knowing about it. In the case of Joel and Maria, their two widowed mothers arranged for their marriage after they had been having sex for only three days.

Of the ninety-nine menstruating or postmenopausal women in the village, sixty women (61 percent) are married, and twenty-nine (29 percent) are women who have not yet married (see table 3-2). Of the remaining 10 percent, three (3 percent) are divorced and living with their parents, seven (7 percent) are widows.

Table 3-2: Marriage of Bakairí Women		
TYPE	N	%
Married women	60	61
Divorced—remarried 1 (1%)		
Widowed—remarried 5 (5%)		
Married once 54 (55%)		
Unremarried widows	7	7
Unremarried divorcees	3	3
Single, never-married women	29	29
Total	99	100

Of the twenty-nine women who have not yet married, twenty-two (75.9 percent) of them are fifteen years or older, which is about the average age for a woman to marry (see table 3-3). Of the twenty-seven young men, twenty-one (77.7 percent) are fifteen years or older, the minimal age for them to marry. Clearly the number of young men and women is nearly evenly matched. Among the Bakairí we do not see large imbalances between the numbers of men and women as we do among groups such as the Yanomamö (Chagnon 1992).

However, I asked informants what happens when there are not enough marriage partners to go around. They replied that a young person could marry a Bakairí from another reservation or a non-Indian. However, both of these options were considered unattractive

Table 3-3: Bakairí Men and Women of Marriageable Age					
	WOMEN			MEN	
AGE	N	%	CUM. %	N	%	CUM. %
12–14	7	24.1	(24.1)	6	22.3	(22.3)
15–17	7	24.1	(48.2)	7	25.9	(48.2)
18–20	7	24.1	(72.3)	7	25.9	(74.1)
21–23	4	13.9	(86.2)	2	7.4	(81.5)
24–26	2	6.9	(93.1)	3	11.1	(92.6)
27 +	2	6.9	(100.0)	2	7.4	(100.0)
Total	29	100	(100.0)	27	100.0	(100.0)

because they might involve the individual leaving his or her home and going to live with strangers.

The age of marriage affects fertility rates. Late marriages have been correlated with low fertility rates in preindustrial Europe (Smith 1988) and in traditional societies in New Guinea (Johnson 1990). However, we might ask how the age of marriage affects fertility when young men and women are sexual from an early age. In these cases, would not unmarried and married women be equally likely to become pregnant? This does not seem to be the case with many indigenous peoples. For example, Canela Indian women between the ages of thirteen and eighteen are generally childless although sexually active (Greene and Crocker 1994:55). Some researchers speculate that this is because young women are traditionally encouraged to have sex with older men who tend to impregnate them less frequently (Crocker and Crocker 1994:34).

Another reason that sexually active indigenous women might not get pregnant until marriage is that episodes of sexual intercourse before marriage are sporadic and infrequent in comparison with marital partners who are regularly available. Instead of having to escape to the gardens or plan for times the girl would be alone in the house, married couples have intercourse at will and sometimes more than once a night. This increases the chances of conception occurring.

A final biological note that might explain why Bakairí women are sexual but childless for the early part of their teens is that early menstrual cycles are sometimes irregular and without ovulation. Many young women experience several years of such cycles, and during this time they are less likely to become pregnant. Certainly this seems to be the case with the Ache Indians. Kim Hill and A. Magdalena Hurtado discovered that young women in this society experienced a period of "adolescent subfecundity" when their cycles were erratic (Hill and Hurtado 1996:307). Similarly Bakairí girls are sexually active but unmarried in their early teens when their cycles might typically be irregular. And the point at which they marry and get pregnant in their late teens corresponds to when we would expect their menstruation cycles to regularize.

Fertility

I looked at fertility in three different ways. First I determined the *crude birth rate* by counting the number of babies born in the village in a year per thousand. Then I determined the *age-specific fertility rate*, which is the reproductive rate of women in specific age groups during the previous year. From it I calculated the *total fertility rate (TFR)*, which is the number of children women typically have in their lifetime, based on projections from last year's data. Last, I interviewed women about their reproductive histories. My goal was to get a sense of how many children women had actually had, not just last year, but during their entire lives. This is called the *lifetime fertility rate*. When I compared this rate to the total fertility rate, it gave me a sense of how things were different in the past.

The Bakairí are inordinately fond of children. If a couple cannot have children or if they have grown children and no grandchildren yet, they ask others in the village if they can raise a child of theirs. Yuka and Beri are good examples. When I first met them, they had two children of their own, and because Beri was not able to have any more, they adopted a little girl who lived down the lane from them. Ten years later, during a subsequent fieldwork session, I noticed they were raising a ten-year-old boy named Marce. When I returned in 1999, Beri and Yuka had two grandchildren by their daughter and two by their son who lived directly next door to them. These children stayed with them for extended periods of time, and Yuka told me with some pride that they preferred living with their grandparents over their parents.

Unlike some societies, the Bakairí believe that only one man impregnates a woman and fathers a child through the act of sex. This belief contrasts with some other South American Indian groups such as the Barí of Venezuela who believe in the secondary-father model. That is, any man who has sex with a woman around the time of conception or during pregnancy is considered a father and helps provide for the child. Stephen Beckerman has found that children with secondary fathers have a better chance of survival than those without (Beckerman 1996).

The Bakairí, on the other hand, subscribe to the single-father model. As soon as a woman determines that she is pregnant, she immediately stops having sex with her partner. The couple must observe this sex taboo for two to three years following the birth of the child. The Indians believe that if they do not comply, then the health of the mother and child may be affected. In fact, it is thought that the child may not learn to walk or talk.

In addition to sex taboos, Bakairí couples must observe strict food taboos until the child is born and the umbilical cord falls off. This is considered a very dangerous time for the child, and parents are typically conscientious about this responsibility. They do not eat fish, meat, chicken, banana, or any of the non-Indian foods they sometimes consume. Instead they eat manioc and drink a beverage made from manioc flour. Sometimes they are allowed a little rice.

To determine the crude birth rate during baseline research between 1979 and 1981, I counted thirteen live babies born in a twelve-month period. That is a rate of 45.1 per thousand. Ten years later, in 1989, I calculated the crude birth rate to be 30.8.

I then went on to complete two kinds of interviews so that I could calculate age-specific fertility, total fertility, and lifetime fertility. I spoke with Bakairí women, and their husbands if they wanted to be present. These conversations were sometimes painful because if children had died, the parents invariable wept or became very agitated when they talked about it. In one poignant case, the husband told me about their daughter who had been bitten by a snake down by the river. With tears streaming down his face, he described how she died despite the medic injecting her with antivenom serum.

To determine the age-specific fertility rate, I divided the seventy-five Bakairí women I interviewed who were under fifty into seven different groups (see table 3-4). I then asked each how many children they had borne during the past year, and divided that number by the number of women in the age group.

Example:

$$\frac{\text{Number of children born to women in age group}}{\text{Number of women in age group}} = \text{Age-Specific Fertility Rate}$$

$$\frac{2 \text{ (no. of children born to women age 15–19)}}{16 \text{ (no. of women in 15–19 age group)}} = .125 \text{ Fertility Rate—Age 15–19}$$

I then went on to calculate the current total fertility rate of Bakairí women which we already know is the average number of children a woman can expect to have in her lifetime. I derived this figure by adding together the seven age-specific rates and multiplying them by five, the number of years a woman is in any one age group.

Example:

(Sum of age-specific fertility rates) x (5 years in age groups) = Total Fertility Rate
(.125 + .364 + .333 + .250) = 1.072 x 5 = 5.36 children in a lifetime

Table 3-4: Age-Specific Fertility Rates and Total Fertility Rates of Bakairí Women

Age Group	N	Number of Children	Age-Specific Fertility Rate
15–19	16	2	.125
20–24	11	4	.364
25–29	15	5	.333
30–34	13	0	.000
35–39	8	2	.250
40–44	6	0	.000
45–49	6	0	.000
Total	75	13	1.072
Number of Years in Age Group			x 5
Total Fertility Rate			5.36

The results of my study indicate that Bakairí women have about five children in their lifetime. However, this estimation, based on data from the previous year, applies to the current situation in which we find these Indians. How does it compare with family size in the past? I went on to complete a second, more comprehensive, fertility interview of seventy-two (83.7 percent) of the women who had been pregnant at least once in their lifetime (see table 3-5). This time I did not focus on children born in the last year. I asked about children born at any time. The mean number of live births reported is three.

If we compare the number of live births reported in the lifetime fertility study (three children) with the current total fertility rate of women (five children), we see a discrepancy. One obvious conclusion we can draw is that Bakairí women are having more children. To better understand the implications of this, I asked how the new rates compared with those of other societies and discovered that the Bakairí's total fertility rate falls into the middle range. Hill and Hurtado (1996) determined the total fertility rate of the Ache Indians of Paraguay is eight, and the Gainj people of New Guinea have a TFR of four. I already mentioned at the beginning of this chapter that Kenneth Campbell and James Wood (1988) have pulled together some cross-

Table 3-5: The Results of Fertility Interviews of Mature Bakairí Women

Variable	N	Mean	Standard Deviation
Average Age of First Pregnancy	72	16.2	3.3
Number of Pregnancies	72	4.5	2.7
Number of Abortions	72	1.3	1.8
Number of Miscarriages	72	0.2	0.4
Number of Live Births	72	3.0	2.0
Number of Infanticides	72	0.1	0.3
Number of Dead Children	72	0.4	0.6
Number of Living Children	72	2.5	1.7

cultural data on fertility in small societies and have given a range of four to eight children for the average woman, with a mean of six.

Although most American women would not consider five or six a small number of children to have, nonetheless when we consider that the Bakairí lack the luxury of modern contraceptive technology such as condoms and birth control pills, it is amazing they do not have more. For example, rural Brazilian women I met had thirteen and fourteen children. How do indigenous women avoid repeated pregnancies?

Nursing, Abortion, and Infanticide

Lactational anovulation, or the cessation of ovulation due to nursing, has been cited as the most significant single factor affecting birth spacing and overall fertility rates (Campbell and Wood 1988). A substantial body of evidence has grown to document this phenomenon. For example, Nancy Howell's (1979) work with the !Kung showed that it is possible to have birth intervals of just over four years, even without birth control, if mothers are nursing their children for extended periods of time. The Yanomamö have birth intervals of just under three years (34.4 months) (Melancon 1982), and the Ache of just over three years (37.6 months) (Hill and Hurtado 1996). Patricia Johnson's (1990) research on the Gainj of New Guinea also supports this conclusion. She calculated that the median interval between births among this population is almost exactly three years (36.5 months).

Recent research encourages us to examine the interaction between nursing patterns and other factors such as nutrition, exercise, and overall health since they may indirectly impact on ovulation and fertility (Hill and Hurtado 1996; McNeilly 1993). However, the key premise remains unchallenged: Breast-feeding suppresses the secretion of hormones that causes ovulation, and thus prevents pregnancy from occurring.

The Bakairí nurse their children for about three years. Weaning takes place gradually, and in its final stages can involve conflict between mother and child. It is not unusual to see four-year-old children aggressively trying to nurse and being equally aggressively rebuffed by their mothers. The mean length of birth intervals between Bakairí children is about four years, which is consistent with findings in other traditional societies.

Abortion and infanticide also affect family size and, indirectly, how rapidly populations grow. Yet these are complicated topics to explore when doing field research, and data on them must be used cautiously. For example, the difference between miscarriage and abortion in an indigenous community is often obscured by how it is reported by the woman. Unlike some non-Indian societies where individuals have abortions in clinics under the supervision of doctors, Bakairí women abort in their own homes using such means as herbs and force. It is frequently only a matter of reporting as to whether the expulsion of a fetus from the uterus is brought on by natural causes, as in the case of a miscarriage, or by other means, as in the case of an abortion. In my interviews, the average number of reported abortions is 1.3 with a maximum value of 10 in several older women. During the year of my fertility study, six abortions reportedly took place in the village.

The question of infanticide is also a complicated issue. The killing of infants, usually at birth, is an ancient way of managing family size, but FUNAI actively discourages such practices so that over the years fewer Bakairí either utilize, or report utilizing, it. This vagueness is consistent with what other researchers have discovered in South American indigenous villages (Flowers 1994). The average number of reported infanticides—.1 with a maximum value of 2—may be underreported or may reflect a trend away from the use of infanticide, or both.

Another factor that affects the reporting of infanticide cases concerns the difference between *indirect infanticide* and direct infanticide (Scrimshaw 1978, 1983; Dickeman 1975). For example, infanticide may consist of strangulation, suffocation, and burying alive, while indirect infanticide is more subtle but equally deadly. It is the underinvestment in a child and takes many forms such as inadequate feeding, neglect, and even abuse. It is typically found in households where there is close birth spacing, a large number of living children, or a single parent living alone. In such situations, a child dies ostensibly of medical reasons, and the reason for death escapes being included in the infanticide category.

A final reason to be cautious about abortion and infanticide data is mathematical in nature and concerns the standard deviation values in table 3-5. Standard deviations are measures of how the averaged numbers spread out around the mean. For example, if the standard deviation is small, the numbers are similar in value. On the other hand, if the standard deviation is large, it suggests that the averaged numbers vary widely. When this occurs, we need to be more cautious about making generalizations. The standard deviations for Bakairí mean number of abortions and infanticide are relatively large compared to the mean values, suggesting that a few extreme observations may be preventing us from making inferences.

Many students ask me how to resolve the contradiction of Bakairí parental behavior. These parents are capable of loving and indulging their children, and of killing them at birth. Anthropologists differ in their views about this subject. Some like Gregor (1988) are convinced that women find the infanticide decision traumatic and that they grieve afterward. Although his Mehinaku informants claimed infanticide did not make them feel guilty, he concluded that the act was "edged with moral and emotional ambivalence" (1988:19).

Others, like Scheper-Hughes (1992), posit that women can draw on a number of protective cultural devices that prevent them from developing maternal bonds with fetuses or with infants until it is certain they will live. Such devices include the decision not to *anthropomorphize* the fetus. To anthropomorphize something is to give it human qualities when these are not in existence or readily apparent. In our society we may anthropomorphize a fetus by giving it a name, talking to it, and planning for its future.

When the fate of the fetus is unclear to a Bakairí woman, she may avoid developing emotional and psychological bonds with it, as predicted by Scheper-Hughes. After it is born, family members frequently step in to help with the final act while she rests after labor. She sees and hears very little of what happens, and there is no discussion of the event afterward. The Bakairí frequently say that is important to leave unpleasantness and sorrow behind.

However, I feel compelled to remind the reader that everything is different when an infant dies after the couple has committed themselves to caring for the child. One of the more painful events I experienced during fieldwork was the death of a boy who was only a month old. The mother was distraught, and her screams could be heard all over the village. When she finally fainted, her exhausted family laid her in her hammock and tried to bring her back to consciousness. For weeks after, she remained indoors weeping. The FUNAI agent and I were extremely worried about her emotional state, but she gradually recovered her spirits. Eventually she became pregnant again and this time her child lived.

Causes of Deaths

To understand the whole picture of how the number of Bakairí Indians has increased over time, we must determine the *crude death rate*, which is the number of deaths in a year per thousand people. During baseline research between 1979 and 1981, I calculated this rate to be 10.4, and in 1989 it was 9.5. In collecting data on 120 Bakairí deaths, I found that slightly more males, sixty-two (51.7 percent), than females, fifty-eight (48.3 percent), died, and more adults, sixty-two (51.7 percent), than children, fifty-eight (48.3 percent), passed away.

Disease causes most deaths in the Bakairí reservation, and infectious disease is more common than chronic. Most infectious diseases that occur in the Bakairí village are the result of the Indians' contact with non-Indians. Tuberculosis, whooping cough, sexually transmitted diseases, polio, smallpox, yellow fever, meningitis, diphtheria, and typhoid are only some of the Old World diseases that have decimated the people of the New World. While I was in the field, yellow fever and meningitis caused the deaths of workers on nearby ranches. The ranch foremen in both cases contacted FUNAI so that within twenty-four hours of the first deaths, a plane with vaccination equipment arrived at the Indian Post.

Of the 120 deaths I accounted for, 40 (33.3 percent) were the result of lung infections of one kind or another. Tuberculosis has always been listed as a major killer of the Bakairí, and deaths from this disease continue even today. Individuals diagnosed with this disease are periodically taken from the reservation and treated in hospitals in Cuiabá.

Sometimes the treatments are not successful due to resistance on the part of the Indians. For example, when victims are adults, spouses do not want them absent for a long time because of the economic impact on the household. Families are also reluctant to allow children to travel to the city for medical attention because the course of treatment is lengthy—usually about six months. Parents do not want their children away from home for this amount of time, and they are skeptical about whether the treatment works. Relapses frequently occur because dairy products such as milk, cheese, and eggs, required for a complete recovery, are not available in the reservation. When the parents see the relapse, they resist authorizing further treatment.

Whooping cough is another lung disease that has affected the Bakairí. It appeared in the reservation in 1960 and was responsible for the deaths of ten Indians. After the epidemic passed, the disease did not reappear, presumably, because of the vaccination program. Pneumonia is a killer of small children in the reservation, and while I was working with the Bakairí, two infants died from colds that affected their respiratory tracts and turned into what seemed to be pneumonia.

Liver and heart diseases reportedly caused the deaths of twelve (10.0 percent) persons. It is difficult to assess the accuracy of these data because symptoms of such diseases are easily confused by laymen, and no autopsies were performed.

Accidents such as burning and drowning killed eleven (9.2 percent), and violence led to the deaths of another three (2.5 percent). The number of deaths from violence over the fifty-five-year period is low. Those that occurred caused consternation in the village. For example, a policeman shot and killed a young Bakairí man in Paranatinga in the 1980s. This was considered an extraordinary event and shocked the community.

Fevers and intestinal disorders led to the deaths of another thirteen (10.8 percent). These infections affect young children more than adults. In fact diarrhea is one of the major causes of death among children in developing areas of the world. It starts as a viral or a bacterial infection and quickly leads to dehydration and then death.

Sometimes Bakairí parents try to cure their sick children in ways that contribute to dehydration. They bundle up the sick in blankets and place them in hammocks over smoldering fires, believing that the heat drives out the spirits that cause the sickness. However, if the illness does not pass rapidly, this folk treatment could actually harm the patient.

Strokes and cancer were responsible for the deaths of six (5 percent). It is interesting to note that as medical attention in reservations improves, cancer is being diagnosed and treated more frequently. For example, there is no record of any cases of cancer prior to 1980. Since that time medics have diagnosed cases of skin cancer and uterine cancer.

Only one recorded measles epidemic occurred in the Bakairí reservation. It took place in 1962, directly after the whooping cough epidemic. Two people died. Since measles usually kills large numbers of indigenous peoples when it first enters their population, it is probable that the Bakairí were previously exposed to the disease.

The Brazilian Indian organizations, SPI and FUNAI, have generally done a good job with small budgets in providing health care for peoples such as the Bakairí. There is a clinic manned by a Bakairí attendant who has some first-aid training, and in the past a two-way radio summoned a small plane when there were life-threatening circumstances. At this time, budgetary constraints unfortunately preclude this service, but if an Indian manages to travel to Cuiabá, FUNAI will provide a medical doctor. Another area that has been quite effective is the vaccination program. The Bakairí are protected against many diseases that could seriously affect the health of their children.

Dentistry and optometry are two areas that need attention. Although more Bakairí are having their eyes tested and being provided with glasses, dentists still recommend that even young people have their teeth pulled out and use dentures. This is standard operating procedure in rural areas where there are no dentists regularly available. In this way they prevent the occurrence of an infected tooth or an abscess that not could not only cause agony but might result in life-threatening blood poisoning.

Population Trends

Table 3-6 and figure 3-2 show that the Bakairí population has steadily increased over the past forty-five years, except for periods in the mid-sixties and early seventies. Although the dip in the 1960s may be the result of the last of the disease epidemics, I cannot account for the decrease in population between 1971 and 1972 in this way. Neither

Table 3-6: Bakairí Population 1954–1999*					
YEAR	POPULATION	YEAR	POPULATION	YEAR	POPULATION
1954	145	1970	215	1977	233
1959	191	1971	220	1978	248
1965	177	1972	207	1980	279
1967	190	1973	224	1981	287
1968	192	1974	227	1989	394
1969	202	1975	232	1999	502
		1976	234		

*Information is from P.I. Pakuera records and from research census notes.

death records nor interviews with older Indians uncovered any significant health problems in the reservation. An alternative possible explanation is out-migration. Individuals may have left the reservation to work at that time.

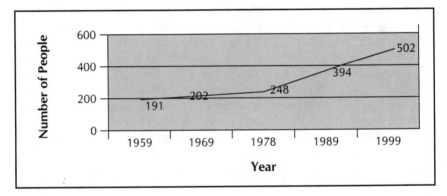

Figure 3-2: Bakairí Population Increase between 1954 and 1999.

If we look at the percentage-increase column in table 3-7, we see that the increments of population-growth rates have shot up dramatically since 1959. Although they are quite high, there have been fluctuations in the numbers over the decades. For example, note that the 1990s' percentage increase is smaller than the 1980s' percentage increase.

The comparison of 1980 and 1989 *rates of natural increase* and *population doubling times* reveals similar fluctuations. The rate of natural increase is the death rate per thousand inhabitants subtracted from the birth rate per thousand inhabitants. It is reported in percentages.

Table 3-7: Ten-Year Percentage Increases of the Bakairí Population 1959–1999 °			
YEAR	POPULATION	NUMBER INCREASE	PERCENTAGE INCREASE
1959	191	—	—
1969	202	11	5.8
1979	264	62	30.7
1989	394	130	49.2
1999	502	108	27.4

Example:

Birth rate per thousand inhabitants	45.1
– Death rate per thousand inhabitants	– 10.4
Difference/10	34.7/10
Rate of Natural Increase	3.47 percent

The doubling time of a population is calculated from the natural increase rate. It is an estimation of how many years it will take the number of people to double in size. Population doubling times are considered to be theoretical predictions because it is impossible to foresee all of the factors that might affect size. For example, how could we anticipate beforehand the huge number of casualties from World War II or the appearance of HIV?

In 1980 the Bakairí birthrate was estimated to be 45.1 and the death rate 10.4. Therefore, the rate of natural increase was calculated to be 3.47 percent per year with a doubling time of twenty years. But in 1989 the birthrate dropped to about 30.8, and the death rate decreased to 9.5 with a rate of natural increase of 2.1 percent and a doubling time of thirty-four years.

Two possible explanations for these variations include out-migration and amplification effects. As we will see in subsequent chapters, more Bakairí are leaving the reservation either temporarily or permanently to work and live in cities such as Cuiabá. Amplification effects are those variations in any system that are heightened when the system is small. That is, because the Bakairí Indians are a relatively small group, the effects of any event, such as disease, economic depression in the region, drought, and so forth, would be exaggerated. Either of these explanations, or the two together, may explain recent population oscillations.

Table 3-8 compares the two doubling times and illustrates what this might mean to the future of the Bakairí Indians. Note that in about 2020 the population of the reservation could be about 790 (if the doubling time is thirty-four years) or about 1150 (if the doubling time is twenty years). Of course the discrepancies between the two population levels grow greater as time passes. In either case, unless

Table 3-8: Comparison of Population Levels With 20-Year and 34-Year Doubling Times					
YEAR	20-YEAR DOUBLING TIME	POPULATION	YEAR	34-YEAR DOUBLING TIME	POPULATION
1980	0	288	1989	0	394
2000	20 (once)	576	2023	34 (once)	788
2020	40 (twice)	1152	2057	68 (twice)	1576
2040	60 (3 times)	2304	2091	102 (3 times)	3152
2060	80 (4 times)	4608	2125	136 (4 times)	6304

something happens to affect these rates radically, children who were born the last time I was in the reservation, in 1999, will certainly experience a dramatically different reservation life than their grandparents did.

As part of my original research, I attempted to understand whether or not the meager resources on the Bakairí reservation could support their burgeoning population (Picchi 1982:361–420). I developed a computer model that accommodated various population doubling times and different types of food production systems. While being aware that events change circumstances in ways we can never anticipate, I made some theoretical predictions about the fate of the Bakairí. I suggested that if they continued to depend upon only traditional methods of raising crops, then their population would never increase beyond four thousand. If they adopted a mechanized agricultural production system, then more people could survive on the reservation, although other factors might severely affect their quality of life and environment.

Hill and Hurtado (1996) approached the effects of population increases on the Ache Indians from a different point of view. There are 750 Ache living on reservations in Paraguay. Hill and Hurtado estimate that they have a twenty-three-year population doubling time and that by the time today's children reach old age, there will be about five thousand of them. Their predictions alarmed these researchers, and they warned that available land and resources could not support such numbers (1996:258, 477).

They cited James Wood and Peter Smouse (1982), who developed a model for detecting and describing the effects of high population density on mortality rates of small children among the Gainj of New Guinea. Wood and Smouse showed that when populations increase beyond a certain level, the response may not be what is expected. For example, one might anticipate fertility rates to decrease or adult mortality rates to increase. This does not happen. Rather juvenile mortality rates increase. That is, children die.

Hill and Hurtado are afraid that Ache infant and juvenile mortality rates will begin to increase if something is not done about family size.

They urge government officials to make family planning technology available to the Ache so that these Indians do not have to suffer unnecessarily from existing population growth rates.

Is this the fate of the Bakairí Indians? If we look at table 3-8, it is clear that sometime during the next century their numbers may well climb to the dangerously high 4,000 mark. Will child death rates begin to soar if this number is approached? If so, how can this be prevented? Certainly Hill and Hurtado are correct in identifying the availability of modern family planning technology as one key factor. Other variables are resources and ways to make a living. We will turn our attention to them in the next chapter.

Summary

The Bakairí Indians are in many ways a "demographic success story" in that the size of their group is increasing rather than decreasing within a reservation that is their own. Many other indigenous peoples are not so fortunate. However, it is important to use the demographic statistics discussed in this paper to monitor the Bakairí in the twenty-first century. Such conceptual tools as fertility rates and rates of natural increase will help us understand how change affects the Indians' health and long-term chances of survival.

The total fertility rate for the average Bakairí woman can be classified as moderate when compared with other traditional societies. Women can be expected to have about five children, and this falls well within the range of between four and eight defined by Campbell and Wood (1988). Their population is increasing at rates of between 2 and 3.5 percent each year, which is not an unusually slow rate, as is the case in the sub-Saharan African "infertile crescent" where there is high prevalence of sterility (Caldwell and Caldwell 1983). Nor is the fertility rate abnormally high, as it is in the case of the Yanomamö who are expanding into new areas (Neel and Weiss 1975).

The Bakairí, like so many indigenous people, manage to keep their population growth rates low by depending on such fertility-inhibiting practices as nursing and sex taboos following the birth of children. Whether or not these traditions are adequate for keeping their numbers low enough for living within the reservation they were given in the 1920s remains an open question.

Chapter 4
MAKING A LIVING, BAKAIRÍ STYLE

"The planting of a Mekranoti garden always follows the same sequence. First, men clear the forest and then burn the debris. In the ashes, both men and women plant [the crops] . . . This gardening technique, known as slash-and-burn agriculture, is one of the most common in the world. The early settlers in North America adopted the method from surrounding Indians, although it had been used in an earlier period in Europe as well."

(Werner 1990:105)

An Ecological Question

The Bakairí Indians make their living in a variety of ways. They depend on food they produce in the reservation and on cash they earn or receive from Brazilians. By far the most significant aspect of their livelihood is the household gardens that they make in the forests that lie along the rivers in the reservation. Harvests provide the Indians with staples, such as manioc, which they eat on a daily basis as well as other important foods such as rice, corn, banana, squash, and beans.

In the late 1970s and early 1980s, FUNAI introduced a number of development ventures to indigenous groups. Many of these projects involved showing the Indians how to use industrial agriculture, which is a way of producing food that contrasts sharply with traditional methods of gardening. The reservations of the Tukuna (Oiveira 1979), Kaingang (Helm et al. 1978), Xavantes (Menezes 1982), the Bororo (Vieira Filho 1981), and Bakairí (Picchi 1982, 1991) became sites for experimentation.

FUNAI officials arrived in these areas, armed with tractors, fertilizers, and pesticides. Their goal was to accelerate the integration of indigenous people into Brazilian society by teaching them how to use the technology and methods commonly found on farms in Brazil and in the United States. It was believed that modern means of production would allow the Indians to increase their harvests and begin to sell surplus crops in urban markets, thus enabling them to participate more fully in the cash economy. FUNAI officials hoped that these experiences would result in stronger links between the indigenous and national economies, and ultimately in the Indians' absorption into Brazilian society (FUNAI 1980).

FUNAI also anticipated that the new technology would help the Indians use their lands more efficiently. Traditionally the Bakairí only garden where the soil is naturally fertile enough for them to grow food without turning over the topsoil or applying fertilizers. This type of land is in limited supply, and FUNAI believed that by supplying the Indians with technology that would artificially improve soil fertility, they would increase the area the Indians could productively farm.

This industrial agricultural project places the Bakairí right in the middle of an exciting controversy that involves thinkers in such fields as anthropology, economics, and environmental science. Some believe that indigenous peoples' traditional ways of producing food are superior to Western industrial methods because they have been used for thousands of years in places like the Amazon without any major irreversible environmental damage. They propose using indigenous food cultivation systems as the model for *sustainable agriculture*, which is food production for indefinite periods of time without major environmental degradation. In fact anthropologists such as Leslie Sponsel go even further, stating that ". . . indigenes are to a large extent the key to environmental ethics, ecological knowledge, sustainable land and resource use and management, and the conservation of bio-diversity, ecosystems, and wildlife" (Sponsel 1995:283).

Others are against creating an "ideology of indigenous sustainability" (Cleveland 1998:333). They believe that we should not assume that traditionally based technology and knowledge are always best suited to conditions or adaptable to change. Robert Netting (1974, 1993) and David Cleveland (1998) prefer that we collect data on a case-by-case basis and tease apart what actually makes up indigenous food production methods. For example, how do traditional farmers know what they know? Do they understand cause and effect? Do they experiment with crop varieties and growing conditions to manipulate effects? Will they innovate with new technologies? Will they use what R. R. Wilk calls "*hybrid technologies,*" a mixture of traditional and modern technologies, to adapt to changing conditions (Wilk 1996)?

Netting (1993) points out that traditional people are often eclectic and practical in their approach to farming. He describes how the Kofyar of Nigeria have adopted modern technology and woven it into their overall long-standing production methods. Cleveland and his colleagues (1995) offer another example of this. The Zuni farmers in the southwestern part of the United States employ global position system (GPS) technology to map their family farms when using traditional agricultural methods.

Both schools talk about morality (Sponsel 1995:281; Cleveland 1998:335). Sponsel is deeply concerned about what he calls Amazonian ecocide, and he is willing to forfeit scientific objectivity and neutrality to help stop the destruction. Cleveland sees the world as being increasingly crowded and interconnected, and he posits that environmental concerns may force anthropologists to jettison one of their most cherished concepts—that of cultural relativity. Soon it may be too much of a luxury to allow every culture to employ its own food producing traditions. We may eventually have to evaluate all local ways of managing resources, including our own, using a global ruler whose size and shape have yet to be agreed upon.

And yet these schools of thought differ on the basis of a key issue. One group privileges an indigenous mode of production, while the other advocates a more pragmatic approach. The former rejects the way most nation-states are growing food, while the latter warns that if local people want to survive physically and culturally, they may need to borrow techniques from the Western world. One school places ecosystem integrity first, believing humans will survive as a consequence, while the other advocates people doing what they need to do to make a living.

How does this controversy apply to the case of the Bakairí Indians? It would be difficult to find an anthropologist or ecologist today who promotes the transformation of Brazilian indigenous food producers into industrial agriculturalists. FUNAI's vision from the 1970s and 1980s of Indian-reservations-turned-into-mechanized-agribusinesses has been largely abandoned after two decades of experimentation (Santos et al. 1997).

Many anthropologists assume that indigenous gardening techniques are more sustainable than industrial ones, and over the long haul, they probably are. The pernicious effects of commercial agriculture tend to show up faster and more dramatically than we ever imagined. And yet the Bakairí continue sporadically to cultivate small-scale rice fields with Western methods. As we will see, the effects have not been altogether positive for either the culture of the Indians or their environment. Should they abandon their new agricultural technology and return solely to their traditional ways? And if so, how will that affect food and cash availability in the reservation?

Readers may remember from the previous chapter that the number of Bakairí Indians has grown significantly in the past twenty years. We need to ask if they as a group can afford the luxury of being purists—that is, of depending only on indigenous ways of growing food. The alternative is an eclectic production system that emphasizes traditional methods of crop cultivation but grafts on some modern technology and knowledge. Such an approach also allows for cash being pumped in from a variety of sources. With it people purchase additional food, material goods, and other necessary items. Employing such a pragmatic approach may buy the Bakairí some time, during which they can better position themselves to survive the twenty-first century.

In this chapter I begin by describing the ecology of the Bakairí reservation and then go on to discuss how the Indians make a living. I map out the various sources of food and cash on which they depend and discuss some of the implications of their approach to earning a livelihood.

The Ecology of the Region

The Bakairí reservation lies on the natural border between Amazon forest and *cerrado* with cerrado clearly dominating the region. Some gallery forest is interspersed along the rivers. In order to understand the composition of the area, I ordered Landsat images from the United States government's EROS Data Center. These are photographs taken by satellites. I measured the relative amount of cerrado, gallery forest, and river and discovered that cerrado makes up most of the reservation. It constitutes about 85 percent of the Indians' lands, while gallery forest composes only 14 percent and rivers the remaining 1 percent.

The Cerrado

The cerrado consists of two distinct layers of vegetation. The first is made up of grasses that reach about 1 meter in height, while the second layer consists of short twisted trees that grow up to 10 meters tall. The grasses grow continuously, resembling a prairie, with trees dotting the landscape occasionally. Every year during the dry season (May–September), the grasses burn and are thus renewed. The fires are started by the Indians, by lightening strikes, and by people outside the reservation.

Cerrado fires are dramatic to see and can be dangerous. I recall being at Pakuera when a fire crept closer and closer to the village over a period of days. People stood outside their houses with their arms crossed, anxiously watching the smoky line move toward us. Eventually the wind changed and moved the fire in another direction, but for days an acrid cloud hung over the village.

I have worked with Indians in cerrado and Amazon forests and believe that living in either kind of environment has its pluses and minuses. However, I prefer the sunny openness of the cerrado. It is true it provides little shelter from the sun, but the vistas are amazing. The grasslands stretch out endlessly until they meet the purple hills that border the area.

Doubtlessly someone with a love for forests would argue eloquently on their behalf. And certainly when I entered into the trees along the rivers in search of one more garden to measure I got the feeling I was walking into a cool green cave. The moist darkness surrounding me was a dramatic contrast to the dry gnarled trees and waist-high grasses outside.

Up to 1980 the Bakairí ignored the cerrado for all practical purposes when it came to gardening. They concentrated their efforts on raising food in the forest and reserved the cerrado for hunting and herding FUNAI cattle. They told me that the cerrado soil had never been any good and that the forest land was far superior.

Although somewhat perplexed by the Brazilians' interest in using the cerrado for crop production, they understood the value of turning over the topsoil with a tractor and applying fertilizers. But it did not surprise them to hear that following the use of intensive agriculture for two or three years, cerrado soils harden, making continued crop production nearly impossible. Brazilians generally introduce livestock into the fields at that point.

During my fieldwork, I decided to see exactly how different cerrado and forest soils really were. I took soil samples from both areas and sent them away to be analyzed. The ground in the forest yielded samples with little problem, but I really struggled with the cerrado part of the study. I have a vivid memory of the temperature being in the 90s with the heat radiating up from the dry earth. I knelt on my hands and knees with the sweat running down my face and gnats buzzing around my eyes.

The earth was like concrete, and I could not make a dent in it. And to make matters worse, I had to dig not one, but fifteen holes, in a zig-zag fashion and mix the soil in a tarpaulin before bundling up about a pound of it to send away to a laboratory. It was only when I went back to the village and found an implement that resembled an ice pick that I made some progress. This is not one of my more pleasant memories of fieldwork, or the cerrado.

My efforts paid off though, and I learned a lot from studying these soil analysis results (Picchi 1982:240–247). In a nutshell, the lab test results supported the Bakairí distinction between the cerrado and forest soils. They confirmed that compared to forest soils, the cerrado consists of less organic matter, or nutrients for growing plants; it has a limited amount of phosphorus in it, something that is important for plant growth; and it contains high levels of aluminum ions, which can negatively affect plant growth.

These findings also reaffirmed what a meager piece of land the Bakairí had been handed in the 1920s on which to eke out a living. Apparently about 85 percent of it was very poor indeed.

The Gallery Forest

Islands of *gallery forests* line the rivers that flow through the reservation. These forests are made up of three distinct layers. The first consists of trees that reach as high as 20 to 30 meters. Their upper branches make up the canopy where such animals as monkeys live. They shed their leaves during the dry season, and this forms a layer of decomposing organic matter on the ground. This thick mat is the source of the soil's fertility.

Belts of dense gallery forest line the rivers in the region. The Indians make their gardens in the fertile soils of these forests. *Cerrado*, where the soil is not as fertile, lies adjacent to the forests.

Shorter trees that grow to about 15 meters make up a second layer, and shrubs and small trees growing to 1 to 2 meters form the bottom layer. The vegetation in these layers does not shed its leaves during the dry season. When the Indians practice slash-and-burn gardening, the underbrush and shorter trees are the first to go. Only if it is absolutely necessary do they attempt to cut down the larger trees, an effort that entails a lot of work and that can be dangerous.

The greatest reservoir of gallery forest in the reservation is where the Paranatinga River intersects with the Bananal River. From the air, the two rivers form a huge S shape with forest thickly growing in all directions. It is no coincidence that this is where the Bakairí chose to locate Pakuera in the 1920s. And it is in the heart of this S that the village still lies today.

Because the Bakairí invariably make their gardens in the gallery forests, they have been forced to farm repeatedly the area closest to Pakuera, wearing out the soil over a seventy-five year period. Normally the Indians allow their gardens to remain fallow for at least ten years after they use them for two- to three-year periods. But the land around the village is rarely allowed to remain unused that long. Its farming value, as a consequence, has been seriously undermined.

Each year the Bakairí travel farther from the village to find lands suitable for crop cultivation. This is undesirable for a number of reasons. They must walk or ride bicycles for long distances to get to their gardens, thus wasting time and energy. They also have to transport harvests home to the village. Carrying heavy loads of manioc, rice, and corn for several miles in the hot sun after spending hours gardening is an obvious drawback.

Another reason to avoid having distant gardens is that animals are more likely to raid crops when people are not around regularly. Capybara, the largest rodent in the world, as well as less exotic creatures such as deer and raccoon can ruin a harvest well before its time. I came to understand this firsthand one afternoon when I was measuring the size of a distant garden. I was quietly moving around the perimeter of the field, absorbed in letting out my measuring ropes and checking angles when I heard a sound. I looked up and saw a pair of river otters, the water still glistening on their dark fur, standing on their hind legs at the edge of the garden. They moved forward and began to feed before they heard me and scampered away. When I told the Bakairí gardeners about this, they became grave because they realized what such animals could do to a harvest in a short interval.

To determine the average distance of gardens from the village, I took a *simple random sample (SRS)* of thirty-six gardens, or 26 percent of the total number of fields used by the Indians. A simple random sample is made up of a selection of members of a group, all of whom were given the same chance of being chosen to be included in the sample. This is achieved by labeling each member and using random digits from a preprepared table to select the constituents of the sample. The use of a simple random sample helps save time and work by allowing us to make generalizations about the larger population from what we find out about the smaller sample.

From my garden sample, I discovered that the average distance of the gardens from the village was 4 kilometers, or 8 kilometers round-trip. There were also clusters of gardens within 5 kilometers round-trip of the village and between 12 and 24 kilometers round-trip. Although families managed to walk 8 kilometers or less, they either used bicycles to travel to the more distant gardens, or they remained in these gardens for days at a time.

The results of my garden study confirmed my suspicions that food cultivation was taking place at a considerable distance from Pakuera and lent credence to the Indians' concern about the lack of fertile lands near the village. And when groups of Indians in the mid-1980s began to leave Pakuera and form new settlements, I was convinced that they were doing so partly in response to this ecological problem, although internal and external political factors also contributed to their decision to relocate.

Cerrado and Forest Animals, Birds, and Insects

There are many different kinds of animals and birds in the cerrado and forest, including anteater, armadillo, capybara, paca, deer, tapirs, peccaries, wild pigs, and agoutis. (For a more complete listing of animals, and their scientific names, see Picchi 1982:110–116.) Animals in the reservation that the Indians avoid are the jaguar, sloth, rabbit, and fox.

A jaguar was once accidentally killed during a community pig hunt and brought into the village where a young man wanted to skin it so he could sell the pelt in the city. An uproar among the elders ensued, and the animal quickly disappeared after the youth was severely reprimanded. The jaguar plays a key role in Bakairí mythology. He is a kind of culture hero who not only helps the Indians but plays pranks on them.

A variety of birds such as quail, seriema, and emu are also found in the reservation. The Indians keep some birds as pets. They like toucans, parrots, parakeets, and macaws, both to have in the house and for their feathers, which are used in body decoration. Sometimes the Bakairí bring land tortoises home to play with for a while before killing them for their shells and meat. They also eat some insects. For example, they like to collect and smoke termites whose large nests dot the landscape around the village. I enjoyed eating them the one time I was offered some. They were crunchy and tasted like roasted nuts.

The Rivers

The rivers in the reservation are the third major component of the Bakairí ecosystem. Five pass through the reservation. By far the most significant one is the Paranatinga River, called the Pakuera by the Bakairí. It is one of the headwaters of the Teles Pires River, which in turn flows into the Tapajós River, a tributary of the Amazon River. According to the Landsat photos, over 45 kilometers of this river twist and turn through the reservation, and the average width is about 77 meters.

Smaller rivers also found in the reservation include the Tuiuiu, notable for its lush forests, the Azul, which the Indians call Paikum, the Vermelho, the Paixola, and the Kayapó. Three of the Bakairí villages are located near the Paranatinga, and three others near the Azul. A seventh lies on the Paixola River.

Although they make up only about 1 percent of the reservation's area, rivers are extremely important to the Indians. Unlike other groups who prefer to live inland, away from the water, the Bakairí have depended on rivers for their livelihood for as long as they can remember. Not only do they garden in the forests that grow on the riverbanks, but they are primarily fishermen. They catch many different kinds of fish, including a variety of freshwater catfish, which the Brazilians call *mandí, bagre, piaba, jaú*, and *piraíba*. There are also small *pacu* and large, fatty *matrinxã*, which resemble salmon. Other riverine animals of significance to Bakairí diet and culture are otters and turtles.

The Bakairí use the rivers for canoeing. Although over the years bicycles and trucks have mostly replaced boats for long-distance travel, canoes are still used for short trips and for fishing. The Bakairí are expert canoers, and even women and children are adept at handling the boats in the water. They make two kinds of canoes. One is of solid wood, and although it has a long life span, it is difficult to maneuver in the water. The other consists of bark. It is light and buoyant, but more fragile. Groups of men join together to make canoes. First they locate and chop down a large tree. If they are constructing a dugout, they hack out the inside of the tree trunk with metal tools, leaving just the wood shell for the boat. They seal the inside of it with smoldering fires. If they are making a bark canoe, they carefully strip off the bark and cure it.

Although the rivers are important for food and travel, they can be dangerous. People drown in them when canoes capsize, and poisonous snakes, attracted by the cool shade, gravitate to them. What the Brazilians call *jararacas* (*Bothrops species*) or pit vipers, as well as boa constrictors, anacondas, and the spectacular bushmaster that grows to twelve feet long, are frequently found near or in the rivers. The first snake-bite case I ever saw was the result of a man coming across a snake on the banks of the river where he was fishing. Within an hour he was throwing up blood and survived only because the

Bakairí medic promptly injected him with anti-venom serum.

The Indians do not eat snakes or sell their skins. One young Indian man who heard that Brazilians thought snakeskin was valuable, decided to try to sell some. After skinning several snakes, he hung the skins to dry, but the powerful smell that emanated from them was so offensive that the villagers forced him to bury the skins.

There are caymans in the Paranatinga River, but the Indians do not hunt them. Nor are they overly afraid of them, as far as I could tell. Having lived in Florida for a while, where newspaper articles recounted stories about alligators making off with toddlers, I was surprised at the almost playful way the Indians interacted with the animals. I was once in a canoe with two Indians, and a cayman passed under the boat. They smacked its tail with their paddles so that the animal thrashed around, bouncing the canoe up into the air. As I held on tightly to the sides and hoped for the best, the men laughed uproariously.

Slash-and-Burn Horticulture and Mechanized Agriculture

Anthropologists contrast two major types of crop cultivation: *slash-and-burn horticulture,* or gardening, and *agriculture,* or farming. Horticulture requires less work, depends on limited technology, and allows land to be used for a relatively short time. It does not change the landscape dramatically, and even gardens that are as young as a year old sometimes blend in with the forest. The process of field preparation consists of people "slashing" away the underbrush, usually with machetes, and cutting down small trees with axes. They then let the vegetation dry before they burn it and plant crops in the ash-covered soil. After two or three years, harvest yields begin to drop, and the families prepare new gardens.

Agriculture, on the other hand, demands more work, as farmers clean-clear the land of trees and rocks and turn over the topsoil with plows, both of which do not take place in horticulture. People may also build irrigation ditches and terraces as well as apply fertilizers and pesticides. Fields are generally well demarcated and look different from the surrounding countryside. And because the soil is improved, farmers use their plots of land for longer periods of time and typically enjoy larger harvests than they do with horticulture.

At this time the Bakairí employ both horticultural and agricultural production systems. Up until the 1980s they used only slash-and-burn gardening, but when FUNAI introduced mechanized agriculture to Indians in the early 1980s, the Bakairí became involved in the experiment. Let's look first at their traditional way of producing food, and then go on to examine their use of agriculture.

Bakairí man harvesting manioc tubers in his garden.

Slash-and-Burn Horticulture

Bakairí slash-and-burn technology is available to everyone. Gardening tools include machetes, axes, knives, hoes, and digging sticks. They purchase the metal implements but construct such items as digging sticks. As is consistent with the classic definition of horticulture, the Indians do not use plows or construct terraces or irrigation ditches. Nor do they clean-clear their fields. At the beginning of the dry season, they clear away the underbrush with machetes and cut down trees with axes. They set fire to the fields after the vegetation has dried for several months, planting around the charred stumps and logs.

Planting takes place when the rains begin in October and November. The Indians raise bitter and sweet manioc, rice, corn, banana, sugar cane, melon, and other crops. They also plant fruit trees sometimes. The rice is harvested in February and March, and the corn crop soon after. They harvest manioc gradually, continuing through the next year. Bananas, which produce for years, and sugar cane are also harvested over a period of time.

The Bakairí normally make new gardens each year, but they keep two gardens up and running simultaneously because of the relatively late harvests of manioc and fruit. After the third year, gardens are typically abandoned unless there are fruit trees there. The Indians try to leave the used garden land fallow for about ten years, and ideally fifteen to twenty years.

Individuals do not own the land they garden, although they consider the crops they cultivate to be their property. This tradition contrasts sharply with the way Brazilians organize their use of land, and sometimes these differences lead to clashes. Once while I was doing research, a group of impoverished rural workers received permission from the Bakairí to make a garden on the border of the reservation. The situation became problematic almost at once when the Brazilians said that since they had cleared and planted the land, they owned it. The Indians explained there was no custom of ownership in the reservation. There were only use rights, and since they were not Bakairí Indians, they technically did not even have those. Tempers flared and I was concerned about the possibility of a knife fight, since the Indian men and rural workers carry eight-inch knives stuck through their belts. However, violence was averted although the workers did not leave the reservation until much later.

In traditional food production, any one household depends on a labor force drawn from the kin group, augmented sometimes by people from the community. Kin do most of the routine work. Everyone participates although men tend to perform more of the heavy work such as chopping down trees, while women do more weeding and harvesting. Entire families generally go to the garden together, and even small children help with tasks appropriate to their size and age. Friends from the village help out when there is a particularly difficult chore to do, such as moving a large tree. Work is defined in social terms. People are not paid with money or goods when they complete the task. Their contributions are recognized as part of a reciprocal arrangement in that their host repays them with similar service at some point in the future when they need help in their gardens.

I already knew that the Bakairí make their gardens in the gallery forests on the Paranatinga, Tuiuiu, and Azul Rivers and that these gardens are on the average 4 kilometers from the village, or 8 kilometers round-trip. But I needed to know more. I wanted information about the average size of a garden, the total number of gardens in the village, and the total amount of land under cultivation by the Indians in any given year. I also hoped to learn about harvests. Armed with these basic facts I would have a clearer picture of how the mechanized agriculture project would interface with the traditional production system.

I chose a simple random sample of fourteen households (26 percent of the newly made fields) and worked closely with these families to collect information on gardening over a twelve-month period. First the Indians took me to their gardens. Typically these fit the width of the gallery forest that lined the river at that point. They measured anywhere from 16 to 60 meters. The length of the garden varied, depending on how much the family wanted to cultivate.

I measured garden size using a method based on premeasured ropes (Gross 1979; Carneiro 1979). Using a compass, colored ropes, and cloth flags, I cordoned off a rectangular area and calculated its size. Odd areas not included in the original rectangle were measured separately. After mapping the shape and dimensions of the gardens, I mathematically estimated the areas using standard geometric formulas.

Based on the above methodology, I discovered that the average size of a first-year garden was about 4,060 square meters. I went on to look at gardens from the previous year and found they were only slightly larger. In addition to these single household gardens, there were three multihousehold gardens, seven separate corn gardens, and two large community gardens. I measured these separately. When I added everything together, I ascertained that although the land newly cleared in a year was about 23 hectares, the total land (first-year, second-year, and community gardens) under horticultural production was 44.5 hectares.

I estimated harvests by measuring off a section of a field and then asking the gardeners to help me harvest what was in that area. From these measurements I was able to estimate total garden harvest. I discovered that much more manioc was grown and harvested than rice. I attributed this to the fact that manioc was a key component of the Indians' traditional diet, while the Brazilians introduced rice to them relatively recently. Other important crops in decreasing order of amount harvested included corn, banana, sugar cane, yams, melon, beans, papaya, and squash. I have summarized estimated harvests of the most important foods in table 4-1. Note that not all gardens grow each crop.

Table 4-1: Estimated Harvests of Five Crops Grown by the Bakairí Indians		
CROP	NUMBER OF GARDENS	ESTIMATED HARVEST (KG)
Bitter Manioc	42	198,941
Sweet Manioc	34	141,879
Rice	40	19,380
Corn	39	14,640
Banana	16	34,481

The Mechanized Agriculture Project

The industrial agriculture mode of production introduced by FUNAI contrasts sharply with the traditional way of producing food described earlier. First, it shifted the focus of crop production from one part of the ecosystem to a radically different one. The gallery forests used to be the only place the Indians grew food. The cerrado was used for hunting or cattle-grazing.

Another difference is that agriculture relies on expensive Western technology that is not available to everyone. Tractors and pesticides are expensive to buy, and not even Brazilian farmers can always afford such purchases. Most Indians would find raising such money for farm equipment impossible because they lack access to credit. If it weren't for FUNAI, groups such as the Bakairí would never be able to buy such things as tractors and seed dispensers.

The tractor given to the Bakairí to farm the *cerrado*.

An additional consideration is who uses the technology once it is inside the reservation. In traditional horticulture, women participate in all phases of crop production and actually control the harvesting part of the work. In the cerrado, men alone do the agricultural work because only they have had the opportunity to learn such skills as driving tractors on nearby ranches where they go to earn wages.

Others who do not have access to the farm equipment are Indian men who have not learned how to use Western technology. Farmers typically use Indians as unskilled labor. They do not teach them how to run complex equipment. Part of the reason for this is that job training is expensive and time consuming, and there is no incentive to proceed with it if the workers are only around for the short term.

But another reason is that most Indians lack the foundation of general knowledge that would allow job training

---

Box 4-1: Ways to Compare Traditional Gardening and the Agriculture Project

Ecosystem Component

Technology
    Expense
    Availability
Labor
    Skill Level
    Gender
    Community Participation
Planting and Harvesting Organization
    Diverse versus Single-Crop Planting
    Gradual versus All-at-once Harvesting
    Pace
    Scale
Harvests

---

to take place. For example, they theoretically know how to read and write in Portuguese since they attend reservation schools, but since they do not use these skills on a daily basis, their proficiency is not developed. Also, Portuguese is not their native language and Western technology is not part of their cultural tradition. Imagine trying to read a label when you do not know how to read very well. Now make it even harder by assuming the words are in a foreign language, and they are describing concepts with which you are totally unfamiliar.

In the final analysis, only a few men worked the cerrado fields. Most men were left out, and women and children provided assistance during the short harvesting period that took place at the end of March. A feeling of alienation grew.

Those who worked on the project did not improve the situation when they demanded most of the rice harvest as payment for services, stating that they had worked the hardest and should receive the lion's share of the crop. A delegation of FUNAI officials had to fly in from Cuiabá to settle the dispute because the atmosphere in the reservation became dangerously tense. The officials tried to strike a compromise by distributing a sack of about 55 kilograms of rice to each household in the village and awarding the project workers bonuses of the harvest.

This might have ended the conflict, except that FUNAI had to ship about 85 percent of the rice harvest out of the reservation to a nearby town where it was sold. Most of the proceeds went to purchase diesel fuel, fertilizer, and pesticide for the following year's planting. This exacerbated the perception that the project did not really belong to the Indians, even though the FUNAI agent tried to make it clear the project was communally controlled. In the end, many Bakairí reported feeling discouraged, and the feeling prevented them from participating in the project over the next several years.

An additional difference between traditional and agricultural ways of producing food concerns the planting and harvesting schedules. For example, in traditional horticulture the Indians plant many different crops in a single small plot of land. They mix manioc in with melons, and squash with beans. Later, they harvest the crops one-by-one over a period of time. In agriculture, a single crop in a large plot of land is planted and harvested all at once.

Furthermore, the scheduling of the rice project seemed compressed to Indians who were more accustomed to setting their own pace. Clearing the cerrado occurred during a two-week period in September, while plowing, harrowing, and planting involved night and day work with two tractor teams composed of three men each, working around the clock. This kind of pace is unheard of in the Bakairí villages.

Still another way in which the mechanized project contrasted with traditional horticulture concerned the scale of production. The amount of land that the Indians typically cleared and cultivated was about 4,000 meters^2 when they practiced horticulture, but 50 hectares, or 500,000 meters^2, for the agriculture project. A related scale problem concerns harvests. Agricultural harvests are theoretically larger and more sustained over time because of plowing and fertilizing, while the horticultural ones are smaller and decrease in size after the first year, thus requiring new garden cultivation. In the case of the rice project, FUNAI officials planned conservatively because this was the first year of an experiment. However, a series of setbacks that included bad weather, missing equipment, conflict, and other problems prevented the Indians from meeting this modest goal. The Indians were to harvest about 1,000 fifty-five-kilogram sacks of rice from the cerrado field, but they ended up with only 450 sacks. As table 4-2 shows, this represents about half of what the gallery forest gardens yielded.

Table 4-2: Comparison of Gallery Forest and Cerrado Rice Cultivation*			
FACTOR	GALLERY FOREST	CERRADO PLANNED	CERRADO ACTUAL
Area in ha	17.78	50.00	50.00
Area in m^2**	177,822	500,000	500,000
Rice harvested (kg)	19,380	55,000	24,750
Rice yield (kg) per m^2	.109	.110	.049

*Information from Picchi 1982:256–258, 344–352.
**One hectare (1 ha) is equal to 10,000 squared meters (10,000 m^2).

Nonetheless, this was still a huge increase over what they were used to. Households generally harvested only five to ten sacks of rice in a given year, if they grew the crop at all. The organizational implications of this were not entirely thought through. Not only was the availability of enough workers an issue, but the coordination of tasks and their timely execution were problematic. Even storing the harvest before it was shipped to town was difficult. The abandoned infirmary was chosen for the storage area, but the pests inside it made it a less-than-perfect solution.

Following the inauguration of the agricultural project, political conflict in the village turned the Indians' attention away from the cerrado. Between 1983 and 1985 Pakuera divided, and people were more concerned with village-related problems than with rice production. But in the late 1980s the village of Aturua obtained a tractor from FUNAI and began to grow rice separately from the Pakuera project. Throughout the rest of the 1980s and 1990s, production took place on two cerrado sites, one near Aturua and the other close to Pakuera.

The amount of land cultivated and the size of harvests fluctuated wildly. The Indians tended to plant far less than the 50 hectares they had previously planted, sometimes clearing as little as 4 hectares. Another interesting adjustment they made was to move the rice fields around, much as they do when they grow food in the forests. Although this is necessary with slash-and-burn horticulture, it is not with agriculture, which involves the refertilization of the soil with each planting. In general, harvests were low, although the Bakairí managers reported two or three good years. The yields ranged between .05 kg/m^2 and .20 kg/m^2.

Today the Indians continue to plant cerrado rice. They sell some of the harvest and distribute the rest in the village. However, as we have seen in other reservations where FUNAI initiated similar projects in the 1970s, these rice harvests are not the most significant part of the indigenous diet. Nor do proceeds from the sale of the rice dominate the Indians' economy. It is just one part of their general food production system.

Fishing, Herding, and Hunting

The Bakairí fish, herd cattle, and hunt in addition to raising crops. Of the three activities, fishing is the most important to them. Fish provide them with important nutrients and, according to a time allocation study I did, fishing is an activity on which they spend a considerable amount of time.

In a study of the Bakairí diet, I examined the extent to which the Indians depend on the three major food groups—fats, carbohydrates, and protein (see table 4-3). I discovered that, like many other groups,

Table 4-3: Grams and Percentages of Carbohydrates, Fats, and Proteins in the Bakairí Indians' Annual Diet*		
FOOD CLASS	**NUMBER OF GRAMS**	**PERCENTAGE OF GRAMS**
Carbohydrates	9.830×10^7	86.9
Fats	$.792 \times 10^7$	7.0
Proteins	$.686 \times 10^7$	6.1
Total	11.308×10^7	100.0

*Information is from Picchi 1982:306–307.

most of their food derives from the carbohydrate class, while much smaller percentages are fats or protein.

Although most of the protein the Indians consume during any one year derives from garden products and is vegetable in nature, a significant amount, 22 percent of the protein grams consumed, comes from fish. Beef from the cattle herds and game from hunting make up the rest (see table 4-4).

To determine how the Indians allocated their time over the course of the year, I followed Allen Johnson's (1975) and Daniel Gross and associates' (1979) *time allocation study* method. This methodology, based on scientific principles of randomness, was developed in the 1970s to determine relative amounts of time people spend on specific activities. During my research with the Bakairí, I made twelve visits each week to houses randomly selected in the village. I also randomly chose times, within a twelve-hour day, as well as days of the week. Upon entering the house I noted what

Table 4-4: Sources of Protein in the Bakairí Indians' Annual Diet*		
PROTEIN SOURCE	**PROTEIN (GRAMS)**	**PROTEIN (PERCENTAGE)**
Gardening	4.27×10^6	62
Fishing	1.53×10^6	22
Cattle Herding	$.599 \times 10^6$	9
Hunting	$.461 \times 10^6$	7
Total	6.86×10^6	100

*Information is from Picchi 1982:306–307.

each household member was doing. If someone was absent, I asked what he or she was doing and then verified what I was told later.

When I finished my research and began analysis, I discovered that I had thousands of observations. If not for computers, evaluating the data would have been incredibly time-consuming. What I found out is that compared to people in the United States, Bakairí adults do not spend a lot of time doing what we would call "working." For example, men and women over fifteen years of age spent about three hours each day in such activities as gardening, hunting, fishing, herding, paid labor, making things, and so forth. Of course, they do not take off weekends as many Americans do. But even taking that into consideration, they still do not work a forty-hour week.

With regard to fishing, herding, and hunting, they spend about half the amount of time performing these activities that they spend on gardening. There is seasonal variation. For example, the gardening frequencies are low in May, June, and July, with July registering the lowest readings. This is the height of the dry season, when the Indians have prepared the fields and are waiting to burn them. On the other hand, most of the hunting takes place during the rainy season in December and January, when it is more difficult to catch fish, and men turn to alternative ways to get food. During other months, time spent fishing tends to be more evenly distributed, with slightly greater frequencies in the dry season.

Fishing

Fishing is a popular activity among the Bakairí. The Bakairí usually use fishhooks and lines, although once in a while they still employ the traditional bow-and-arrow method of fishing. The Indians purchase line and hooks in stores in town, or from Brazilians on nearby ranches. They make the bows from hardwood they find in the forest and from cotton they grow in their fields. Arrow shafts are made from palm.

Before going out, men prepare themselves for the event by using fish-scrapers. Their mothers or wives use fish teeth attached to a piece of wood to vigorously scrape their wrists and forearms. After they draw blood, the women apply an astringent herbal solution to the scratches to stop the bleeding. They do this to give the limbs strength so that they will be successful in their endeavors.

They fish in all of the reservation rivers, but they depend the most on the Paranatinga, Azul, and Vermelho. The Indians also fish in lagoons or meadow lakes that form when the rivers flood the fields and then recede during the dry season, leaving trapped fish. They organize community expeditions that involve even children. The men travel to the lagoons early in the morning and beat the juices of a vine into the water. This asphyxiates the fish, and they then float to the top of the lagoon. When the women and children arrive, they splash around, gathering up the stunned fish. This is a festive event, with people laughing and joking and generally having a good time.

These lagoon expeditions often provide a perfect opportunity for men and children to practice bow-and-arrow fishing. This technique requires a great deal of skill, and from an early age, boys are encouraged to practice shooting birds and other small animals. Whenever a child kills a fish, everyone stops to compliment the youngster on his prowess.

Although the Indians depend on fish throughout the year, they are most successful during the dry season. During the rainy season, fish are less prone to bite at baited hooks because they feed off of the organic matter that washes into the water. For those Indians using bows and arrows, the fish are less likely to be visible because the water is muddy and opaque.

Although men do most of the fishing, women occasionally use baskets in shallow waters or lagoons to catch small minnowlike fish. After the fish are brought home, the women clean and cook them. The fish are boiled and served with manioc or rice or roasted over the fire.

The Bakairí also eat turtle eggs. When the river water is at its lowest, the adult female turtles move to the sandbars and beaches where they lay their eggs at night. After about a month, the eggs hatch, and the baby turtles make their way to the river water. The Indians search for the caches of eggs, which they dig up and smoke over the fire. Geri, the woman who made my meals, offered to scramble some for me because she knew I had cravings for my American diet. I used to dream about cheese, eggs, and bread. The scrambled turtle eggs were tasty but very different from the chicken eggs I eat at home.

Herding Cattle

In the late 1970s, about 400 head of cattle grazed on the cerrado in the reservation. FUNAI technically owned the herd, and the agency paid two Bakairí men to care for it. But the Bakairí community considered itself the de facto owner, and when the Indians slaughtered a steer, the meat was distributed throughout the entire village. I have

Bakairí cattle.

already mentioned that the beef from the herd was a more significant source of food for the Indians than was game.

In the early 1980s, FUNAI slowly transferred total control of the herds over to the Indians. Each settlement was allocated a specific number of cattle. By 1989 this process was complete, and I noticed another development under way. Individual Indians were building their own herds as sources of capital and cash. They acquired cattle from the community herds and from nearby ranches.

This trend was interesting because until recently the Bakairí did not recognize private ownership of resources such as land or animals. As a general rule, they believed in community ownership. The emergence of this new way of looking at things was fraught with tension, and cattle owners tried to disguise what their resentful covillagers perceived of as "greed" by hiding their animals in distant parts of the cerrado. Only in the far reaches of the reservation where people could not be sure of what was happening was the accumulation of private herds possible. There, ambitious Bakairí household heads escaped the pressure on them to redistribute the cattle to their kin and friends.

Table 4-5: Number of Heads of Cattle Located in Bakairí Villages*		
VILLAGE	**PRIVATELY OWNED CATTLE**	**COMMUNITY- OWNED CATTLE**
Pakuera	101	80
Aturua	98	43
Cabiceira do Azul	30	6
Kaiahoualo	30	0
Sowapo	30	0
Paikum	10	0
Paixola	0	0
Total	299	129
Reservation Total	428	

*I gathered data on Pakuera cattle during a cattle census that took place when I was there. Information about other villages is from interviews with headmen and from key Pakuera informants.

We can better understand the implications of the process of privatization of once community-owned resources by referring to the concept of "the tragedy of the commons" (Hardin 1968) and its corollary, *"the tragedy of the commoners"* (McCay 1984). Garrett Hardin wrote about what happens when each individual in a group seeks to exploit a communally held resource to his or her greatest advantage. He predicted the inevitability of the tragedy of overexploitation if three conditions were met. The first is that the users must be selfish in their interest to exploit the resource at the expense of the larger group. The second is that the resource is limited and that use exceeds its replenishment. And the last is that the resource is collectively owned and thus freely open to any user (Berkes 1985:199).

Bonnie McCay (1984) applies this ecological concept to a political-economic process and renames it "the tragedy of the commoners." She shows how inequities emerge when a resource that was previously in the hands of the group, which she calls "the commoners," becomes concentrated in the hands of a few, thus denying the majority access to the resource. The Bakairí cattle herds are a good illustration of how this works. They were communally held but now they are being taken over by a small number of households. In fact in 1999 a FUNAI agent told me that a Bakairí living in Aturua owned three hundred head of cattle, almost as many as there were in the entire reservation in 1980. As these cattle reproduce, the size of such privately owned holdings will grow, and so will the inequities in the reservation.

Although full analysis of this problem requires more research, one obvious question to ask is why traditional ownership rules, such as the ones that allocate garden lands and fishing territories, are not applied to cattle. It is possible that traditional Bakairí values and norms manage only those resources that have long been a part of the indigenous economy and that are central to the Indians' survival. Gallery forest land and rivers fall into this category. The Indians will apply the new model of private ownership only to recently introduced resources that are peripheral to the indigenous economy. Cattle are such a resource as is cerrado-produced rice. However, in time, if the market economy permeates their world, private ownership may well become the norm.

Hunting

The Indians hunt in the forests and on the cerrado, where they kill such animals as white-lipped peccary, wild pig, capybara, paca, deer, armadillo, and anteater. Using .22 rifles that they purchase from the Brazilians, they usually hunt alone or in pairs.

Once in a while they organize groups to hunt bands of wild pig. For example, in December and January the community prepares for the corn festival that takes place every year to celebrate the corn harvests. Up to forty men go off for a lengthy hunting trip that takes as long as five days. They sleep in the forest for several nights, eating only what they catch, supplemented by the manioc pancakes they carry from home. They smoke the game they catch to preserve it and bring it back to the village, where groups of women roast it over huge open fires. What is not eaten during the festival is distributed in the village.

In sifting through my research notes in preparation for writing this chapter, I found an entry that indicated that these trips are not all fun for the men. I was visiting a woman when her husband returned from one such hunt. He was totally bedraggled and obviously miserable. He said it had rained the entire five days they had been in the forest and that sleeping in a hammock without cover had been horrible, and they had been unable to keep any fires going, so they could not keep warm or cook any food. They were unable to smoke any of the game they killed, which meant they brought little back to the village.

Men generally take their dogs with them when they hunt. Each house has as least one dog, and I found these animals to be different from most dogs in the United States in that they are diseased, starved, abused, and vicious. They guard the homes of the Indians, snarling and trying to bite anyone who comes near. On hunting trips, they are invaluable because they are fearless in their pursuit of game.

Men bring the meat back to the village, where women prepare it. Because sharing is important in their society, the Bakairí either call their relatives to eat some with them or send a child over to their houses with part of the kill. Game is eaten with manioc or rice, and what is not consumed is smoked so that it does not spoil.

The Bakairí and Sources of Cash

Cash links between the Bakairí and non-Indians have existed for some time. In recent history, between 1955 to 1975, Indian men regularly left the reservation to work on nearby ranches to earn small amounts of cash that enabled them to purchase basic necessities such as sugar, soap, flashlights, line and hooks for fishing, and so forth. After 1975 the number of Indians working on ranches began to decline because FUNAI discouraged the practice. Also the number of ranches decreased as businesses concentrated small land holdings into large mechanized enterprises that did not require a lot of unskilled labor. Although some Bakairí continue to work for wages on ranches even today, the numbers are much smaller than before.

When the Bakairí find jobs, they do so only on known ranches with reliable foremen and tolerable work conditions. There are many horror stories about working in slave conditions known to both Brazilian and Indian workers. For example, a Brazilian man and woman arrived on foot in the reservation one night with their children. They told us that they had worked for a rancher in the area for weeks before they had become suspicious about not getting paid. They confronted him about their wages and not only did he refuse to give them any money, he told them that if they did not leave immediately he would kill them. They were terrified and fled with only their clothes. I asked why they did not report him to the police in Paranatinga, and they said they felt powerless and afraid.

Once the Bakairí make arrangements with a reputable foreman, they travel in small kin groups to the establishment, where they remain for several weeks. They are hired to do a particular job rather than paid to work by the hour or day. After the job's completion, the foreman pays the Indian who made the arrangements, and the Indians then distribute the cash to the other men. Tasks assigned to Bakairí work teams may include fence building, land clearing, sacking rice, or caring for cattle.

In one season a Bakairí working in a small team can earn the equivalent of around $100, and if he works two jobs, he can double his pay, receiving by Bakairí standards a substantial sum of money. In a one-year period, I counted thirty-seven men who left the reservation at least once to work on ranches. Seven left twice. They brought in about $4,200.

A second source of cash for the Bakairí is the FUNRURAL payments, which arrive every three months in the village. FUNRURAL is a social service organization that pays retired people or their widows an annual stipend. FUNAI assumes responsibility for the paperwork and for sending the money to the reservation, where the Indian agent distributes it to the recipients. Twenty-five Bakairí receive these payments on a regular basis. Altogether their income amounts to $7,539, nearly double what the men earn on nearby ranches.

Another source of income is FUNAI, which pays salaries to its Indian workers. From the mid-1980s through the 1990s, Bakairí worked as Indian agents, schoolteachers, and cattle herders. But even before that they worked as medics and maintenance men. At one point their combined income was more than that of the FUNRURAL payments. By the late 1990s the FUNAI payments outstripped all others.

In the last ten years a number of Indians have left the reservation temporarily or permanently to work in cities such as Cuiabá. This trend will be discussed in further detail in the final chapter of the book; however, for our purposes here we can say that they work mainly for FUNAI for wages. These people contribute to the reservation's cash economy when they loan money to their families and friends who visit them, and when they visit the reservation themselves.

At one point during my field research, I added up all of the money that Indians had earned or received that year and estimated that they had available nearly $20,000, or $325 per household at that time. About 17 percent of village households did not have a direct income. However, this does not mean that they lacked access to cash. Kinship networks, political faction formation, and ritual all served to redistribute whatever cash flowed into the reservation.

What do they do with this cash? Certainly their expenditures are radically different than the typical Americans. They do not have to pay for housing, and they raise most of their food. They do not have furniture, using only hammocks they make themselves from the cotton they grow.

They do not own cars, and there are no modern appliances such as refrigerators in their homes. At this time, they lack electricity and phones, although the governor of Mato Grosso intends to provide power to more isolated ranches and villages in the near future. They do not have to pay for water, sewage, and garbage disposal because they depend on the river for water, the forest and latrines for waste, and have a minimum of trash. Nor do they pay taxes or worry about insurance.

Nonetheless, they spend their cash almost immediately. Whatever saving exists takes the form of investment in bicycles, guns, expensive knives, machetes, and watches, all of which can be sold later. They also purchase items that they use on a daily basis. These include kerosene for lanterns if they have one, ammunition for their guns, cloth from which to make clothes, soap, salt, coffee, sugar, and lard if they use it for cooking rice.

The Bakairí make these purchases in nearby towns. They travel to these places in FUNAI's truck, which is available for Indians to use, although everyone who rides in it must pay a fee. Once in the city, Indians sleep in the truck or stay with family or in church-run hostels. For a small amount of money, these hostels provide space for them to hang their hammocks.

There used to be a small store in the reservation. It was organized by FUNAI in 1975, and it sold such goods as matches, soap, ammunition, and sugar. This store was to save the Indians from having to travel to towns to make their purchases. Later a Bakairí took over the operation, but he abandoned the project after several years because it proved to be divisive. The shop disappeared.

Summary

A political process has clearly resulted in significant changes in the way the Bakairí use their environment. A "top-down" government-sponsored project targeted their reservation, and others like it, for development in the 1970s and early 1980s. The project introduced agricultural technology and know-how, pesticides and fertilizers, and monocrop production. This new model of production also involved exporting harvests for sale, something the Bakairí had never done before. A second related political process concerns the decision to disperse the cattle to individual communities and ultimately to private owners. What was once a source of food is now a way for Indians to acquire wealth and build capital.

One thing I hope I have made clear in this chapter, and the others that preceded it, is that no two Bakairí Indians have responded to these changes in the same the way. Although macrolevel political forces are indeed in operation, affecting both people and ecosystems, the human actors who inhabit the indigenous landscape confront the reality of day-to-day life, with all its problems and opportunities, in very different manners. The men who work the project tractors and the family that has amassed so many head of cattle have obviously opted to work within the capitalist system that they see becoming increasingly important to them. In subsequent chapters we will see how other actors face the challenge of the twenty-first century.

Chapter 5
LIVING AND WORKING IN GROUPS

".. . the Mundurucú help to remind us that marriage and kinship are more than conventional means of reaching useful ends; they are also the basic criteria and conceptual bases for the division of society into its parts and for the reamalgamation of these parts into a unity."

(Murphy and Murphy 1974:145)

There are a number of important principles that structure Bakairí social relations. They organize the Indians into groups and ensure that they live and work together successfully. We examine four types in this chapter—those based on age, gender, marriage and family connections, and non-kin associations. Among the Bakairí, there are no class or caste differences.

Daily Social Life

A Child's Life

Bakairí children are typically indulged. What disciplinary action takes place tends to be verbal, and I heard or saw few examples of physical punishment. As is common in many societies, girls are encouraged to play a quieter, more demure role, while boys are allowed to be louder and more aggressive. Once when a Brazilian medic and I were walking in the village, a three-year-old boy playfully threw himself against our legs, shrieking loudly. His father laughed as he watched this performance, and the Brazilian ruefully called out that his son was a *danado*, literally "one of the damned" or "a madman," but translated in vernacular American to mean "a hell raiser."

Both girls and boys are expected to do chores around the house and to travel to the gardens with their parents to help out. Boys fish with their fathers and carry manioc home from the garden. They also practice shooting bows and arrows; when they are somewhat older, they use guns. Some learn horseback riding so they can help their fathers herd cattle. One vivid memory I have is of a tiny boy astride, what seemed to me to be, a huge horse. As I watched fearfully, his father patiently taught him to handle the reins.

Girls help their mothers get water from the river, wash clothes, and prepare food. They learn early in life to process bitter manioc and to turn it into manioc flour. They also learn to spin cotton into twine with which they make hammocks and to thresh rice with huge wooden pestles. Some Bakairí households now have sewing machines that are powered by a foot peddle. Older girls learn to make shifts for themselves and other family members out of fabric purchased in town.

Both boys and girls run errands for their parents, giving people messages or fetching things. And both help with child care. Although little girls frequently lug around infants nearly as big as they are, boys also watch younger brothers and sisters if their mothers run down to the river for a quick bath or next door to visit someone.

Children go to school in the morning for part of the year. They learn to read and write in Portuguese and to do some arithmetic. Prior to the 1980s, teachers were Brazilians who spoke no Bakairí, but since the 1980s, all teachers in the reservation are young Bakairí men and women. They are extremely proud of their accomplishments and of the contributions they are making to their people.

Adolescent Adventures

By the time boys and girls reach their teens, a few of the better students, who have families that are supportive of them leaving the reservation, are chosen to study in boarding schools in nearby towns. These young men and women study in the equivalent of our high schools and sleep and eat in religious hostels where nuns and priests carefully supervise them. They come home for holidays and for the summer months.

However, they are a minority. Most teenage men take on additional gardening and fishing responsibilities in anticipation of having a wife and children to feed by the time they are in their late teens or early twenties. They also play soccer with others their own age; perform the mask dances that I will describe in the next chapter; sit in the men's house, listening to their elders; flirt with young women; and travel. Young men in particular are always on their way somewhere—to Paranatinga, Cuiabá, or a nearby ranch. While in the city, they make purchases for their families, take messages to FUNAI offices, and visit relatives.

Sometimes they have adventures. They drink alcoholic beverages and get drunk; they have sex with women and contract gonorrhea; and they get robbed. Once I was staying in a hotel in Cuiabá when the desk manager telephoned my room and urgently asked me to come down to the lobby. Three young Bakairí men, completely drunk, were waiting for me. Amidst the curious stares of other hotel guests, we visited for a while before they drifted off into the night, I hoped, to go back to their hostel. Another time, a youth reported to me what sounded like the classic symptoms of gonorrhea, and we went to the FUNAI offices to find a doctor. Countless times, FUNAI officials and I have helped out Bakairí men who report having been robbed. Indians have had very little experience in protecting themselves from city predators, and they are easy marks for pickpockets.

Young women do not have these kinds of experiences because they travel less frequently outside the reservation and because they are discouraged from experimenting in this way. Their adult routines are established earlier, and by fifteen or sixteen they are marrying, having their first child, and involving themselves full-time in the management of their homes. However, as we will see, the role of women in Bakairí society is changing. They currently have more choices, and young women in particular are considering the value of getting an education, working outside the reservation, and earning wages.

Adult Routines

Bakairí days begin early by most American standards. People wake up at about 4 A.M., and by the gray light of dawn, they are on their way to bathe and get water from the river. Women heat up coffee and food, such as rice or manioc from the day before. Although everyone has a fire in their kitchen area, a few families have propane stoves, too.

By 7 A.M. the men have gathered at the men's house or are on their way to the gardens. Most people try to do heavy gardening work before the humid heat of the day sets in. They clear their fields of brush, weed, plant new crops of cotton, move manioc cuttings around, and harvest manioc tubers to take home with them. If they do not need to go to the garden to weed or harvest crops, then they go fishing or work on such projects as basket making.

Women do housework, sweeping a layer of dust from the hard dirt floors with palm fronds. They may go to the gardens with their husbands if there is weeding or harvesting to do. If not, they go down to the riverbank where they spend hours washing clothes, watching the children play, and gossiping with their friends.

By noon, most people return to the village to eat something and then to rest during the hottest part of the afternoon. The heat shimmers on the paths as people swing in hammocks and sit in doorways letting the breeze from the cerrado cool them. As children either doze or play, women and men work on projects such as hammock making and bench carving.

By about 3 P.M., it begins to cool off and the pace of the village noticeably quickens. Everyone goes down to the river to bathe before engaging in mask dancing, if they have ceremonial obligations, or in visiting friends and family. A light meal is usually eaten as twilight sets in. Bakairí families do not eat meals together sitting at tables. Rather, individuals eat when they are hungry or when food is prepared.

If it is a moonless and rainy night, people turn in early, sometimes at 7 P.M. right after it becomes dark. They rest, chatting and swinging in their hammocks. Elderly people tend to smoke a cigarette they have rolled themselves from tobacco they grow in their fields. They smoke only at night, using the substance as a soporific. I once had an interesting conversation with an elderly woman who told me the reason smoking harmed the health of non-Indians and not that of the Bakairí was because we do not know *how* to smoke. We smoke all of the time, rather than just one cigarette before sleeping.

If it is a bright moonlit night, people sit out in front of their houses and visit with each other. Young men gather in front of the men's house and sing, and children run up and down playing. On such nights, people do not retire to their hammocks until late by Bakairí standards, but when they do, the village becomes silent. A dog might bark occasionally, or an owl might hoot, but generally everything is still until about 3:30 or 4 A.M. when the villagers begin to rouse themselves again.

Bakairí Time Allocation

In table 5-1, there is a summary of the results of the time allocation study I completed while I was in Pakuera. These kinds of summaries are difficult to compile because they do not reflect the level of nuance most researchers would like to see. An excellent example concerns what I will call "river work." Many things happen when women go to the river, and they spend hours there each day. They bathe, get water, wash clothes, care for their children, gossip, and talk. Yet, time-allocation studies require us to code the activity in one category or the

Table 5-1: Bakairí Time Expenditure in the Average Twelve-Hour Day by People Over Fifteen Years of Age*		
ACTIVITY	PERCENTAGE OF TWELVE-HOUR DAY	NUMBER OF HOURS:MINUTES
Visiting, Conversing, Engaging in Political Activities, Resting, Thinking, Being Idle	38.0	4hr:33min
Gardening, Fishing, Hunting, Cattle Herding, Gathering, Paid Labor, Transporting	25.3	3hr:2min
Cleaning the House, Preparing Food, Eating	16.1	1hr:56min
Caring for Children	5.4	39min
Performing Miscellaneous Activities, Being Sick	5.4	39min
Bathing, Grooming, Hygiene	4.6	33min
Performing Ritual Activities	4.1	30min
Doing School Work	1.1	8min
Total	100.0	12 hr or 720 min

*Data compiled from a time-allocation study done over a twelve-month period.

other, which means that the data do not reflect the full range of what is going on. When I was faced with such dilemmas, I attempted to use my common sense, choosing the code that seemed to reflect the predominant activity taking place.

The data suggest that the Bakairí spend most of their time engaged in three major types of activities: (1) interacting with each other in some kind of social activity, (2) engaging in an economic activity, and (3) doing what we would call housework. Richard Reed (1995) discovered similar kinds of allocation of time among the Chiripá of Paraguay. He grouped together tasks according to whether they involved *productive labor*, which ensured the survival of the household, or *reproductive labor*, which allowed society to continue over generations. The former included activities such as gardening, hunting, wage labor, and fishing, while the latter involved child care, cooking, and household construction (1995:92 after Minge-Klevana 1980).

Over half (about 56 percent) of Chiripá time was spent in productive and reproductive labor, compared to slightly less than half (about 47 percent) of Bakairí time. About 45 percent of the rest of Chiripá time was spent resting, socializing, and attending to personal needs, compared to about 43 percent of Bakairí time.

Table 5-1 presents averages of percentages and of numbers of minutes and does not reflect daily or monthly fluctuations. For example, if we look at how time of day affects activity, at 6 A.M. I frequently found people engaged in cooking and eating, but at 10:30 A.M. people tended to be gardening or washing clothes. With regard to monthly variations in activities, ritual activities peak during the dry season, while most hunting occurs in December and January.

There is also variation by gender and age. I found no evidence that women ever cut down trees, cleared underbrush, or burned dried vegetation. Nor did boys under the age of fifteen perform this type of work. My data indicate that this is solely the responsibility of men—fifteen years and older. In fact, I discovered that men, in general, are three times as likely to be found doing garden work when compared to women, although women tend to harvest crops. One reason women are not involved more in these activities is that most Bakairí gardens are located far from the village. Women, who are generally the primary caretakers of children, find it difficult to travel regularly such long distances. If they did, they would have to either carry their children or leave them with others for long periods of time.

These findings are corroborated by Stephen Gudeman (1978) and Richard Reed (1995), who found in their studies that age and gender affect time allocation dramatically. Reed, for example, notes that men perform over 60 percent of gardening activities and virtually all of the forest clearing and brush cleaning. Outside of agriculture, men perform over 90 percent of the hunting and wage labor, while women spend most of their time on household chores (Reed 1995:93–94).

Male and Female Differences

Although it is true that men and women spend their time differently, there are other important ways in which they differ. Two of these discrepancies concern the public nature of their lives and their mobility. Men claim the soccer field that lies near the abandoned infirmary as well as the central plaza where the men's house is located. They occupy highly visible, public arenas. Women, on the other hand, avoid the soccer field and do not approach the central plaza or the men's house. Maintaining a low profile, they skirt public areas and use the back paths that connect the houses to the gardens and the river.

Thomas Gregor (1977), whose research owes a great deal to Erving Goffman's analysis of performance and role, notes that, in small societies, people typically label others on the basis of how they use space. In the Mehinaku village where Gregor studied, the central plaza area readily contrasts with what Gregor calls "the trash yard," which is the area in back of the houses. "The trash yard" is the domain of women, while men dominate the plaza.

If we look at the Bakairí village, a similar pattern of space use emerges. What Gregor calls the "trash yard," but what I will call the backyard area, readily contrasts with the plaza. Women are identified by their use of the backyard space, and if they inappropriately venture into the plaza, they are socially sanctioned by gossip. At times, when there are important ritual events in the plaza, the women ring the periphery of it, making sure not to move off the sidelines. Men avoid the backyard area except to set up clandestine meetings with women, and if they are found there too often, then their manhood is publicly questioned. As Gregor puts it, "a man who is of little account . . . is appropriately called a trash yard man" (1977:54).

The mobility of men also distinguishes them from women. Men in general, but young men especially, have many opportunities to take trips outside the reservation. When they are young, they travel out of curiosity, and when they are older, they go to Cuiabá and even Brasilia for political and financial reasons. They also go to ranches to earn wages. They remain there for days or even weeks before returning home. Women are discouraged from traveling outside the reservation. Child-rearing responsibilities, the inability to speak Portuguese as well as men, and their alleged shyness prevent them from leaving the reservation.

This is not unusual in traditional societies. Michelle Rosaldo (1980) described gender differences based on opportunities for adventure, travel, and worldly knowledge among the Ilongot of the Philippines. Ilongot men, who used to be headhunters, visit distant places where they acquire knowledge that they describe in public oratory. Being well traveled, informed, and articulate brings men prestige and contributes to their social power. Women lack opportunities to have such experiences and to share them publicly, and thus they do not have access to prestige and power.

Recently this has changed among the Bakairí. In the late 1980s and 1990s, I noticed that women were working for wages both inside and outside of the reservation. Some work in Cuiabá in shops and at FUNAI headquarters as domestic helpers, and a smaller number have assumed more responsibility working as teachers and medical attendants. A Bakairí family I know has three talented and bright daughters. One of them was FUNAI's Indian agent at Pakuera for several years, an extraordinary achievement considering that women do not become community or religious leaders in traditional Bakairí society. Another is working on college courses in Cuiabá, and a third (the only daughter who married and who has children) travels to Cuiabá regularly where she works temporary jobs before returning to the reservation where her parents live.

Most Bakairí women do not seek careers. Rather, they generate cash to help support households that are in need. They do this by working as teachers in the reservation or by selling cotton artifacts they make.

Generally these are homes where there are no husbands and where family support is attenuated, but other economic factors we discussed in previous chapters are also responsible. The expanding number of Bakairí Indians has placed pressure on the mix of production activities in the reservation. Wage earning by men, and now with increasing frequency by women, supplements the incomes of households where traditional gardening and cerrado-produced rice are not enough.

What this will mean for the next generation of Bakairí women remains to be seen. Certainly one possibility is that as their economic contributions to the household increase, their social and political power will also expand. This would be consistent with Ernestine Freidl's (1975) position that explains the subordinate role of women in society in terms of their household contributions. She led the way for a school of feminist scholars in the 1980s and 1990s to seek connections between gender on one hand, and social, economic, and political power on the other. Their research findings confirm that, in at least some cases, social and political power increase when women contribute more to the household income (Morgen 1989; Llewelyn-Davies 1996; McKee 1997).

However, just the opposite could occur. Recent research in Latin America and other regions has documented how integrating indigenous and peasant communities into larger national economies can have severely negative effects on the status of women. Relatively egalitarian gender systems may be transformed into hierarchical ones in which men have more control over the household, the economy, and politics. Consequences of such a transition include women working harder and producing more, while at the same time becoming more subservient and marginalized (Silverblatt 1987, 1988; McKee 1997).

Marriage and Families

Kinship includes relationships through blood and marriage and refers to the set of rights and responsibilities each person has as a result of his or her connection to family groups. In the United States and other industrialized and postindustrialized societies, the importance of kin groups has diminished when compared to other groups that organize our social relationships.

This is not to say that we do not recognize the importance of the family. Of course we do. However, other associations based on common interests, careers, and community concerns frequently siphon our time and energy away from that spent with kindred. Job-related travel and relocations exacerbate this tendency by requiring people to live far away from their families. In other societies, such as the Bakairí, it is just the opposite. Family relationships dominate the social scene, and those with non-kin groups represent less important bonds.

Monogamy

A hundred years ago, when von den Steinen first visited the Bakairí, they practiced *polygyny*—that is, men had more than one wife. Usually they married sisters because they believed that related women got on better. They also practiced what anthropologists call *the sororate*. This means that when a man's wife dies, he is required to marry her sister, if he has not already, in order to maintain the marital connection between his family and that of his dead wife.

Today the Bakairí are no longer polygynous. They practice *monogamy*—that is, marriage to one spouse. Pressure on them from FUNAI agents, missionaries, and others caused them to alter their traditions. Crocker and Crocker (1994) describe how such changes were imposed on Indians. They established in their research with the Canela that mid- to late-adolescent women without children used to sleep in the plaza, enjoying sex—often sequential sex—with men other than their husbands. In an attempt to stop them from doing this, government Indian agents got up each morning and publicly and angrily shamed these women, and presumably their partners. In time, the women stopped sleeping in the plaza (Crocker and Crocker 1994:37–38).

Although the sororate is a less controversial custom than polygyny, it is no longer as commonly observed as before, either. Although the Bakairí report that they practice it in hypothetical cases, sisters are frequently already married and thus unavailable when a death occurs.

Marriage Partners

We already established in chapter 3 that marriage takes place in mid- to late teens and that families play a critical role in the selection of a marriage partner. What are some of the criteria they use?

Before Pakuera broke apart in the 1980s, the Bakairí were considered *village endogamous*—that is, they preferred to marry someone from their own village. Two other alternatives existed. They could marry an Indian from P.I. Santana, the other Bakairí reservation, or they could marry a non-Indian. Several marriages between Bakairí from the two reservations took place, but they did not last. The husbands and wives, especially in the early years of their marriage, both wanted to spend time with their own families. Eventually the couples split up.

FUNAI actively discourages Bakairí from marrying non-Indians. They are concerned that the relatives of the Brazilian spouse would move into the reservation and eventually take over indigenous lands. Several Indian women currently have Brazilian husbands. There have been none of the problems FUNAI anticipated, possibly because these men have little or no family of their own. More recently, a few Bakairí

Bakairí woman with her non-Indian husband.

men have married Brazilian women. They live in the reservation but frequently travel outside of it to visit the wife's kin.

Since Pakuera divided, marriages between individuals from different villages routinely take place. As the number of Bakairí in the reservation grows, it will be interesting to see if any marked patterns of village-specific marriage emerge. At this time, the situation is fluid because couples change their village residence frequently.

Extended and Nuclear Families

The Bakairí also prefer that marriages take place within the *extended family*. An extended family consists of two or more individuals related by blood and their spouses and children. Extended families tend to be organized around the males or the females in the group. Among the Bakairí, they are typically organized around the female side of the family. Women, their married daughters, and granddaughters make up a tightly knit core of individuals who are loyal to each other. They share a residence for a good part of their lives, accompany each other to the river several times a day to bathe and wash clothes, work together in the gardens, and defend each other's interests in the community.

In some societies where such groups are named and culturally marked in significant ways, we would say that lineages (social groups based on descent traced through a line of ancestors of one gender) are present. Lineages frequently control important resources such as permanent land holdings, herds of valuable animals, or even sacred sites. But because of the informality of Bakairí extended families and because garden lands and cattle herds are controlled by individual household heads, I would say that lineages among the Bakairí are absent. This is consistent with what we see in the rest of Amazonia, where these kinds of descent groups do not appear to exist. John Bodley (1994) accounts for this by pointing to the mobility of Indian villages that are dependent upon slash-and-burn horticulture. He posits that the constant relocation of villages in search of fertile land prevents the emergence of lineages (Bodley 1994:57–59).

The presence of extended families does not mean that *nuclear families* are nonexistent or unimportant among the Bakairí. Nuclear families, consisting of a married couple and their children, are important for reproduction, residence following the birth of the first child, child rearing, and economic activities. Although embedded in the larger extended family, they operate in a semiautonomous fashion.

In Bakairí extended families, members distinguish two kinds of cousins. In contrast to the way North Americans lump first cousins into one group and call them "cousins," these Indians distinguish between *cross cousins* and *parallel cousins* and use marriage rules to manage mating practices with them. Cross cousins are the children of opposite-sexed siblings of parents—that is, children of either mother's brother or father's sister—while parallel cousins are those of same-sexed siblings of parents—that is, children of either mother's sister or father's brother.

Parallel cousins tend to be lumped together with siblings, and marriage between them is forbidden on the basis of incest rules. Cross cousins, on the other hand, are encouraged to marry each other, a tradition that reinforces solidarity within the extended family. Although not all Bakairí marriages are between cross cousins, some are.

Marriage Ceremonies

A Bakairí wedding is a relatively simple affair. The parents and extended-family members of the groom take him by his arms and lead him, carrying his hammock, to the bride's house. The entire village follows the group and stands outside the bride's house, listening as the father of the groom presents him to the other family and extols his virtues. Then the groom's hammock is hung above the bride's, and the ceremony ends.

Although not required, some couples choose to embellish this procedure by involving FUNAI officials and serving refreshments. For example, at one wedding I attended, the parents of the bride asked the agent to document the union in his records book. Others serve coffee or something to eat. Older Bakairí shared with me that when they married, it was different. The young man, carrying his hammock, simply went to the house of the bride and stayed there.

From time to time, an elopement occurs. Usually this happens when one of the individuals is married. The couple flees to the gardens and stays there, in a hut, for several days until people calm down. Family members keep them informed on how things are going in the village and let them know when it is safe to return home.

No gifts in the form of dowry or bride wealth change hands when two Bakairí marry. However, the bride's family can expect the performance of *bride service*. This is when a young man works for his future father-in-law in exchange for his marriage rights. Although the Bakairí do not rigorously observe this tradition today, it remains a part of the process of marriage that must be at least discussed by the bride's and groom's families.

Residence after Marriage

After marriage, a couple typically lives with the wife's family until they have their first child and build their own house. This is called *matrilocal residence*. However, sometimes for practical reasons, the couple ends up living with the husband's family for a while. This happened when Yuka's son married. He brought his wife home to live with Yuka and Beri because the bride's mother had just given birth to a baby.

Eventually Bakairí couples set up their own households, but they are never far away from their parents by North American standards. Yuka's son built his house directly next door, and other couples generally live only a house or two down the path from their families. When Pakuera divided, some of the most painful and emotional moments came when couples, sometimes married for twenty years or more, confronted the reality of their respective families living in different villages and having to decide where to live themselves.

Due to the strong bonds between family members, the parents of one or both of the spouses can expect to live with the family when the elders are too old to care for themselves. Beri's parents moved in with her and Yuka many years ago. The last time I was in the reservation, I discovered that her father had died, but her mother, now blind, continues to live with them.

Divorce

Divorce occurs among the Bakairí, and the reason is almost always that an extramarital affair has resulted in a pregnancy. An extramarital affair itself is not grounds for divorce, but a resulting pregnancy is, because it entails responsibilities that detract from the original married couple's union.

The actual divorce involves no lengthy legal procedures such as we find in many non-Indian societies. Rather, it consists of spouses either gathering up their possessions and moving back into their parents' home, or collecting their mate's belongings and dumping them outside the door of their home. I have witnessed both types of divorce. In the first instance, a woman with her newborn baby stormed across the village upon finding her husband's lover was pregnant.

In the second, more theatrical, case, I was looking out my window when I saw the young woman who lived across the path from me come out of her house and violently throw some of her husband's belongings on the ground. She did this several times and then ran back inside and slammed the door with a great show of displeasure. The husband did not show up to claim his possessions immediately. They remained in front of the house, in a heap, until nightfall when they disappeared.

Following a rupture between a couple, there is usually a cooling-off period during which the families try to get the two back together. Sometimes their efforts are successful, but when they are not, the individuals seek other mates, while their families smooth over the tensions in the village.

With regard to the children, in the case of a newborn, the mother invariably keeps the child. When there are several offspring, she usually does not take all of them. When she leaves her marriage, she typically returns to her parents' home, and the economic burden on their household would be too great if she brought a lot of children with her. Neither does the father take them. Rather, the children are parceled out to family and friends. This is generally considered a good time to adopt a child if one's children are grown. Older women stop by the house of a newly split couple and happily lead away a young child by his or her hand. This is not as heartless as it sounds because Bakairí villages are small, and adopted children see their parents every day. In many ways it is more like they have gained a second set of parents rather than lost one.

The Kinship Terminology System

Anthropologists refer to the way the Bakairí classify their kin as the *Iroquois kinship terminology system*, which is one of the six or seven major terminology systems found in the world. When kinship experts study people's relationships with family members, they use a single individual as a reference point and refer to him or her as "Ego." They then go on to document the terms Ego applies to his or her relatives and to organize them into a chart.

The location of Ego in a kinship chart makes a difference in the kin term applied to any one member of the family. For example, if I am designated as Ego, then I call the woman who bore me Mom. But if my niece, Michelle, is Ego, then she calls my mother Granny. My mother and her granny are one and the same people, but they have different kinship terms because the location of Ego moved in the chart.

Kinship studies frequently contrast how people from different societies view family members. For example, let's compare how North Americans and Bakairí refer to relatives in their own generation. If we use my family as an example, we see that I have several sisters, each of whom I call Sis, and a brother, Steve, whom I refer to as Brother. I also have seven cousins—four are the daughters of my mother's brother, Ron, one is the son of my mother's brother, Geof, and two are the sons of my father's brother, Ed. I call each of these cousins, Cousin.

One difference between United States and Bakairí kinship systems immediately stands out. We already know that the Bakairí differentiate two kinds of first cousins. Parallel cousins are the children of same-sexed siblings of parents, and Ego applies the brother/sister term on them. If I were a Bakairí woman, I would refer to my Uncle Ed's two boys as Brother, just like I do with my brother Steve. Mating with them, or marrying them, would be considered incestuous in Bakairí societies.

Cross cousins are the children of opposite-sexed siblings of parents, and the term cousin is used with them. Although we in the United States would not allow sexual relations or mating to take place between these relatives, the Bakairí prefer people to marry their cross cousins. Thus, if I were living in their society, they would expect me to marry my Uncle Geof's son, and they would also place some pressure on my brother, Steve, to marry one of Uncle Ron's daughters.

Another difference is how the Bakairí employ gender- and age-specific kinship terms to relatives in their own generation. What this means is there are two completely different sets of kinship terms used—one by women like myself and one by men like my brother, Steve. Just to make things a little more confusing, individuals recognize older and younger status of same-sexed siblings. That is, men like Steve use two different terms on their brothers—one for older brothers, *paigo*, and one for younger ones, *kono*. And, in turn, women like me use one term for older sisters, *ia*, and one for younger, *idi*. There is only one term for opposite-sexed siblings in both the cases of men and women. I would refer to Steve by the term *wi* (brother), while he would call me *ko* (sister) (see tables 5-2 and 5-3).

The terms used for cross cousins are gender specific, but they do not register age differences. Men call their female cross cousins *iwiâpâ* and their male cross cousins *pama*, and women call their female cross cousins *iseambi* and their male cross cousins *yerudu* (see tables 5-2 and 5-3).

Table 5-2: Bakairí Kinship Terms in *Female Ego*'s Generation	
RELATIVE	**BAKAIRÍ TERM***
Younger Sister or Female Parallel Cousin	*idi*
Older Sister or Female Parallel Cousin	*ia*
Brother or Male Parallel Cousin	*wi*
Male Cross Cousin	*yerudu*
Female Cross Cousin	*iseambi*

*Partial Bakairí orthography—a as in "ma," e as in "bet," i as in "beet," o as in "go," u as in "blue," ai as in "pie," â is not an English phoneme, that is, a meaningful sound in English; for readers who have linguistic training, it is a nasalized unrounded mid sound. The only consonant to call to the reader's attention is designated as w but it is not the same as the English w. Rather, linguists would call it a voiced bilabial fricative.

Table 5-3: Bakairí Kinship Terms in *Male Ego*'s Generation	
RELATIVE	**BAKAIRÍ TERM**
Sister or Female Parallel Cousin	*ko*
Younger Brother or Male Parallel Cousin	*kono*
Older Brother or Male Parallel Cousin	*paigo*
Male Cross Cousin	*pama*
Female Cross Cousin	*iwiãpâ*

Let's go on to compare how North Americans and Bakairí refer to relatives in their parents' generation. Most North Americans distinguish between Mother and her sisters and between Father and his brothers. We refer to our parents' siblings as "aunts" and "uncles." However, the Bakairí use the same term when referring to Mother and mother's sisters (*seko*), or Father and father's brothers (*shogo*). And their relationships with these same-sexed siblings of their parents resembles the close, supportive ones that they enjoy with their mothers and fathers. Mother's brothers (*kugu*) and Father's sisters (*yupâri*), on the other hand, are set apart from these relatives, and Ego's relationship with them is distant (see table 5-4).

Table 5-4: Bakairí Kinship Terms in Ego's Parents' Generation	
RELATIVE	**BAKAIRÍ TERM**
Mother and Mother's Sister	*Seko*
Father and Father's Brother	*Shogo*
Mother's Brother	*Kugu*
Father's Sister	*Yupâri*

Kinship Terminology's Functions

Many times the study of kinship terminology seems to be an obscure mental exercise. However, anthropologists have discovered that kinship lies at the heart of the social organization of a traditional society. It also helps us understand how other cultural institutions, such as politics and economics, function. This is because kinship rules organize related individuals into such clusters as political factions and labor groups. It also coordinates their activities (Nanda 1994:27–281).

For example, Bakairí kin groups serve sociopolitical functions in that they are the building blocks of political alliances that organize the community. Individuals related by blood, in particular grown siblings, make up clusters that are effective in achieving consensus and setting goals. Families joined by the marriage of two of their members also form interfamilial alliances. The bonds between them are weaker than those between blood relations, but they, too, are capable of coordinating group efforts.

In Pakuera, blood relatives descended from the same female ancestor play a vital role in the organization of the village. For example, the

Elderly Bakairí woman who is very influential because of the number of adult sons and daughters she has living in the village.

entire village is structured geographically and politically around seven major kin groups. The strongest two are located in the north and south of the village. Elderly women, now in their eighties, are the heads of families made up of eight and six grown married children with grandchildren. These women, situated at opposite poles, do not overtly direct events in the village. Rather they influence the younger members of the family to work on behalf of the family's interests.

In the 1970s and 1980s the members of these two extended families built their houses near each other so that close relatives now dominate the northern and the southern parts of Pakuera, providing a geographic coherence to the village. Other families filled in the gaps in the rest of village. Although smaller in membership or made up of younger individuals, they also organized people to perform specific activities and achieve community goals.

In the 1980s and 1990s, Pakuera fissioned mainly along the fault lines of these kin groups. Clear extended-family affiliation was evident in Paixola, Aturua, Paikum, and Kaiahoualo. Related people gathered up their household goods and moved to new locations where they built their homes.

Gender-Based Groups

Gender is another principle on which groups are formed. Among the Bakairí, males are organized into two different non-kin groups, but women lack a comparable kind of association. Their solidarity, based on kin connections, is strengthened through a lifetime of cooperation and shared experiences in the domestic sphere.

The Ear-Piercing Age Set

Men who pass through the puberty rite of ear piercing at the same time make up a ritual age set. The ear-piercing ceremony takes place approximately every five years when the number of boys between the ages of fourteen and nineteen warrants it. Passing through this ritual signals to the community that one is an adult. Prior to its completion, boys should not engage in sexual activities, although they sometimes do, and they cannot marry.

My informants compared it to the onset of menses. The similarities are striking. For example, the flow of blood is central to both events, and there is fear and anxiety associated with it. Also the two are irreversible. Once menstruation begins, it only ceases temporarily with pregnancy and permanently with menopause. Similarly, pierced ears cannot be made whole again once they are perforated. And most important, menstruation and ear piercing herald a new developmental phase in an individual's life. Men and women both assume new responsibilities and have different expectations than before. Women look forward to having sexual relations, getting married, and managing their own households, while men do more fishing and gardening in preparation of beginning their own families. Upon passing through puberty, both men and women are taken more seriously by the other villagers.

The ear-piercing ceremony takes place in the men's house and is performed by elders who know the appropriate songs. It requires a large running river to meet the needs of the spirits who are involved in the transformation of the boys into men. If this condition is not met, then the boys may become ill. Once, an ear-piercing ceremony took place in Kaiahoualo during the dry season. The river had shrunk to the size of a small stream, and the men argued about whether it would be dangerous to conduct the ceremony. They decided to go ahead, and later the son of one of the village leaders became ill. It was blamed on the spirits who had not been satisfied with the water in the stream.

The ear-piercing ceremony takes two days. The young men go to the men's house on the first day and spend the night there together with their elders. Their upper arms, wrists, and ankles are bound with cotton twine as is common when traditional rituals are performed. Their faces and bodies are painted with the black juice from the fruit of the *genipap* tree and the oily red paste from the *urucu* berry that the Indians cultivate in their fields.

The next day the ceremony takes place. The boys' heads are held by an adult man, and their ears are pierced by an elder with the bone of an emu, an ostrichlike bird of the cerrado. Pieces of wood are stuck in the holes. The actual operation is different than ear piercing in the Unites States in that the holes are much bigger, allowing a plug the size of finger to be forced in. Also Bakairí ritual specialists do not pay attention to sanitary conditions, as we do in the United States, so that the ears of the boys typically become infected. Sometimes the infection is so bad that it spreads down the neck of the young man.

I questioned Yuka's son, Nai, who had recently had his ears pierced, what the ceremony was like. I asked if it had hurt and if he had been afraid. He said it had not been painful, which caused his grandmother to make sounds of disbelief. His report that he had not been afraid was supported by Yuka, who was in the men's house during the ritual. Yuka volunteered that they did not have to hold Nai's hands during the piercing of his ears because he had kept them calmly folded in his lap, something not all of the youths had managed to do.

Men who have their ears pierced at the same time comprise a loosely organized age set. Although their responsibilities toward each other are not rigidly defined, they tend to fraternize, hunt, and assist each other in garden projects more frequently than they do with those in younger or older cohorts. They also compose a type of political interest group in that they share common experiences, aims, and concerns that are different from other men's. And they work together toward achieving their objectives, taking similar positions in the village political arena.

They also marry and have children at about the same time, and move simultaneously through other developmental stages such as the death of parents. Their demeanor toward each other is playful. This is quite different from the respectful way they must interact with the elders and from the mentoring way they tend to act toward those younger than they. Men in the same age set may find their sense of solidarity temporarily affected by village disputes and rivalries, sexual jealousy, and personal animosity. Yet relationships between members remain strong and usually endure until death. On the other hand, they never eclipse, or even compete seriously with, those blood relationships that claim an individual's allegiance.

Elenore Bowen, the nom de plume of anthropologist Laura Bohannan, wrote extensively about her work in West Africa where the institution of age grades is extremely well developed. The age mates she studied had strict, formally defined rights and responsibilities that could not be violated. One of the more dramatic passages in her book describes the terrible moral and emotional dilemma of a young man torn between avenging his father, one of whose wives had been unfaithful, and defending his age mate, the man with whom the wife had sexual relations (Bowen 1954:132–143). Such confusion and pain would never have occurred in Bakairí society, because without a moment's hesitation the son would have sided with the father against the age mate.

The Men's House

In many societies in Melanesia, Africa, and South America, men's associations play a dominant role in the political and religious lives of the people. Young men are initiated into adulthood through such ceremonies as ear piercing or circumcision. They are then allowed to participate in a meaningful way in the key activities that take place in this house. The men's house, in such societies, is usually the largest and most distinctive structure in the community. It is shrouded in secrecy, and women are forbidden to enter it on penalty of death, rape, or some other terrible thing. Inside, men store sacred and/or musical artifacts and ritual masks, and they perform rituals, one of which I just described.

The Bakairí men's house, called the *caduete*, is a rather typical example of such an association. The structure itself stands out in the center of Pakuera's plaza. It is elliptical, unlike the houses of the Indians, which are square. Fashioned like traditional long houses used in the Xingú culture area, the men's house has one low door and no windows.

It represents the political and religious heart of the village. There is a bench in front of it, around which the men gather in the morning and evening to discuss events and make decisions.

Unlike age-related ceremonies that divide men into groups based on when they complete the ritual, the men's house unites them and places them in opposition to the women. Not only are women not allowed inside the men's house, they are threatened with, as one of my informants put it, rape by at least thirty men, or death, whichever comes first. All that takes place in or around the house is a secret, and one of the first things a male child must learn is that he cannot tell girls about these mysterious events.

Beyond uniting men, what purposes do men's associations serve? Gregor (1979) has done a considerable amount of work on men and their secret societies. He developed an ecological/psychological model initially presented by Whiting, Kluckhohn, and Anthony (1958). This model suggests that such institutions are found where male sexual identity is not clearly differentiated from that of females. Such a blurred definition typically occurs in those societies that have low-protein diets, and subsequently, prolonged infant nursing and exclusive mother-child sleeping arrangements to facilitate nursing on demand. As a result of these child-rearing practices, children consequently grow up identifying with their mothers.

In the case of little girls, this is not a serious problem, because they will assume their mothers' roles in a timely fashion. However, in the case of little boys, there is a problem because they must ultimately assume very different rights and responsibilities from their mothers'. It is only through the strict application of cultural traditions such as male initiations and men's houses that they are wrenched away from women and their world.

The Mehinaku Indians whom Gregor studied, and the Bakairí whom they resemble, fit this model. Both societies depend upon manioc, a low-protein carbohydrate, for their staple food, and although both consume fish as an important source of protein, we know that most of the Bakairí's dietary protein is vegetable in nature. Vegetable protein is inferior unless eaten in careful combinations to provide all of the essential amino acids.

In addition, Mehinaku and Bakairí mothers sleep with their children in the same hammock, which facilitates nursing on demand. Children nurse until approximately their fourth year, and weaning is a difficult, stressful process for both the mother and child. Sexual taboos following the birth of a child sometimes last for years, allowing the child to control his mother's time and energy in a nearly unchallenged fashion. In general, the parent and child are virtually inseparable until a younger sibling begins to compete actively for the mother's attention.

Gregor concludes that men suffer from what he calls an "incomplete identification with the masculine role" (1979:267). In fact he posits that the Mehinaku do not believe that men and women are naturally different. The Indians think that the two are distinct socially and politically only because men possess sacred flutes and occupy the men's house. He points to Mehinaku transvestite rituals and ear-piercing ceremonies in which men bleed from their ears, or "menstruate" like women, as proof of the mutability of gender identity.

The men's house thus becomes an artificial device for dramatizing the differences between the sexes and for providing men with a stage for performing these differences. The exclusion of women, the punishment of gang rape, and the secretive nature of what transpires around the men's house are not in and of themselves important. Rather, as Gregor succinctly puts it, ". . . a good part of this business turns out to be confirming the identity of its members and differentiating them from those who are refused admission" (Gregor 1979: 269).

Summary

The continuation of society depends on the organization of individuals into social groups that will work and live together. Every community needs what Murphy and Murphy call "glue" to bind people together so that they forget their individual differences (1974:145). The reproduction of cultures, as well as of people, requires that we overcome our natural isolation and assert, not our independence, but our dependence upon each other. In traditional societies such as the Bakairí's, kinship and marriage are extremely important for the social organization of the group. And if we measure the power of the two—kinship and marriage—many anthropologists, such as Murphy and Murphy (1974), believe that marriage, rather than blood, is more effective in integrating people into larger units. That is because it links together groups that previously had no connection whatsoever.

This may well be. However, as we have seen in this chapter, Bakairí society embeds individuals in webs of rights and responsibilities in a variety of ways. They are "glued" together through their affiliation with nuclear and extended families, matrilocal residence, their spouse and their spouse's family, gender-based associations, and age-affiliated groups. Even the very kin terms they use lock them into tightly knit groups.

Chapter 6
THE BAKAIRÍ AND THEIR DANCING MASKS

"The sounds of their voices, the movements of their dancing bodies recalled the memory of the immortal creators who, as Warodi told in his dream narrative, had given him their songs. As they sang and danced the songs with the creators in mind, the performers brought them into the present. The sounds, movements, and bodily images offered sensible proof that the creators continued living."

(Graham 1995:223)

Excerpts from My Field Diary

Saturday—Pakuera

Tonight the masks are saying goodbye to the village because now that the rains are coming, they will not dance anymore—at least not until the dry season begins again. I must say that it's spectacular out. There is no moon to see the masks so that even if a woman looked outdoors, which is absolutely forbidden, she wouldn't see anything except perhaps a dark shape if it were close up. There is only a very starry sky with the milky way clearly marked . . .

The men sat outside the men's house for a while. I could hear their voices as they joked and laughed. But then there were only muffled laughs when they went inside to put on their masks and costumes. After a while, *kwamba* masks appeared, and a few began to stamp and chant. Then the sound swelled, and the chanting grew in every part of the village—there were *kwamba*, and then *yakwigado* masks, all over, chanting, chanting, until it seemed there was no more space for sound.

Now all I hear is the swish of their costumes as they move, their feet stamping rhythmically—and I am amazed at the power that they generate and the emotion they evoke in me . . .

Sunday—Pakuera

I'm exhausted and going on only coffee, cigarettes, and nerves. I hardly got any sleep last night because of the masks. They stopped at about 4:30 A.M. and began again at 6:00 A.M., stopped at 7 A.M. and began at 9:30 A.M. It is nearly 2 P.M. and they are still at it. We women can now come out and see the performance since it is daylight. I saw one *kwamba* collapse, flat on his face. I don't wonder. Jere said that the spirit of *kwamba* stole his mind . . .

Later

The masks dance in circles around each of the mask owners' houses. Following them are groups of boys and men not in masks. Old men like Kamiare and Nunes, their arms locked with younger men, sing in low rhythmic tones in back of the masks. Many of the women are crying, and I feel choked up too. It will be very sad in the village now, they say, and the masks will only be reborn next year . . .

Later

They have been dancing for almost 24 hours now with only two rest periods. I can't believe it. Their endurance levels are amazing. The men are starting down to the river, and we women have been instructed to go indoors again. Some of the women are running to their houses. We won't be able to look until the men come back. Jere tells me that the men will detach the masks and wash the costumes really well before cutting the palm into tiny pieces and scattering the shreds in the water. The masks are put in sacks and hidden . . .

Later

It's dark now, and I am lying in my hammock, feeling strung out, thinking about it all. The way the ritual disturbed me . . .

The above is an excerpt from my field diaries. My field notes and field diaries are two very different sources of information. In the former I recorded as accurately as I could systematically made observations about research-related questions and events, while in the latter I wrote down my perceptions, opinions, emotions, and general observations about many unrelated topics.

My impressions of the ritual in which the Bakairí put their masks to sleep are just that—subjective impressions. However, so powerful were they that I felt compelled to investigate mask dancing in a more systematic way at a later date. In this chapter, I report some of my findings. I make a few brief observations about ritual power and its roots and then go on to discuss the history of the masks and the ways in which they function in Bakairí society. Although these artifacts are clearly beautiful expressions of an indigenous belief system, they also play an important role in the Indians' economy and social organization.

A "Ritually Powerful Event"

Jonathan Hill (1993) wrote about an experience he had while working with the Wakuénai in Venezuela. The thrust of his research was different than mine in that he studied how religious leaders draw on their knowledge about the histories and characteristics of spirits to create powerful imagery. The Indians use these images to fashion moving artistic performances.

Hill establishes that *ritual power* depends on spoken, chanted, and sung explorations of key myths. But although a shaman's ability to imbue ceremonies with energy builds on his knowledge of myths and his skill at embroidering images around mythological narratives, it also relies on the community's receptivity to what is being communicated. Not only must people possess the breadth of knowledge to understand the meanings, they must share a similar context.

At one point, Hill attended a ritual held for a dead child. He was impressed by the extraordinary power exercised by the shaman who musically gave voice to the grief shared by people who knew the individual. The ceremony galvanized a community that had received a severe blow and helped it confront with courage those natural processes, such as birth and death, that so profoundly affect us all.

Unlike Hill, I did not target ritually powerful speech in my research (Hill 1993:7). However, without a doubt, what I witnessed was what I will call a "ritually powerful event." In its simplest form, this event linked the Bakairí, as a vibrant community of people holding common traditions, to the natural world. The natural world, in this case, is not represented by death as it was in Hill's work. Rather, the mask celebration encompassed a wider set of processes in which we might find such themes as the joys and pains of beginnings and endings or an embracing of the essential relationship between humans and the rest of the universe, represented by the animal faces on the masks. The extraordinary musicality of the mask chants as well as the undercurrent of songs by the men and boys who followed them through the village provided a poignant backdrop for the enactment of these themes.

The disorientation and disturbance I felt must have been minor compared to what the weeping women and exhausted men experienced during that event. After all, it was they who lived the cultural context and possessed the mythological knowledge, both of which are indispensable for total immersion in what Hill so aptly calls "a musically produced space-time" (1993:2). My understanding was superficial and intellectual, while theirs was profound and emotional. Only my ability to empathize allowed me to glimpse how much I was missing.

The History of the Masks

I was amazed the first time I saw the Bakairí masks, and I asked myself where they had come from and what they were for. Through subsequent library research on historical documents and interviews with some of the Indians, I discovered the following.

The Bakairí masks are part of an enduring tradition. Mask making and dancing have a long history, which reaches back until at least the late nineteenth century. In an 1887 visit, von den Steinen (1940) described seeing the Bakairí in what is now Pakuera, dancing in masks to honor the *matrinxã* fish. And Paul Ehrenreich (1929) reported at around the same time that the Bakairí in the Xingú headwaters possessed masks that were so huge that he could not transport them back to Europe.

Mask dancing among these Indians probably continued sporadically through the first part of the twentieth century, although the Bakairí were suffering through the worst phase of contact at that time (Krause 1960). In interviews with older informants, I heard that they gave up the ritual for a time in the 1950s, but not for long. They resurrected it in the 1960s at Pakuera when they presented the masks and their dances to a visiting missionary (Wheatley 1966). The tradition has continued uninterrupted since that time, and certainly when I began field research in 1979, one of the first things I saw was an enormous yakwigado mask, making its stately way down a village path.

Kwamba, the Playful, and *Yakwigado*, the Dignified

Bakairí masks are one meter long and a half of a meter wide. Kwamba masks are oval, and yakwigado are rectangular. They are made of wood or tree bark and decorated with black, red, and white colors. The black is derived from crushed charcoal or *genipapo*, a berry; the red is from another berry called urucu, which the Bakairí cultivate. The white is from chalk that the Indians scrape from deposits in the nearby river.

A group of *kwamba* masks clusters around the camera.

When the masks dance together, kwamba usually come first with yakwigado following. Three important kwamba are *Nuianani-Mak-wala*, *Tãnupede*, and *Kwalobi*. These masks are named in Bakairí after fish. Their faces are painted dramatically with distinguishing marks that can be seen even at a distance, and they are attached to "hair" and "clothes" made from palm.

The ownership, storage, maintenance, and use of the masks involve complex and contradictory traditions. For example, while the women technically own the masks, it is the men who store and guard them. The women pass the masks down from generation to generation through the female side of the family, but the men resurrect the masks each season by repainting the faces. The women know the chants of the masks by heart and teach young people to sing these songs, but these same women pretend they do not recognize the masks when they see them perform, and they look the other way if they stumble on a man maintaining a mask, since that kind of work is supposed to be done in secret. All of this involves a certain amount of discretion and even theatre. However, the Bakairí are equal to the task.

Dangerous Dual Personalities

The two kinds of masks represent distinct personalities. Kwamba is a trickster and a joker. He chases children and plays tricks on elders. He steals and hides things, provoking people to yell at him and even to chase him. The yakwigado, on the other hand, is dignified and serene. This mask moves slowly, chanting in a deep voice. Unlike the kwamba, he never runs, begs, or steals things.

Owners typically choose young men to dance inside the kwamba and more mature men for the yakwigado. When a young man dances for the first time inside a mask, he must learn the chant he will sing. Elderly women and men teach him the lyrics by repeating the words until the young man can successfully sing the entire text alone. Prescribed chants are associated with each mask, but people are also allowed to improvise lyrics. For example, they may sing about events that have taken place. Although the songs are supposed to be respectful and fitting for a guardian spirit to sing, sometimes kwamba masks sing in a suggestive manner.

Once inside a mask a man temporarily adopts the name and identity of its spirit. From the moment he dons the costume, he is technically the guardian spirit of the animal the mask represents. These spirits are dangerous. They can injure or kill people. For example, while making a mask, a man discovered his wife was pregnant. He

The older woman standing to the right of the *kwamba* mask is its owner. Her family join her to pose with the mask.

turned the project over to a friend rather than risk causing his wife to miscarry. Female owners of masks refuse to sleep in the same hut as a mask while it is being prepared for a dancing season out of fear that its spirit will force sexual relations upon them.

The Dances of the Masks

The men prepare the masks during the rainy season. When the time draws near for their ritual debut at the beginning of the dry season, the dancers take the masks out of hiding, and under the cover of night when everyone is asleep, carry them to the men's house. In the morning, they dramatically introduce each one to the villagers. The masked dancer bursts from the men's house and rapidly spins around the central plaza where he remains chanting and stamping his feet. When all of the masks stand in the plaza, they form a line and walk down the village paths, visiting the houses of the mask owners. There, they sing their special ritual songs before moving on to the next house.

After their introduction, the masks and costumes are stored in the men's house for the season. The dancers take them out on a daily basis in the morning and the evening. Each mask leaves the men's house and visits his owner's home where he performs for five or ten minutes. The owner, in turn, prepares a packet of food and slips it under his costume or has a male child take the package to the men's house. When the dancer returns to the men's house, he sheds his costume and shares the food with the others. Several times a season, the masks dance all night. These rituals generally take place on moonless nights. During these vigils, the masks dance from house to house, singing in front of each one.

Women are forbidden to go inside the men's house to see the masks, or from attending some of the rituals associated with them. For example, during the all-night vigils, they must lock themselves inside their homes after the sun sets and not look out the window. The threat of gang rape ensures their cooperation. When the women explained the rules to me, I asked if anyone had recently between punished in that way. They said that they did not know of anyone.

This was apparently one prohibition from which I was not exempt. Before the first all-night vigil I experienced, I did not move indoors quickly enough, and one of the men came over to me and, nervously looking over his shoulder, told me to get inside. Thereafter, I was careful to move respectfully indoors in a timely fashion.

In November, when the rains start again, the masks are put to sleep in a grueling celebration that lasts several days and nights. The entire village is involved, and men, women, and children dance, sing, and eat with the masks until people begin to collapse from exhaustion.

Yakwigado mask entering the men's house backward, in keeping with the ritual, carrying a packet of food from its owner's house.

The ceremony culminates with the men dancing down to the river, where they shred the palm costumes and throw them into the water. They whisk the masks away into the forest and return with them at night when everyone is asleep.

The Masks Organize the Bakairí Economy

Mask traditions relate to ecological and economic aspects of Bakairí culture. The rhythm of their appearance and disappearance in the village mirrors what is happening in key parts of the Bakairí's natural world, and their painted faces, representing birds and fish, call attention to the resources that are vital to the Indians' survival. Furthermore, they ensure the equitable distribution of food in the village because they act as conduits of food from individual households to the communal men's house.

The Rhythm of Producing and Dancing

Masks dance in the Bakairí village mainly during the dry season. If we look at production activities, dancing commences directly after the

Indians harvest rice and corn, and at the time they begin to gradually harvest manioc. During this time, the Indians already have identified and cleared their gardens and are waiting to burn the vegetation and to plant their fields. Ritual dancing coincides with this lull.

The masks retire after the gardens are planted. Seeds go beneath the ground, and mask spirits fade into the river and air. The crops grow as the mask spirits rest, both increasing their life force. The disappearance of the masks and the fish also occurs at the same time. During the rains, when the fish are more difficult to catch, the Indians believe that they are resting and growing in size in much the same way that the plants and spirits are.

The masks effectively tie together ritual activities and the two most important food producing activities of the Bakairí: gardening and fishing. When the men dance, they discharge their life force as well as the energy of the fields and rivers. The Bakairí consume this energy either symbolically or physically. A regeneration period follows.

Resources, Distribution, and Change

Masks not only amplify the pulse of food production in the village, but they also mark crucial resources used by the Indians. For example, the faces on the masks represent animals that are part of the everyday life of the village. The most widespread type is the fish, and abstract expressions of them are found on two-thirds of all masks. The Bakairí illustrate fewer masks with birds, and they avoid using terrestrial animals altogether. The connection between their diet and the masks is clear. Fish is the Bakairí's most popular food, while birds and game are consumed much less frequently. In placing the likeness of important animals on masks, the Indians honor those resources that are so important to their survival.

Mask dancing serves yet another function: that of providing for equitable distribution of food and other goods. Men in masks dance in the morning and in the evening, receiving gifts of food from the mask owners' houses at the same time. Although not every man has a mask, all are allowed to eat the food brought to the communal area. Furthermore, male children who help carry food from the owners' houses are given bits of food to take home to the women, who are forbidden to approach the men's house.

At a fundamental level, mask dancing results in a general pooling of all surplus food in the village and in a reallocation of the resources to the entire group. It reflects an indigenous economic system predicated upon sharing wealth and relying on relatives and friends in times of need. Yet, the Bakairí world is clearly changing. We know that many, if not all, households in the reservation have access to cash with which they purchase foods such as sugar, peanut butter, and canned fruit. These food supplements sometimes contribute to the indigenous diet.

The Indians have introduced these foods into the mask dance without violating the integrity of the masks. When a kwamba or a yakwigado goes to its owner's house to collect a gift of food, it may receive some freshly roasted fish wrapped in a piece of manioc bread, which is the preferred traditional meal. But it may also receive a piece of manioc bread spread with peanut butter. This substitution does not appear to detract from the ritual's power.

The Masks Bind Bakairí Society Together

Masks are an important source of social solidarity among the Bakairí. They call attention to divisions that create conflict and dissension in the village, while at the same time, revealing interlocking aspects of indigenous society.

Men and Women

Compared to many other societies, Bakairí men and women are dependent on each other. This is, in part, because responsibilities and rights associated with each gender role are more rigidly defined among these Indians than they are among people in industrial societies where overlapping is tolerated. For example, Indian men perform such tasks as fishing and hunting, while women cook and wash clothes. Women are not allowed to hunt, and men do not cook or wash clothes. This clear distinction between male and female work means that unless there is a member of both genders present in a household, significant inconvenience, even hardship, results.

This contrasts sharply with contemporary life in North America, where most people are capable of performing a wide variety of tasks. Many American men are excellent cooks and know how to wash their own clothes, while women earn wages and do yard work. This flexible nature of role definition contributes to independence and self-sufficiency as individuals. But it also detracts from interdependency between the genders.

Why don't Bakairí men and women learn to do each other's jobs? Readers may recall from previous chapters that society sanctions them if they adopt inappropriate behaviors. This clear definition of gender roles may well frustrate those who seek a more comprehensive way of life. But, at the same time, it contributes to the functioning of a society in which components are firmly interlocked.

This does not mean friction is totally absent. *Sexual antagonism* exists among the Bakairí, as it does in the United States and other Western countries. And we see reflections of it in the mask rituals. The very way in which masks are used illustrates this point. Once they are taken out of hiding and given fresh coats of color, men take these artifacts out of the hands of their female owners and hide them in the men's house where women cannot see them. Furthermore, during some rituals women are not allowed to leave their houses and to even look outdoors. The threat of gang rape, an unusually harsh penalty by our standards, forces the women to comply with these rules.

Another way in which masks illustrate sexual antagonism concerns the content of their chants, which frequently alludes to specific sources of tension between men and women. Texts of the songs constitute a running commentary of daily confrontations between the genders. Sometimes the themes are traditional in nature. But others reveal how contact with non-Indians has exacerbated conditions.

In one incident, men from a nearby ranch came to visit Pakuera, and the Indians killed a steer to recognize the festive occasion. The younger Bakairí women, dressed in their best clothes, flirted with the Brazilians during the course of the afternoon and evening. There were rumors that some even had sex with the men. The Bakairí men resented the women's friendliness toward the Brazilians, and as a consequence, the masks sang highly critical songs about the women for a week. The women were very angry and complained about the unfairness of the public and controversial nature of the denunciation of their actions. However, retaliation against the masks was impossible.

While the masks reveal some of the sources of friction between men and women, the ways in which the masks are created, maintained, and used show how the genders rise above conflict and cooperate with each other. While men make and wear the masks, women own them and hand them down from generation to generation through the female side of the family. Both women and men must work together to store and to resurrect the masks annually. They refurbish the faces of the masks and manufacture new palm costumes together. Women choose the men who dance inside their masks, and the oldest women teach the chants to new male dancers. While men occupy center stage when they perform the mask dance, women provide an indispensable audience and prepare gifts of thanks for the work they have done.

Mask rituals provide evidence that Bakairí existence is contingent upon cooperative and harmonious relations between the two genders. Both the physical and social reproduction of their world hinges on their successful articulation. Men and women depend on one another to make families, sharing the responsibilities of rearing and educating their offspring. And they both work to create and express cultural traditions that make their way of life so distinctive. Clearly a united front is necessary not only in the religious domain, but in all aspects of life.

The Old and Young

The mask dance also illustrates the differences between the old and young as well as their reliance on each other. A division of labor based on age is seen in the execution and organization of mask rituals. The elders have certain responsibilities not shared by their juniors, while the young are allowed to behave in ways denied the old.

Assignment of masks to dancers occurs on the basis of age. Young males usually are chosen to dance inside the oval kwamba masks. Typical behaviors associated with this kind of mask are similar to those connected with unruly children. A sixteen-year-old boy dressed up as a kwamba gives the impression of being in constant motion.

A group of *kwamba* masks fooling around in front of the men's house.

When he is not racing around the village or dancing with great speed and agility, he rapidly stamps his feet. In addition, the kwamba is a trickster and a joker. He chases children and sneaks up behind elders and scares them. He steals and hides things, tempting people to run after him to retrieve their possessions. Frequently reckless and uncontrollable, he can do damage by breaking or setting fire to things.

Yet the Bakairí view the kwamba with indulgence and amusement, much as they respond to their own children. People tolerate him and even seem to enjoy his behavior despite the fact that it may inconvenience them. Always capricious and unpredictable, the kwamba provides the village with a provocative kind of entertainment.

On the other hand, older men are given rectangular yakwigado masks. They behave in a dignified behavior, moving slowly and chanting in a deep voice. They are regal in their bearing. In contrast with the kwamba, yakwigado masks never run, beg, or steal. In fact, they appear to lack any sense of humor at all.

Yakwigado is accorded a great deal of respect. When asked to compare the chants and the dances of the two, people invariably prefer yakwigado over kwamba because the former has more complicated songs and body language and typically performs them with greater precision. For example, yakwigado is required to enter the men's house backward, not an easy feat to perform with a huge wooden mask that obstructs one's vision and puts one off balance.

The differences between the behaviors of the yakwigado and kwamba are marked and call to mind the distinction between old and young people. While children are allowed to run and play, grown men are not. Society expects them to have work and other important tasks to attend to. Children may provoke and tease, but adults should exhibit a sense of decorum. And although the young can destroy things by mistake, and society may forgive and indulge them, the Bakairí world holds different expectations for adult men and women, who are punished for carelessness.

Yet kwamba and yakwigado masks rely on each other. They chant and dance together on a daily basis and during key rituals, such as when masks are put to sleep for the duration of the rainy season. In fact, without each other to perform as foils, their performances would lack the vividness they now hold. Kwamba's vivacity would pale without yakwigado's solemnity, and yakwigado's deep voice would lack resonance without kwamba's shrill tenor.

The masks illustrate the concept of ritual age reliance by underscoring the importance of the young and old working together both in ritual contexts and in other areas of village life. The young rely on their seniors to teach, nurture, and protect them, while the old depend on their juniors for physical strength and vitality and for care after they pass their prime. Both the old and young rely on each other for the continuation of a familiar and predictable social world.

The Masks Reflect a Living Belief System

Ritual mask dancing is related to the Bakairí ideational system, which is that aspect of culture dealing with intangibles such as ideas and values. One key part of this system is the *sacred* domain, which concerns spiritual, religious matters. It differs from the *profane* area, which has to do with the secular, nonreligious world. The masks help us understand how the Indians distinguish the sacred from the profane. In fact, they epitomize the Indians' sacred world while defining values that are important to the smooth functioning of the profane part of their lives.

The Bakairí believe in the existence of a sacred realm that is inhabited by supernatural beings who live inside such things as animals and plants and who behave in much the same way as humans do. These beings can be seen by people, but they typically stay hidden. We call this belief system *animism* and contrast it with other religious beliefs on the basis of how it depicts spirits. For example, spirits are viewed as lesser beings who are not necessarily all-knowing. They can be tricked in much the same way that humans can—something that would never happen to a Judeo-Christian God.

Chagnon relates a Yanomamö myth that illustrates this essential difference. When Yanomamö die, their souls travel up into one of the upper levels of the four parallel layers that make up the world. They move down a path until they come to a fork where a spirit, the son of Thunder, waits. This being asks if they have been generous or stingy during their lives. If they have been generous, they are allowed to proceed to a place of tranquility, and if they have not, they are sent to a fiery region. Chagnon reports that the Indians are not particularly concerned about this spiritual "moment of truth." They blithely told him that if they have been stingy, they intended to lie to the spirit (Chagnon 1992:103).

Spirits sometimes can be contacted and even manipulated by *shamans*, who are religious semispecialists. These individuals, through long and arduous periods of training, learn to contact and direct specific spirits with whom they have special personal relationships. Through the intercession of these supernatural beings, shamans are able to cure diseases and to perform sorcery against their enemies.

According to the Bakairí, each mask represents a guardian spirit of all of the spirits who reside in a particular animal or fish type. The power of these spirits is very strong and ultimately derives from the river, which is why the Indians return ritual paraphernalia to the water, following a season of dancing. It is there that the mask's force resides.

The mask spirits are somewhat demanding and vengeful. They require people to offer them a reasonable amount of food each season, or they retaliate by sending sickness to the village. Sometimes when it is apparent that the Indians will not have enough time or food to give to the masks, they let the spirits rest, rather than endangering themselves by disappointing these supernatural creatures.

When a person puts on a mask, he allows his body to be used by this guardian spirit. Sometimes people faint when they are dancing, and the Indians believe that when this happens the spirit has actually taken possession of the body and mind of the person. Because a dancer gives up his identity when he comes under the control of the mask spirit, he adopts its name. The community is aware of this and addresses him as if he were the spirit. Although almost everyone in the village knows who is inside a given mask, they are careful to avoid revealing his true identity. Usually a man is set free by the spirit when he takes the mask off. However, sometimes he becomes ill because the spirit will not totally abandon his body. At that point, a shaman must be called in to cure him. He does this with the assistance of a supernatural being with whom he has a particular relationship.

Men who are weak or ill avoid mask dancing because they are especially susceptible to spiritual possession. And the power of the spirit goes beyond the mask wearer, affecting those who are close to him. This explains why men give up mask dancing if there is someone ill in their family, or if their wives become pregnant. The sacred world is a dangerous place from which the weak must be protected.

Unlike supernatural beings in some societies, Bakairí spirits are sexual. We have already established that women refuse to sleep in a house with a mask in it, afraid that it will make sexual advances. Even mask owners are at risk. While a mask is being refurbished and taken away by its dancer, the female owner usually sleeps in the home of relatives.

This is one of the reasons that the masks are kept inside the men's house once they begin to dance. The elderly, women, and most children do not enter this structure and thus are protected from the mask spirits. Also, men do not sleep inside except under special ritual circumstances, so they, too, are afforded some safeguards.

Danger and secrecy are two important characteristics of the sacred realm, and the masks are tangible representatives of it. They are beings who must be treated in a respectful manner, and the Bakairí use the utmost care in dealing with them. Yet masks represent more than an awe-inspiring sacred world. They also provide guidance for the Indians as they lead their daily life. In their chants the masks publicly set forth society's values and ideals. Furthermore, they are agents of social control because they are capable of leveling public critiques.

The mask chants compliment such behaviors as generosity and humility and condemn stinginess and laziness. Stinginess is arguably the greatest sin that can be committed in an Indian village, and everyone is expected to share what they have. Humility is also highly valued. People are not supposed to call attention to themselves or to boast about their accomplishments. They are expected to downplay their contributions to their family and to the group. Those who brag are ridiculed.

Mask chants frequently admonish individuals for their bad behavior. I have examples of texts where masks criticize a man who buys things in the city for women other than his wife, a woman who wants to marry her uncle, a mother who is badgering her daughter to marry prematurely, a young man who broke the confidence of his friend, a daughter-in-law who talked back to her mother-in-law, a wife who won't feed her husband because he is having an affair with another woman, and so forth. The lyrics make specific references but also call for general kinds of behavioral changes.

The masks also review Bakairí interactions with Brazilians. They frequently discourage the adoption of Brazilian ways by advocating traditional values and by criticizing those who do not exemplify them. Critiques are leveled at men and women who have sex with Brazilians as well as at those who involve themselves too deeply in Brazilian traditions.

A Final Word about the Masks

Connections between the ritual masks and the Bakairí's economic, social, and ideological institutions are apparent. The masks function to remind the Indians, on a daily basis, of the many important values that set their culture apart from others. The rituals also serve tangible and practical purposes in that they influence individual and group behavior. The Bakairí Indians are under tremendous pressure to adopt Western traditions, and whether mask dancing survives remains to be seen. We will return to this question in the final chapter of this book when we examine the issue of ethnicity.

Chapter 7

LEADING THE BAKAIRÍ INTO THE TWENTY-FIRST CENTURY

"The headman's leadership is subtle: he leads by soft persuasion and quiet example. Rarely does he raise his voice to harangue his kinsmen; rather, he strokes them lightly with words, never talking too much . . . His is not the ability to coerce, but to persuade or, perhaps more accurately, to lead his kinsmen gently to consensus."
(Kensinger 1995:175–176.)

Contact between the Bakairí and non-Indians transformed the political stage on which indigenous leaders, or *headmen*, act. Significant long-term changes in demographic, economic, and social circumstances have altered not only how leaders come to power, but also their job descriptions and the skills they need to do their jobs successfully. In this chapter I show how the political behaviors of the Bakairí Indians have changed in recent years, and I go on to discuss what kinds of headmen will lead these Indians into the next century.

In presenting my arguments I am following Robert Murphy's example of exploring "the micro-domain of everyday life" by showing how individuals experience structure (Murphy 1978:239). I provide historical and political nuances by combining aggregate data and detailed case studies about how specific leaders make decisions as they cope with complex situations brought about by cultural contact and change.

Leadership and Ecology

Demography

We already know from chapters 2 and 3 that, in the first part of the twentieth century, epidemic diseases caused the Bakairí population to decrease and that this trend was exacerbated by out-migration to towns in search of wage-paying jobs. During the second half of the century, better medical attention became available, and the number of Indians increased. Simultaneously, as a result of economic conditions in the region during the 1970s and 1980s, some Bakairí returned to the reservation to live. Between the time of that baseline research (1979–1981) and a 1989 restudy, the number of people in the reservation grew by 36.8 percent, from 288 to 394 individuals, and by 26.9 percent, from 394 to 500 between 1989 and 1999. The growing number of people at Pakuera, coupled with other factors (Picchi 1995), led to the division of this settlement and the formation of other villages.

How have the above factors affected Bakairí political leadership? First, there were far fewer candidates for leadership. Deaths from epidemic diseases during the first half of the century decreased the number of potential candidates for the headman's position. Headmen used to inherit their titles from their fathers, but as gaps appeared in the demographic structure, such successors became more difficult, and ultimately impossible, to find. Migration out of the reservation in search of jobs only shrank the available pool further.

R. Brian Ferguson (1992) and Napoleon Chagnon and Thomas Melancon (1983) have commented on another, less obvious, way that demography affects political process. The disruption in family life and in the village world caused by disease-related deaths is enormous. The long-term effects on kinship ties and marriage alliances are not easily repaired. Yet it is such relationships that form the political factions, without which headmen cannot effectively manage communities. Chagnon and Melancon use the word "chaos" to describe the shattering effects of disease on the Yanomamö (1983:73), and while the Bakairí Indians' current situation is not chaotic, they may well have endured such a time before World War II.

More recently, turmoil and conflict have plagued the reservation as the number of Indians increased and Pakuera split into several settlements. This division certainly caused disruption and even anguish by separating extended families and rupturing political factions. For example, in 1989 a middle-aged wife of a man who wanted to move to the village where his brothers and mother lived confronted him publicly in tears because she wanted to remain in Pakuera with her mother.

On the other hand, opportunities were created because additional headmen were needed to lead the new communities. By 1989 seven men emerged as consensual leaders in as many different villages. No murders or major sorcery cases marred the transition, although gossip and backbiting, lower-level mechanisms for coping with conflict, continued well after the settlements were formally established.

Ecology and Technology

Along with the demographic changes, there has been a process of ecological depletion and damage that occurred as a result of Western contact and the concomitant introduction of new technology. The Bakairí case is complex and involves a number of factors. The first concerns the occupation of the area around the village of Pakuera for an unusually long time, leading to overexploitation of the gallery forests. There also has been a depletion of fishing resources as a result of non-Indians fishing, legally and illegally, in the area. And there are reports of pollution, as a result of the use of pesticides and fertilizers, both in and around the reservation. Run-off from these chemicals has flowed into the rivers, negatively affecting the water and fish supplies.

With regard to the first factor, much has been written about what Ferguson calls "the *anchoring effect* of Western outposts" (Ferguson 1992:205). Certainly the Bakairí have experienced attraction to, and coercion by, SPI and FUNAI officials, missionaries, anthropologists, and other visitors, all of whom provided medical attention, technology, manufactured goods, and so forth. As a result of their relationships with these outsiders, the Indians have remained in the same area continuously since at least 1930, when Petrullo (1932) visited them.

Anchoring the indigenous community to one location for a long period of time has damaged the ecology of the reservation, particularly in the vicinity of Pakuera. We have already discussed in chapter 4 how the gallery forests, which are necessary for slash-and-burn horticulture, are so overused in that area that the Indians are forced to travel long distances to reach their gardens. Although some Bakairí formed new villages closer to fertile lands in the 1980s, the problem continues to plague those who remain in Pakuera.

The relatively small amount of gallery forest available in the reservation coupled with the long occupation by the Bakairí of the general region, much of the time at Pakuera, may account for the decrease in the number of gardens that household heads made between 1981 and 1989. In 1981, only 16.9 percent (ten of Pakuera's fifty-nine households) did not make traditional gardens, while in 1989, that percentage rose to 48.4 percent (twenty of Pakuera's forty-one households). Although other factors contributed to decisions not to grow crops, I would argue that the ecological depletion of soils in that part of the reservation was a key reason for the decrease in the number of Pakuera gardens.

A second, but less well-documented, question involves the Bakairí perception that the fish supplies in their reservation have diminished in recent history. Some complain that the non-Indians in the region have illegally exploited fish resources, while others blame the mechanized agriculture project for polluting the rivers and killing the fish. A certain amount of circumstantial evidence exists to support the first complaint. The tremendous population growth in the region, which caused the creation of a new state in the 1970s and new municipalities in the 1990s, has increased the demand for fish. Also, anecdotal evidence supports the Indians' contention that non-Indians are illegally fishing in their rivers. In chapter 2 I described how some Bakairí men discovered a group of Brazilian fishermen using nets inside the reservation. Not only was their unauthorized presence in the reservation against the law, but the use of fishing nets was prohibited.

With regard to the third issue—that of river pollution—some of the younger Bakairí who are better informed about environmental issues claim that the mechanized agriculture project as well as the agribusinesses in the area are polluting the rivers that flow through the region. They believe that heavy rains flush poisonous fertilizers and pesticides out of the fields and into the waters. Reports of the Paranatinga River turning murky, and dead fish floating on the surface of the water, are common in Pakuera.

It is ironic that while the long-term dangers associated with such Western technology as fishing nets and chemical pesticides are well known by the Bakairí people, the attraction of such goods remains strong. The Indians lobby heavily for better access to such things as vehicles and tractors. In recent years these demands have proliferated because each village that split off from Pakuera sent delegations to FUNAI to request its own set of equipment. Every community wants a jeep, truck, tractor, disk plow, disk harrow, planter/fertilizer, and pesticide dispenser. Although not all villages have been successful in obtaining what they want, many requests have been honored. The upshot is that, at the same time the Indians are complaining about the impact of non-Indians on the ecology of their reservation, they themselves are contributing to the worsening situation.

Techno-Ecological Change and Its Effects on Leadership

In what ways have these developments affected Bakairí political leadership? They have created a new set of requirements Bakairí headmen must fulfill in order to succeed. Indigenous leaders must possess a better-than-average understanding of the complex non-Indian world with which they interact. The ability to speak Portuguese is indispensable for such interactions. Although many Indians speak some Portuguese, most do not speak the language well enough to allow for comfortable communication with Brazilians. Headmen tend to be among the most proficient Portuguese speakers in the reservation.

The ability to speak Portuguese is not the only skill needed for interacting with non-Indians. General knowledge of Western culture is also important. Information about bureaucracies, agricultural and medical technology, banking, and the media are only some of the areas in which headmen need to be informed. For example, Yuka works competently with non-Indians. The combination of an excellent command of Portuguese and an acute understanding of the FUNAI bureaucracy in Brasilia, which he visits regularly, allows him to function efficiently on behalf of his people.

He claims that during the late 1970s, he persuaded FUNAI to initiate the industrial agricultural project in the Bakairí reservation. Although this is an exaggeration in the sense that FUNAI planned to introduce mechanized agriculture to many reservations in the region, there may be some truth to the story in the sense that the Bakairí reservation is relatively small when compared to other indigenous reservations that received equipment. For example, the Xavante agriculture project was begun on the Pimental Barbosa Reservation, which was made up of over 200,000 hectares, or about four times the size of P.I. Bakairí.

There was concern that the Bakairí would be bypassed for other groups where more adult men could learn to use the technology and more people in general would benefit from the food produced by it. Yuka may have played a decisive role in demonstrating that the Bakairí could manage the project successfully. When the equipment arrived in the village in 1980, he took charge of it and played a key role in determining where the rice field would be located, how large it would be, and when the various phases of cultivation would take place. Indeed he was better informed about mechanized agriculture than the FUNAI agent who resided at the Indian post at that time.

Knowledge of Portuguese and about Western culture allows headmen to cultivate relationships with Brazilians who live near their reservation. Although some Bakairí are not interested in the outside world and have never left the reservation, most headmen travel to ranches in the vicinity where they visit with Brazilians who live on them. They even cultivate relationships with Brazilians who live illegally within the border of their lands. In fact, several headmen have participated in Christian ceremonies where they became godparents of the children of posseiros (landless farmers).

Conklin and Graham's (1995) study of the association between South American Indians and environmentalists offers insights into the relationship between the Bakairí headmen and non-Indians such as FUNAI bureaucrats. They employ Richard White's (1991) concept of *the middle ground*, implicit in which is a rejection of the subordination/domination model that frequently characterizes interactions between indigenous and Western peoples. According to this model, Indians and non-Indians both perceive that their respective goals are being met through the process of negotiation and trade. The so-called middle ground is the arena where this intercultural communication takes place.

Conklin and Graham (1995) apply the middle ground concept to the alliance between South American Indians and environmentally concerned people from "the first world." These two groups share the controversial assumption that the indigenous way of using resources is consistent with the Western conservation principle (p. 696). As a result of this perception, new forms of communication and cooperation have benefited both Indians and environmentalists. Yet Conklin and Graham identify "fault lines" in this middle ground as they point out that the stereotypes of Amazonian Indians, so valuable to environmentalists as symbols, misrepresent both the diversity of indigenous cultures and the reality of how they manage their resources (1995:705–706).

This analysis of White's model is pertinent to a discussion of the Bakairí Indians' relationship with FUNAI agents. FUNAI's commitment to a philosophy dedicated to the preservation of Indian culture and to the health and education of Indians (FUNAI 1988) provides a protective shield between the Bakairí and the outside world and engenders a sense of power and control in the Indians. The Bakairí people's recent memory is one of a long and placid association with organizations such as SPI and FUNAI, punctuated by few major altercations, and their perception is that FUNAI accommodates their demands once their headman articulates their needs. Yuka's conviction that he persuaded the FUNAI bureaucracy to begin a mechanized agriculture project in the reservation is a good example of the decontextualized information with which the Indians construct their world.

Middle grounds, however, are mutually constructed accommodations. FUNAI agents also perceive that their goals are being met and have characterized the Bakairí to me as *manso* or tame. Contrasting them with the somewhat more assertive Xavante and Kayapó, some FUNAI personnel report that the Bakairí have successfully completed "the pacification process." And in Cuiabá at the regional FUNAI offices, I was told they are a success story because of the degree to which they ostensibly have adopted Western culture. FUNAI officials cite as role models for other groups the Bakairí men who learned to drive tractors and to work on the agriculture project producing sacks of rice to sell in regional markets. Although FUNAI frames its commitment to the future of Brazilian Indians in terms of cultural integrity, assumptions about Western-style economic development permeate its offices (FUNAI 1988:38–41).

The role of indigenous political leaders is clearly a key one in the process of constructing any middle ground and of situating their people within it. Negotiating the terms of exchange and the joint political positions shared by Indians and FUNAI agents is done in Portuguese, in bureaucracies, and in cities, all foreign entities to the Bakairí. Indian headmen manage to cope not only with these disadvantages, but also with foreign cultural constructions, which they then interpret and take back to their communities.

Yet the temporary nature of middle grounds cannot be ignored. There is a warning implicit in the description of the relationships between Native Americans and Europeans during the previous century that applies to South American Indians and environmentalists today. The middle ground that White defined in reality preceded a preliminary stage for unjust and even brutal treatment of Indians in North America. Many Native Americans died, and those who lived were isolated on inferior reservations.

Conklin and Graham's work resonates with these historical observations. They describe the way ecopoliticians turn on Indian leaders who fall out of fashion. For example, these researchers point out that in the 1970s and 1980s, environmentalists embraced the Xavantes as the perfect symbol of "The Indian." However, they eventually rejected the Xavante leaders and adopted Kayapó ones instead. Conklin and Graham show that time and again, Western ecopoliticians abandoned indigenous leaders for failing to meet their own expectations, sometimes leaving an Indian headman exposed and vulnerable after encouraging and helping him to take controversial stands (1995:706).

Carlos Frederic Mares de Souza's (1994) recent overview of the tenuous web of relationships between Brazil's Indians, courts, military, and politicians, all under the umbrella of the 1988 constitution, underscores the illusory quality of the middle ground model. The five hundred or so Bakairí who inhabit their tiny reservation are not powerful, nor do they exercise a great deal of control over their own destiny at this point. For now, the agendas of organizations such as FUNAI and the environmentalists are dovetailing with the very real and practical needs of such groups as the Bakairí. But this situation may well change in the future.

Leadership and Socioeconomics

Economics

Ferguson's (1992) analysis of how contact affected Yanomamö warfare levels provides a starting point for our discussion of how the influx of Western goods in the Bakairí reservation, and more generally the penetration of the cash economy, have affected reciprocity and redistribution systems. Assuming that sharing is the foundation of village solidarity, he establishes that Indians tend to prevent Western goods from flowing through traditional reciprocity networks because these items are scarce and valuable. As a result, tension surrounds these objects and causes widening social rifts that result in atomization, conflict, and violence.

Switching to a macrolevel regional perspective, Ferguson develops his model even further. He suggests that the villages that remain anchored for extended periods in close proximity to "Western outposts," such as centers for missionaries, government officials, businesses, and anthropologists, have major advantages over isolated communities because they can more easily acquire and retain valuable Western goods. Inequities evolve even further and lead to more intervillage violence (Ferguson 1992:206–207.)

With regard to the Bakairí, the tradition of sharing is certainly fundamental to village life. Furthermore, it is clear that one of the key aspects of the headman's role has been, until the recent past, ensuring that *redistribution* networks worked. Such networks act to spread out goods in the village so that nobody goes without and no one has too much. However, the penetration of the cash economy into the reservation has resulted in the breakdown of many of these systems and has led to a redefinition of this dimension of leadership.

What sources of cash do the Bakairí tap? We already know from chapter 4 that the Indians acquire cash by working at nearby ranches, receiving social-service-type payments from the government, and earning FUNAI salaries. The majority of households in the reservation have direct access to cash from one of these sources. However, some have more money than others, and some have none at all. As with Ferguson's description of the Yanomamö, the resultant tensions and friction disrupt village life, causing conflict and strife.

Ideally, headmen smooth over such problems by facilitating redistribution of valued goods so all households have at least some access to them. However, this is not what is happening in Bakairí villages today. Both in Pakuera between 1979 and 1981 and in various villages in 1989 and 1999, examples of headmen using their positions for privileged access to cash and goods led to the development of incipient stratification as certain families accumulated more cash than others. Some manifestation of wealth differences currently include ownership of cattle, living in houses made of concrete instead of traditional materials, and having possessions such as watches, bikes, clothes, and knives.

One of the more egregious examples of this trend was when a headman took over a small store started in 1975 by a FUNAI agent. The original intent of starting it was to reduce the time and expense Indians spent on traveling to Paranatinga, the closest town, to purchase

A house made of concrete
rather than traditional
materials marks a wealth
difference in the village.

necessities. By 1979 the FUNAI agent had left the area, and the headman assumed responsibility for the store. A male kinsman used the
FUNAI truck to purchase supplies in the city and to transport them
to Pakuera. The headman then sold these goods to the Bakairí for a
profit. In a one-year period, I ascertained that $2,138 worth of goods
were sold at the store. However, I am convinced that was the bare
minimum since the headman was decidedly unenthusiastic about my
documenting the flow of goods in and out of his store. What began as
a community solution to the problem of unavailability of goods to villagers became one man's opportunity to get rich. And he got that
opportunity because he was headman.

If we follow Ferguson's example and switch to the macrolevel regional
perspective, similar inequities emerge between villages. For example,
the number of cattle owned by individuals and by communities varies
(see table 4-5). Pakuera and Aturua maintain the largest numbers. In
fact the Bakairí in these two settlements control three-fourths of all the
cattle in the reservation, while the Indians in Paikum have about ten

head and those in Paixola have none. And other kinds of material culture are distributed differently in the reservation. Concrete-walled houses, treadle sewing machines, dirt bikes, and propane-gas stoves are more frequently found in some villages than others.

Ferguson's model relates the presence of manufactured goods to the concept of Western "outposts," or communities where Indians regularly have contact with non-Indians. Among the Bakairí, I was able to distinguish three kinds of villages: ones with relationships with officials from Indian agencies, ones with connections with businesspeople, and ones with no regular interactions with non-Indians.

Pakuera is an example of the first group. People who live in this settlement clearly have many interactions with non-Indians because the FUNAI agent resides there, and medics and missionaries visit. These people have jobs to do in the reservation, but they also trade items and even give Indians goods without recompense. This type of contact is less likely to occur in settlements that fall into the second category. Border villages such as Sowapo and Kaiahoualo abut the ranches near the reservation. The ranchers operate on the basis of the profit motive, so their relationships with the Indians are different from that of FUNAI officials. The Bakairí depend on the ranchers both for cash, which they obtain by providing services, and for occasional rides, for which they are required to pay.

Bakairí villages such as Paikum and Paixola fell into the last category until fairly recently. These settlements were isolated and possessed few Western goods, having only occasional opportunities for contact with non-Indians. Paixola remains like this, but two American missionaries are currently working part-time in Paikum. Building on work begun by Protestant missionaries in the 1960s, they are working on a project to translate the Bible into the Bakairí language. Their part-time presence ensures a flow of manufactured goods into the village.

Ferguson's model is valuable in that it helps us understand the process whereby modes of political leadership change as headmen of groups such as the Bakairí not only obtain Western goods but modify their behaviors to maximize access to them. Additionally, the notion of "outposts" provides a conceptual tool for ranking villages in a region according to wealth and possessions.

Kinship

Inheritance of titles, number of adult male relatives, and marriage exchange used to constitute a key set of factors in determining leadership talent. Inheritance rules played a key role because fathers passed their titles down to their sons, and the number, age, and solidarity of related men figured heavily into determining the identity, and tenure, of a Bakairí leader because the support of kin was crucial to a leader's ability to lead. Currently inheritance rules are not applied, and the significance of kin relations has diminished. What has become paramount in determining who assumes leadership roles in the reservation is how effectively individuals work with FUNAI personnel and interface with non-Indians.

Bakairí headmen previously inherited their titles through the male line. Generally, sons followed their fathers, and male parallel cousins could inherit in the absence of a biological son. (See chapter 5 for a discussion of parallel cousins.) This practice is consistent with the findings of many anthropologists who have worked with indigenous peoples in South America (Price 1981; Kracke 1978).

However, the last Bakairí headman to inherit his title in this manner was named Milao, and he relinquished his responsibilities in the middle of the 1970s due to illness. He died in 1988. His two sons, who normally would have followed him as Bakairí leaders, left the reservation to work for FUNAI even before his death. For the first time in their recent past, the Indians were left without a "legitimate" headman.

FUNAI's solution to this problem consisted of introducing Jeffersonian democratic procedures. Agents encouraged the Bakairí to nominate two men, and then instructed the Indians on how to vote with colored paper ballots. The man for whom adult men and women cast the most ballots won the election. Under this system, however, tenure became an issue because traditionally headmen remained in office for extended periods of time, until they became ill or died. As it turned

A Bakairí headman.

out, the elected leader only remained in office for two years before being toppled by a rival. Following the somewhat disruptive experiment, the Bakairí abandoned this type of democracy and, when conflict between factions marked the beginning of a transition, a new leader emerged by consensus formation to assume the title.

The number and age of relatives also contribute to headmen's success, although in recent years the significance of these factors has diminished. Anti, an older headman, spoke at great length about how important brothers and parallel cousins used to be in establishing and affirming the legitimacy of a leader. He described an incident in which he was accused by members of another faction of stealing community cattle and selling them to non-Indian ranchers in the area. His antagonists tried to convince the other villagers that Anti should be ostracized from the village for several months as punishment. His five brothers and two male parallel cousins, all adults, organized around him, thwarting his enemies.

Older Bakairí leaders, in contrast to younger headmen, are more likely to be members of families in which *double marriages*, consisting of two siblings marrying siblings from another family, have taken place. For example, Otav, ex-headman of Pakuera and present headman of Aturua, solidified the connection between his and his wife's family by encouraging his sister to marry his wife's brother. Another headman achieved the same effect by marrying two of his sons to two sisters. These unions clearly help to ensure affines' loyalty to a headman.

Although there is no doubt that large numbers of kin contribute to the effectiveness of Bakairí headmen, other skills and qualities recently eclipsed the significance of this factor. In 1989, two young headmen lived in separate villages in the reservation. One had four mature male brothers and the other had no brothers or classificatory brothers. Neither of them had sons or nephews old enough to contribute to their efforts. One would predict that the headman with kin would be more prestigious, influential, and powerful; yet he was not. The other leader was more respected because of his cooperative and close relationship with FUNAI officials and with nearby ranchers, that is, he had skills that made him successful in dealing with non-Indians.

As Bakairí headmen face new and complex situations, other qualities and skills come into play. Examples include organizing journalists to come to the reservation to film a Bakairí mask dance, which was later shown on national news in 1989, and traveling regularly to work within the FUNAI bureaucratic system in Cuiabá and Brasilia to secure additional vehicles for the reservation.

In trying to evaluate how contact has affected the role kinship plays in the selection of leaders, Roberto Da Matta (1976), Dennis Werner (1982), and R. Brian Ferguson (1992) discuss how indigenous leaders exploit their relations with outsiders, using the goods Westerners bring and the prestige associated with these foreigners to enhance their own power. On the other hand, Anthony Seeger (1981) and Michael Brown (1993) emphasize the role played by non-Indians in actually creating indigenous leaders. In the first case, traditionally defined leadership qualifications are not necessarily affected in the sense that headmen continue to work within indigenous parameters, using their contacts with missionaries, anthropologists, and government officials only to facilitate their jobs. For example, Werner (1982) notes that contact does not disrupt Mekranoti-Kayapó inheritance rules. Rather, the presence of outsiders makes it easier for a Kayapó chief to inherit his father's position because members of the chief's family become "culture brokers" (1982:343).

However, in the case where contact situations result in the creation of leaders, traditional qualifications such as kin relations and inheritance rules are circumvented, and individuals who would not normally assume positions of power are given this opportunity, either consciously or unconsciously, by Westerners. It is clear that more Bakairí men than ever before now have the opportunity to become leaders of their communities. Inheritance of titles is no longer a requirement, nor do they have to cope with the complexity of marriage exchange. Furthermore, the kin-based factions they used to depend on to support them are not as indispensable as they were in the past.

Yet, if the qualifications for political leaders have changed, then so has the job description. Community members require their headmen to interface effectively with such parties as journalists, FUNAI agents, local ranchers, anthropologists, and intruders into the reservation. I would also argue that relative effectiveness is measured in terms of factors such as land security, health care availability, agricultural technology, availability of vehicles, and other such services and goods.

Brown (1993) calls our attention to a phenomenon we are only beginning to appreciate. Many indigenous leaders, who have recently assumed the responsibility of traveling outside their territories and interfacing with politicians and journalists for their people, have found their authority challenged when they are absent from their constituents for long periods of time. The double-edged sword of serving as a headman in a modern national context challenges indigenous leaders, and as Brown notes, the most successful of them "return to the idioms of traditional authority" when necessary (Brown 1993:312).

What Bakairí Headmen Say

In a series of interviews I did of past and present headmen, Bakairí headmen told me what qualities they thought were most important for ensuring a successful tenure. This section examines some of these and illustrates how deficiencies in one or several of these areas could prevent headmen from taking advantage of such benefits as a large kin base or a willingness to advocate Bakairí culture.

I was told that the single most important characteristic of a good Bakairí leader is his ability to remain calm. A good headman is not expected to lose patience or to get angry at members of the village no matter how they behave. He must be able to control his feelings so that they do not influence his decisions. A capacity to tolerate the daily drama of village life while remaining objective is critical for a headman's success.

Otav, one of the most stoical headmen, said that this quality was difficult to cultivate. And yet without it, political allegiances and social relations clouded his judgment. For example, Otav's brother-in-law disliked a Brazilian nurse who visited the reservation for a few weeks during an epidemic. The brother-in-law met several times with Otav to convince him to expel the nurse from the village. The situation became emotionally charged over time as agitated groups took sides. Otav seemed caught between doing what was best, healthwise, for the villagers and satisfying the demands of his increasingly provocative kinsman. In the end, he allowed the nurse to complete her work and, at the same time, avoided alienating his brother-in-law by remaining low-keyed and patient.

Controlled aggression is another important headman characteristic. In some ways it seems to contradict the attribute described above. However, leaders need be able to "read situations" and ascertain how to behave within certain contexts. For example, it is necessary for a headman to know how and when to fight. He is not expected to engage in physical altercations because they generally take place between younger men. Nor is he expected to do spiritual battle. Tradition does not require a Bakairí headman to be a shaman. However, under certain circumstances, he cannot compromise but has to defend his position. The example Gilo gave to illustrate this was that of a headman defending his people's lands from invasion by posseiros. He stated that if posseiros entered the reservation, the headman must go at once to the squatter settlement and speak with the non-Indian leaders, or he will be perceived as lacking in courage by his people.

Bakairí headmen clearly see themselves as men of peace in spite of the need to behave assertively. They readily contrast their behaviors with those of the Kayapó Indians, who are known for their public demonstrations of aggression. The Bakairí perceive these Indians as behaving inappropriately and attribute their behavior to the tribe's relatively recent contact and pacification.

Shrewdness and canniness are other traits vital to the success of a headman. Verimo, another leader, stated that a headman must be able to thwart factions that want to overthrow him, or he will not survive long as a leader. When he perceives he is in danger, only a clever and rapid response will defeat his opponents. For example, Kwigi verbally attacked Palo, a shaman and headman. After one difficult interaction, Palo publicly reported that he had gone home and ingested enough tobacco to induce a trance in which he contacted his spiritual guide who helped him cure people. He said that this spirit was so angered by Kwigi's behavior that he wanted to send a huge storm to destroy him and his followers. But Palo claimed he pleaded Kwigi's case, and the spirit relented.

Palo achieved several goals when he publicly recounted this story to the villagers. He warned Kwigi that he was crossing the bounds of acceptable behavior and that further action on his part could lead to violence. At the same time, Palo revealed himself to be a benign leader and a man of peace even to his adversaries because he forestalled a catastrophe. Kwigi lost face, and public opinion turned against him.

Circumspection is another key characteristic of a successful headman. For example, Yuka said that although one must not appear uninterested, discretion in a small society is highly valued. Anti added to these observations by evoking the metaphor of spillage. A headman cannot "spill out" every thought or feeling he has about a subject. That would destroy the illusion of neutrality. On the contrary, he must keep his own council and listen to what others have to say about things.

Headmen are usually generous people. An example I witnessed was when some Bakairí from Paixola wanted to use Pakuera's truck. Many of Pakuera's men objected because the Paixola driver was not a popular man. However, Pakuera's headman argued that any reservation resource belonged to all of the Indians. He said it would be unfair to refuse Paixola's request.

Bakairí leaders are also conscientious and responsible people, and they habitually do more than other villagers. They try to motivate people by setting a good example. One year FUNAI organized a statewide cattle vaccination program that involved the Bakairí reservation. The Indian agent told Otav that he needed to know how many cattle there were in the reservation so that adequate medicine could be ordered. Otav organized some of the men to round up the cattle. They began work, on horseback, before dawn. As the day wore on, the men disappeared one by one until, at sundown, only Otav remained seated on his horse, laboriously completing the task. The following day his leg muscles were so sore that he limped down to the river to bathe.

It is imperative that headmen maintain a reliable flow of information between themselves and their constituents. One way headmen keep informed is by carefully and regularly consulting with all factions in the village. Successful leaders make it their business to meet with all the men in front of the men's house during the early morning before the people go to their gardens, and in the evening prior to going to sleep.

Informal discussions appear at first glance to dominate the meetings. However, the men actually are forging compromises about how to manage the village. They also spend a great deal of time conferring with FUNAI agents and other non-Indians in the area. When ranchers arrive in the reservation, they usually go directly to the headman's house.

The headman's wife is an invaluable asset in that she not only defends his positions to the women and younger men, but she also gathers information. The most effective way to access news quickly is to go to the river when the women are washing clothes. This activity requires individuals to spend several hours at a time in one location, allowing for involved discussions. If the morning and evening meetings of the men at the headman's house represent brief, up-to-the-minute news broadcasts, then doing the wash constitutes in-depth analysis of issues. All of this information is funneled back to the headman, who synthesizes and evaluates it.

Headmen who do not regularly consult with their constituents leave themselves open to criticism. They are perceived as being uninformed and uncaring. Additionally, the Bakairí are convinced that if someone is not being open, then it usually means they are trying to benefit themselves at the expense of everyone else. For example, Ago was a headman of a small village on the Sowapo River. A number of Brazilian posseiros moved into the reservation over the course of a year and a half. They built small houses near Ago's fields, which were located some distance from Sowapo. The people in his village complained that they did not know why these non-Indians were in the reservation.

The mystery was solved to the satisfaction of the villagers when they discovered that the squatters were raising pigs for Ago. He planned to sell these animals when they reached maturity to ranchers in the region. Ago illegally authorized the squatters to make slash-and-burn gardens in the reservation in return for doing him this favor. Eventually the non-Indians were forced out of the reservation, and the FUNAI agent warned Ago not to do that again.

A second method used by headmen to increase communication concerns the use of *silence*. Anti emphasized the importance of a leader remaining quiet. He said that a man who talks too much will never be heard. Rather, a headman should be silent because only then will people listen when he speaks. Otav provides the best example of the way in which silence can be used. He seldom speaks, and when he does so, he generally echoes in a low voice what another person has just said. This technique serves the purpose of affirming the speaker's point.

Reliance upon a soft voice is another related technique depended upon by successful headmen. The Bakairí associate a loud voice with anger. Compared to non-Indians, they generally speak in quieter tones, and leaders speak in even lower voices as they attempt to maintain the impression of someone who is humble and unassuming.

Many researchers have commented on the important role *oration* plays in lowland Indian societies (Gregor 1977; Seeger 1981; Graham 1995). The Bakairí also employ formal speech making in order to communicate their positions on key issues. Although any man may speak in front of the men's house, a headman's words undoubtedly carry more weight.

The Bakairí reserve the use of oration for important occasions. For example, when the Bakairí found professional fishermen in their reservation and confiscated their fishing equipment, representatives from IBAMA, the environmental branch of the Ministry of the Interior, and from FUNAI came to the reservation to try to resolve the conflict. Many Bakairí men took the opportunity to stand in front of the men's house and orate about the event. Headmen from several of the Bakairí villages spoke, but Gilo, headman of the largest village, addressed the group last and summarized many of the arguments presented by his colleagues.

The incident described above also illustrates another technique used by headmen to maximize their influence. Waud Kracke (1978), David Price (1981), and Jonathan Hill (1984) have commented on the importance of flexibility in leadership style. Altering one's management style is critical to the survival of the headman. Most indigenous leaders stress *consensual leadership*, a leadership style stemming from the consent of both parties involved in a decision. In this case, the headman might be one party and the group of constituents the other party. This is by far the most popular mode of leadership among the Bakairí. However, more headmen are becoming adept at assuming an authoritarian leadership style, which consists of making unilateral decisions without consulting one's followers.

Bakairí leaders claim their power is rooted in concessions the villagers make. And, in fact, headmen are allowed by the Bakairí people to do only so much. Yet the ability to act decisively in times of crisis is tolerated by the Indians. For example, when the fishing boats illegally entered the reservation, Ji, a relatively young headman, confronted the fishermen and took their boats despite the lack of village consensus on what should be done. In fact many of the Bakairí were not even aware of what happened until after the event took place.

Jere, another leader, demonstrated this same rapid shift to an authoritarian political mode when the Bakairí contested the occupation of part of their territory by cattle-raising ranchers. He played a major role in organizing the Bakairí to stage a sit-in at the regional FUNAI headquarters, and later, when the Indians returned to their reservation, to go into the Paixola area and burn down the buildings on two of the ranches.

Ensuring a regular flow of information between a headman and his constituents continues to be the mainstay of the finest leader's repertoire. Contact with non-Indians has not diminished the significance of such techniques. Yet reliance upon different management styles constitutes an increasingly important aspect of a leader's craft. The number of crises precipitated by contact with non-Indians may lead to greater reliance on the authoritarian style at the expense of the traditional consensual style.

Summary

The Bakairí culture, like all other cultures, is constantly changing. During the 1700s, we know that Europeans contacted the ancestors of today's Bakairí. Although many Indians fled into the headwaters of the Xingú River, they could not escape European explorers forever. Today they live in permanent contact with non-Indians. Many Bakairí speak Portuguese, and some know how to read and write. They wear clothes and possess Western goods such as bicycles and watches. And they earn and spend money.

The shift from a subsistence-based economy to a capitalist system of production probably began soon after the Bakairí moved to their present location. However, over the last three decades, the rate of change accelerated as the Brazilian frontier moved farther west. Ranchers and farmers now surround the reservation. The Bakairí actively participate in the regional economy. Although they do not technically own the land on which they make their slash-and-burn gardens, some Indian families now own small herds of cattle. Furthermore, FUNAI has made modern agricultural machinery available to them as a group, and while several men have the skills to utilize this equipment, others are at a disadvantage because they lack these competencies. Finally, a number of Bakairí are amassing capital, while others are not.

These modifications in the economic system, as well as demographic and ecological changes, have transformed the Bakairí's political system. The Indians have redefined both the process whereby Bakairí leaders assume power and the requirements for indigenous leaders. Headmen work in two different arenas: the village and the nation-state. Successful performance in both ensures their tenure, while failure in one leads to a loss of power and influence.

James Flanagan (1989) and Lin Poyer (1993) discuss the importance of documenting the process whereby indigenous peoples adopt hierarchical modes of leadership. While they warn against "naturalizing" egalitarianism, or assuming that egalitarianism is a natural state that need not be documented or accounted for, they note the ambivalence toward inequality in a society that traditionally redistributes power and wealth. Poyer goes on to point out that a fundamentally egalitarian society can undergo a partial transition to a hierarchical type of society. Egalitarian and hierarchical contexts evolve with rules governing access to strategic resources in each arena. There is a tension between the two, and by focusing on this tension and allowing public discourse to take place about it, the existence of at least some egalitarianism is guaranteed for the time being.

A fieldwork anecdote sums it up. Yuka and I, along with about fifteen other Bakairí, took the FUNAI truck from P.I. Bakairí to Cuiabá. Under the best of conditions, this trip is long and arduous. At a certain point, we stopped at one of the roadside bars, so popular in that area. Yuka confided that he was hungry, and surreptitiously showing me some cash he had, he said he wanted to buy something to eat. In the end, he decided against it, explaining that if he bought food for himself, he would have to buy it for all the Bakairí in the truck. Caught between two value systems, he could neither generously share his wealth as his father would have done, nor could he defy village traditions and eat alone.

Chapter 8
THE BAKAIRÍ:
INDIANS, ETHNIC MINORITY, OR BOTH?

"For centuries the white man has been the Indians' most imposing 'significant other.' Far from being 'peoples without history' with 'totemic' minds, the Indians are and have been engaged in interpretations and reinterpretations of contact."

(Ramos 1988:230)

The Bakairí in a Global Context

In 1999, twenty years after my first visit to the Bakairí reservation, I returned for a follow-up study. I could have taken a bus from Cuiabá to Paranatinga and then waited for the Bakairí truck to come and pick me up. The roads between the two towns are now paved, and the bus trip takes only ten hours. But I decided not to risk it because of the rainy season. The dirt roads between Paranatinga and the reservation would still be muddy, which meant I could count on that part of the trip taking five hours, and on the truck being stuck in the mud at least once. I rented a small plane and flew in.

Yuka and Beri, now with two grandsons, were flying with me in the extra seats. They were returning from Cuiabá where they had been visiting their daughter who had married a non-Indian. Yuka looked

157

great. I had met him at the FUNAI offices in Cuiabá and immediately noticed his new jeans and eyeglasses. Glasses in the reservation used to be uncommon, but I was to discover on this trip that many Bakairí now wear them.

Beri and I stood near the air hanger and caught up on news while the pilot weighed us and our bags. Her mother was still alive, but her vision was failing; Nai, her son, and Rea, his wife, were enjoying the new home they had built next door to Yuka and Beri's; Nilda, her daughter, had gotten a divorce but then remarried; she now had two sons, and so on.

Once in the air, I peered down and noted that although there were still huge stretches of green cerrado and gallery forest, it was clear that much more land than I remembered had been farmed or turned into pastures. Roads crisscrossed the fields under us, and ranch after ranch went by. Since I first began working in Mato Grosso, many things had changed. I recalled some background reading I did before my trip. Agricultural products account for 90.4 percent of the total exports of Mato Grosso, whereas minerals represent only about 5 percent. This is quite different from the colonial period described in chapter 2. During that period, it was the desire for minerals that fueled the exploration of the region. Farming took the back seat.

Fields and farms now dot the region in which the Bakairí reservation lies.

The Mato Grosso economy has a lot of room to grow. Statistics indicate that 28 percent of the state is judged arable, but only 3 percent is under agricultural use. The main crop is soybean, and the state's economy is heavily dependent on the export of it or derivative products such as soy oil. In the last five years, production has increased by a whopping 75 percent, and soybean sales generated U.S.$925 million. Because of their high quality they are competitive on the international market, and Japan is one of the principal importers (Atanes and de Lamonica 1998:8–10).

Some economists express concern that Mato Grosso is too dependent on soybean production and have advised businesses to diversify. They are attempting to do so and now grow other crops such as rice, cotton, and even grapes from which they manufacture jelly. Unlike soybeans, these products are sold only on the internal market at this time (Atanes and de Lamonica 1998:8-10).

Mato Grosso is also fighting for its share of the tourist industry that Brazil is developing. Between 1990 and 1995, the number of tourists visiting Brazil each year increased by 55.9 percent from 1.09 million to 1.70 million. About a million of these come from Argentina and Uruguay, which are located geographically close to Brazil, but the next largest number, about 370,000, travel from Europe. Germany and Italy far outrank other European countries in terms of the number of tourists, but many Spaniards, Portuguese, and French also visit Brazil for pleasure. North America lags behind with only about 133,000 U.S. and 11,000 Canadian tourists (Embratur 1997).

Most visitors head for the beautiful coastal cities of Rio de Janeiro and Bahia, but a growing number are opting to travel to Mato Grosso to visit the *Pantanal,* or as it is called in Brazil, *O Grande Pantanal* (the Big Pantanal). This unique natural area cuts across the states of Mato Grosso and Matto Grosso do Sul as well as Paraguay and Bolivia. Similar to the Everglades in Florida, it is swampy and filled with rivers, lakes, and ponds. And it teems with exotic and beautiful wildlife. A recently published tour book describes it as follows.

> Although nearly obscured by the eco-media's blitz on the Amazon rainforest, the Pantanal—an immense kidney-shaped swampland in Western Brazil—is perhaps the country's greatest natural resource . . . Simply, what the Amazon is to flora, the Pantanal is to fauna. If you want to see Brazilian wildlife at its most exotic, come to the Pantanal. (Bloom 1997:671)

The Pantanal is the largest wetland area in the world. It is home to such mammals as the jaguar, tapir, giant otter, giant anteater, wolf, giant armadillo, and the highest concentration of caymans anywhere. Bird watchers are attracted by the huge number of birds, many of them relatively unknown. This area has not been studied seriously by scientists, and only recently the first serious academic work about its ecology was published (Por 1995).

Mato Grosso is attempting to woo tourists from the coastal cities by offering them ecotours of the area. I noticed that a wide range of such tours were available when I was in Cuiabá in 1999. Tourists have a choice of accommodations in rustic lodges on ranches or in luxurious guest houses that boast pools and satellite-dish TV. Package tours include horseback riding and canoeing, and all promise glimpses of wildlife.

A young Brazilian woman in a shop in Cuiabá symbolizes the energy of the Brazilian west.

Not coincidentally a new television miniseries called *Pantanal* began in 1998 and was still in progress in early 1999. The story line included a romance between a woman born in the Pantanal and a man from cosmopolitan Rio de Janeiro, with all the assorted tensions and problems one would expect in such a relationship. However, it was clear that the real hero or heroine of the series was the Pantanal itself, which figured predominantly in each episode.

Concerns about the future of the area have recently surfaced. The Pantanal has been identified as a preferred site for a massive government-sponsored development project called *the Hidrovia*. Plans are shaping up for the construction of a huge shipping channel that would connect the Pacific and Atlantic Oceans so that ships could take a short cut from the east to the west coasts as they carry cargo to Asia. Slicing through these wetlands and dredging the area would clearly transform the region beyond recognition. Regular shipping traffic such as we see passing through the Panama Canal would do even further damage (Eckstrom 1996).

Brazil, like the United States, is a huge, diverse country with many different and competing interests. Both in the national political arena as well as in regions such as Mato Grosso there are conflicting notions about what is best. Whether one should develop ecotourism in the Pantanal or build a shipping lane are questions being debated in the halls of government and in the press. Although we may not know at this time what will happen to the Hidrovia project, we can be certain about one thing. The economic profile of Mato Grosso is changing rapidly, and the population of the state is growing.

This is the complex world in which the Bakairí live. How they survive this challenge depends to a great extent on how they view themselves and their opportunity to participate in it.

Arriving at Pakuera One More Time

The first thing that struck me when I initially arrived in the reservation was the heat. This time it was the presence of Este, a Bakairí man whom I had not seen in a long time. Frequently outside the reservation, he lived for a while in both Brasilia and Cuiabá. Now he had returned. As we walked off of the landing strip, he told me that FUNAI radioed that morning from headquarters about my arrival.

He was currently the FUNAI Indian agent, or as he put it, "the FUNAI agent for the time being." He added casually that the entire agent concept was under review, and that in his opinion a new model was needed, one which involved the withdrawal of FUNAI from the Bakairí reservation altogether and the establishment of an autonomous indigenous area which the Bakairí would administer themselves.

I had not been on the ground for five minutes, and I was already groping for my tape recorder and asking Este if I could tape an interview with him. He agreed and led me to the house of Gilo, the headman. Gilo was not home, but his wife brought me a tiny cup of cafezinho, which she quietly asked me to accept. It reminded me of so many years ago when I first visited Yuka, and Beri had shyly entered the room to offer me coffee.

Este and I sat for about an hour and had an extraordinary conversation. During that brief time, he sketched key events that had affected the Bakairí in the recent past and the direction in which he believed the group was now moving. He began by telling me about a UNESCO-sponsored tour that over twenty Bakairí men had gone on in the late 1990s. For six weeks they had toured Europe, performing, what UNESCO called, folk dances with a number of other European and Latin American groups. Este reported liking Europe, but he had been frustrated because he could not talk to Europeans as much as he wanted. So few of them spoke Portuguese, and none of the Bakairí spoke any other European language.

Este and his sisters Dora and Daral also had opportunities to travel to international indigenous conferences and exchange programs. I was amazed when he reported to me that he had been to what he called *Novo Mexico*, or New Mexico, where he had attended a conference in the Navajo Nation. He was extremely impressed with them and asked me if I knew of a way to set up an exchange program so that he could do an internship with them.

My impression was that he, and many other Bakairí I met on that trip, were intensely curious about the outside, and intensely open to experiencing it. This perception was confirmed when I asked if the Bakairí were still selling cultural artifacts in the FUNAI stores in Cuiabá and Brasilia. He said that the Cuiabá store no longer existed, and that the Bakairí had dreams of opening their own museum shop independent of FUNAI. They wanted something that would both educate visitors about their culture and make a profit. He mentioned the town of Chapadas dos Guimarães, a town about an hour outside of Cuiabá, as a possible site for this venture. He observed that ecotourism was becoming very popular in that area and that tourists might be interested in learning about Bakairí traditions.

Eventually Este elaborated on his belief that FUNAI would be playing a less significant role in indigenous reservations than it had during the last two decades. He speculated that grassroots indigenous organizations would take its place. One such organization in the Bakairí reservation is the *Kura–Bakairí* Association, which was born in Pakuera in the 1990s. It is made up of representatives from all seven villages in the reservation. Gilo is currently its president, and Este the secretary.

Este outlined the objectives of Kura–Bakairí. They include: (1) to guard and preserve the cultural traditions of the Bakairí, (2) to support the use of the Bakairí language, (3) to try to recover customs that have been lost over time, and (4) to protect those natural resources that play a special role in Bakairí culture. He illustrated his last point by explaining that the burutí palm, native to the cerrado and not found in the Tropical Rainforest, was in limited supply in the vicinity of the reservation due to overexploitation. And yet this palm remains crucial to Bakairí culture because it is used in the manufacture of the mask costumes and of roofs for traditional houses.

Este and the other members of Kura–Bakairí are not alone in their concern about the future of community resources such as palms.

What is called *sustainable social forestry* in the literature is being closely examined in many parts of Latin America where community organizations are acting as gatekeepers in the production, preservation, and marketing of tropical-forest products (Stanley 1990).

In the case of *babaçú* palm nuts, poor Brazilian farmers in the state of Maranhão have created an entire industry centered on the gathering and sale of palms and their nuts (Anderson, May, and Balick 1992). However, whether they can maintain this industry, or whether they will be forced to move on into virgin Amazonian forest beyond Maranhão, depends on the preservation of these palm forests. And there is even more at stake than the livelihood of these farmers and the Amazon. Apparently, following germination, the babaçú palm's leaves appear aboveground only after an incredibly long time—fifty years.

Kura–Bakairí Roots

I was surprised at first to hear Este describe the Kura–Bakairí Association because it sounded so Western in its concept to me. The equal number of representatives from each village and the clearly stated objectives implied a different kind of political organization from the indigenous headman system to which I was accustomed. And yet I should have been prepared for its appearance in the reservation. Over the past thirty years, a powerful social revolution has quietly taken place in Brazil, and organizations like Kura–Bakairí are the legacy of this movement.

In the 1960s Pope John XXIII called on Vatican Council II to reformulate the social mission of the Church (Garrison 1993). Brazilians took this charge very seriously, and almost immediately activist priests, nuns, and layworkers fanned out and organized an estimated one hundred thousand community-based groups to help the poor, the marginal, and the disenfranchised. By the 1970s the first *Grassroots Support Organizations* (GSOs) emerged to support and advise such local groups as rural cooperatives and neighborhood associations. *Conselho Indigenista Missionário* (CIMI), a progressive branch of the Catholic Church, organized the first regional Indian assemblies, and by 1980, the Brazilian Indian Movement (*União das Nações Indígenas*) was created (Ramos 1988:214).

These GSOs articulated the growing sense that it was necessary to bypass top-down, state-centric development models and to conceive of alternative policies and methods for instigating change. They advocated the notion of *praxis*, the idea that theories and models must be grounded in social reality for them to be valid. Stressing the importance of community involvement in the process of planning for the future, Brazilian GSOs became famous for implementing services through one or more of six different activities: (1) grassroots organizing, (2) information sharing, (3) coalition building, (4) public policy advocating, (5) applied research, and (6) on-site training and technical assistance (Garrison 1993:6–7).

During the 1980s the process of GSO formation accelerated. Leaders of such organizations as the Brazilian Indian Movement buckled down to, what Alcida Ramos has called, the unspectacular, long-term work of consciousness-raising in communities, with an emphasis on the preservation of the Indian identity (Ramos 1988:231–32.) Although these organizations generally have avoided direct confrontation with the government, they have at times been dramatically visible. For example, in 1988 Brazil committed itself to writing a new constitution. GSOs provided the means whereby convoys of marginalized people came to Brasilia to be part of the process. Street children, Indians, housemaids, and rural workers traveled in buses and trucks to the capital to appear before congressional subcommittees and be heard (Garrison 1993:4).

By the early 1990s, a study done in Brazil estimated that there were over one thousand Brazilian GSOs and that 85 percent of them had been organized in the last fifteen years (ISER 1992). They all shared the desire for institutional autonomy and space so that they could be free to develop methods for change tailored to the needs of their constituents. Partially in response to this objective, they began to seek financial support from international organizations such as church groups and private foundations that were not overtly controlled by any one country. They have been successful in their efforts, and by 1991, 78 percent of them managed budgets of $500,000 or under, while a growing number reported budgets in excess of $1 million (Garrison 1993:5).

These initiatives ultimately dovetailed with work being done outside of Brazil among indigenous peoples and their supporters (Bodley 1999:145). Groups in North America, South America, Europe, and Africa were experimenting with political strategies that allow them to negotiate more effectively with the nation-states in which they lived. For example, the Dene Indians and the Inuit, both located in Canada, built self-determination movements that have made significant gains.

Since the mid-1970s when the First Circumpolar Arctic People's Conference was held in Denmark, indigenous peoples have also become active in the organization of multiethnic international conferences (Bodley 1999:165). Their attempts to forge links between cultures and continents has paid off as their increased visibility has attracted interest and sympathy.

The Kura–Bakairí Association was not the anomaly it appeared to me to be at first glance. Rather, it belongs to the best tradition of Brazilian GSOs. Grounded in praxis, it is rooted in the practical realities of the reservation. Organized by the people who face these challenges daily, it seeks to better serve their needs. Its leaders are now trying to establish concrete connections with other indigenous peoples such as the Navajo. By networking, the Bakairí plan to learn new ways to administer their lands and defend their culture.

FUNAI's Dilemma

Kura–Bakairí's interest in reducing relations with FUNAI occurs not coincidentally at the same time as the government is making deep cuts in FUNAI's budget. Although such budget crises are historical and recurring, those taking place in the late 1990s come at a time when the organization is under review. There is intense debate in Brazil about whether the government should abolish it or transform it into something radically different.

When I arrived in Cuiabá in January 1999, the headlines of the *Cuiabá Gazete* were that FUNAI was facing an "unprecedented crisis" and that since 1997, its budget had been reduced by a third. The situation worsened through January and into February because the government was forced to devalue the *real*, Brazil's currency. At the beginning of January, a real was worth about a dollar. However, its value plummeted to as low as $.50 and, since the price of goods and services in Brazil is connected to the value of the dollar, that meant the cost of living essentially doubled. In an interview I had with a FUNAI administrator before I traveled to the reservation, I was told that the situation was so bad that FUNAI was having trouble paying for security and cleaning services. In some cases it was in arrears by as much as 20,000 *reais* (about $18,000 at the time).

Responsible for twenty-one thousand Indians inhabiting fifty-six different areas in the Mato Grosso region, FUNAI officials were frantically seeking ways to provide for basic services such as health provisions, the completion of demarcations of lands where needed, and community development projects. I asked an administrator about a news article that said that FUNAI was also paying for "water, light, and telephone services" in indigenous lands (*Cuiabá Gazete* 1999:1C). He responded that the newspaper was mistaken and that FUNAI was clearly not interested in providing that level of services in reservations. What he was concerned about were fundamental things, like making sure Indian children were vaccinated.

One avenue FUNAI was exploring was the establishment of partnerships with other Brazilian government agencies that had larger budgets. For example, they had contacted institutions such as *Fundação Estadual do Meio Ambiente*—the State Environment Foundation—(FEMA) and *Universidade Federal de Mato Grosso*—the Federal University of Mato Grosso—(UFMT) in an effort to develop a multi-institutional approach to program development in indigenous lands.

They were having some success with this approach. Last year the Bakairí had been one of five groups to have agricultural projects funded by World Bank monies dispersed to *Programa de Desenvolvimento Agroambiental*—Agricultural Development Program—(PRODEAGRO) and *Programa de Apoio às Iniciativas Comunitárias*—Support Programs for Community Initiatives—(PADIC). There are hopes that other projects might also find supporters outside of FUNAI. One idea being floated was to designate the Bororo reservation in Barão de Melgaço as a possible ecotourism site. Tourists on their way to visit the Pantanal could stop off and visit the Bororo Indians, who would give them a tour of the village and sell them cultural artifacts.

Such a concept is quite controversial of course. Tourists bring diseases and can be disruptive. The fact that an organization founded on the commitment to protect indigenous peoples and their cultures would consider opening up a reservation to the tourist industry underscores the seriousness of the pressures on FUNAI officials at this juncture. After a generation of trying to protect Indians, some FUNAI agents are being put in the untenable position of developing initiatives that may well act against the interests of the people they are trying to serve.

But as I sat in Gilo's house listening to Este, I thought that just possibly such efforts may well buy indigenous peoples such as the Bakairí more time. These people are straddling two worlds—the Western one and their own indigenous world. To deny that they are at the mercy of what Ehrenreich has called "the hegemonic forces" of global capitalism and patriarchy would be naïve (Ehrenreich 1997:vii).

Visiting Brazilian farmers and Bakairí Indians pose in front of the Bakairí men's house during a celebration. (Starting from the left, the farmers are the third, fifth, and sixth men.)

However, as research on indigenous peoples all over Latin America continues, there is the growing realization that Indians in the Andean Mountains, in the lowlands of South America, and in MesoAmerica are responding to the Westernization of their worlds with what Mary Weismantel (1997:51) calls "a lively dialectical imagination." They are incorporating alien elements into their own culture but have avoided losing their identities. The result is different than it was before but essentially indigenous.

For example, we know that during the mask dance, men go to the houses of their masks' owners and collect food to share in the men's house. Traditional foods such as manioc and fish are commonly offered to the singers; however, the substitution of a Western food such as peanut butter sometimes takes place. Although this shows the influence of non-Indian cultural processes in the reservation, it does not necessarily transform the entire custom.

The Bakairí have been in contact with the outside world for many years, and they have through their own ingenuity and flexibility put in place a cultural synthesis that has allowed them to maintain their traditions while, at the same time, accommodating Western influences.

Peasants, Small Farmers, and Indians

Years ago I had to go before a committee for an interview about my doctoral dissertation. One of the first questions a senior member of the committee asked me was, "So, are the Bakairí still Indians?"

It was an excellent question, and I am sure I fumbled the answer. Up to that point I had assumed their indigenous identity without examining any of the other possibilities. This professor challenged me to think about whether fifty years of contact had transformed them into a group of *peasants*, or *small farmers*, or something altogether different.

Another related question concerns how the Bakairí view themselves as well as other people with whom they interact. What does it mean to be *Indian* to them? How do they see themselves as being different from, and similar to, non-Indians? In the following sections we will examine some of these issues.

Peasants and Small Farmers

Eric Wolf's work (1966, 1969) on peasants deeply influenced many anthropologists' way of thinking. He described a kind of rural people who are found all over the world, from China and Egypt to Peru.

Nation-States   Wolf began by stipulating that peasants are cognizant of the fact that they live within the confines of a nation-state. They

---

Box 8-1: Characteristics of Peasants à la Wolf (1966, 1969) for Comparison with Small Farmers and the Bakairí Indians

Nation-State—an existence within the confines of a nation-state.

Relationship with the Land—an existential, emotional relationship with the land.

Relationships with People—a narrow but strong range of kin and community relations within which to derive social status and make decisions.

Means of Production—the restricted use of the means of production, such as land, technology, and labor.

Intensive Agriculture—the practice of intensive agriculture on permanent fields through which they produce food mainly for consumption.

Market Economy—the participation in the market economy through the sale of surplus crops.

---

do not believe that their society is entirely independent and autonomous. Through such experiences as taxation, economic activities, or military exploits, peasants feel the presence of the larger political unit.

Relationship with the Land   Another distinguishing characteristic they share is that they are "existentially involved in cultivation" (Wolf 1969:xiv). This refers to the connection between peasants as individuals and their fundamental identification with the land on which their survival depends. Wolf made the strong case that people who work the land to survive have a qualitatively different relationship with it than those who farm for income.

Relationships with People   Peasants are also dependent on a narrow range of social relationships from which they derive social status. This trait refers to the societal context in which peasants make choices and decisions that are grounded in strong kin and village relationships. The sense of community that evolves from these connections provides peasants with social status and other means for emotional and psychological satisfaction. Wolf thought these relationships were narrowly defined because, compared to those who interact with larger populations in cities for example, peasants seemed to him to be focused on only a limited number of family members and neighbors.

Means of Production   Although peasants are agricultural producers who make autonomous decisions about cultivation, they are not free agents. The means of production on which they depend, that is, the land, technology, and even their labor, are restricted because these individuals are typically found in economically and politically subordinate positions. For example, in order to work their lands, peasants may be required to pay rent or a percentage of their harvests, or to make labor donations.

Intensive Agriculture   Peasants practice intensive agricultural production on permanent fields where they use such technology as plows, draft animals, and irrigation systems. They produce enough food to live on and generate a surplus to sell in markets. It is through buying and selling in regional marketplaces that peasants participate in larger economic networks even though it is risky for them to do so because of their precarious financial position.

Market Economy   Wolf contended that they only participate in the market economy when they are sure they have raised enough food for their families. However, subsequent research has discovered that peasants are sometimes forced to work for cash whether their crop harvests warrant it or not. They need to earn wages to pay rent and taxes, and when these demands threaten their access to their fields, they are compelled to seek employment (Tax 1953; Dalton 1972; Hopkins 1987; and Kearney 1996).

Wolf believed that some of the characteristics of peasants appear, at first glance, to be shared with *farmers* who live in industrialized countries such as the United States. However, he argued that the two groups are different in significant ways. Farmers lack the fundamental relationship with the land that is so vital to peasants. That is, they depend on land for income rather than for survival and therefore do not experience the same emotional connection to it that peasants do.

Compared to peasants, the context in which farmers make choices is broader and less constrained by social relationships. In the first place, they are able to gather information from a wider range of sources, including the media and extension services. In addition, their decisions do not come under the same family and community scrutiny that peasants' decisions do. For example, farmers may arrange, without group consensus, to grow different kinds of crops, or use another kind of technology, or even sell off part of their land.

At this point I feel compelled to add a footnote to Wolf's discussion. Farmers in the United States make up a complex group that includes anything from CEOs of huge impersonal agribusinesses to owners of small family-run farms, although statistically speaking the latter are in the minority. The kind of relationship individuals have with the land, and the role of relatives and community members, varies based on what kind of farm they work. About a fifteen-minute drive from my house is a farm that sells vegetables and plants. It is famous in the area because it has been owned by the same family since the early 1600s. I suspect that the son who recently took over managing the farm may well have a strong emotional connection to it that rivals any peasant's, and he probably works within a set of powerful family and community constraints, just like peasants do. However, as I said, such establishments are not the norm in our country.

Although many farms in the United States are mortgaged, rented, or leased, those who work the land tend to have more control over it than do peasants because they have access to legal and financial institutions that protect their interests. With regard to the intensity of farm- versus peasant-agricultural production, farmers employ more technology than do peasants, having more access to it and to the capital for investing in it.

Farmers in industrialized societies are fully involved in buying and selling what they produce on the market economy. This is how they make a living, unlike peasants, who consume most of what they produce. This is also how they maximize their profits, an important goal in the United States but not, according to Wolf, in peasant societies. While farmers may improve their lot by increasing their returns on investments and amassing gains, peasants increase social status in their worlds by achieving collective goals set in the community.

The Bakairí Compared to Peasants and Farmers

Do the Bakairí fit either of these categories? Certainly they share certain characteristics of peasants in that they also have an existential relationship with the land and the community, which are essential to their survival and even imbued with social and mythological meanings. The gardens they make in the forests along the rivers are indeed important for meeting their nutritional requirements. But they are also significant because of the spirits who inhabit the rivers, waiting to be called to animate the dancing masks.

The social context in which these Indians live their lives, consisting mainly of relatives and close friends, determines many of the choices they make, and this range of relationships is narrower than many people's, especially those who live in towns and cities. As we know from chapter 5, their daily routines and the organization of their labor and time are strongly influenced by other members of their extended families and, in the case of men, gender-based groups. The tight formation of the Bakairí male and female labor force is in part the result of strong family and community ties. Decisions about how to use resources are made with their collective input.

Like peasants, the Bakairí are food producers who consume most of what they harvest, but they sometimes buy and sell goods in nearby markets. They also work for wages although for different reasons than peasants. While the latter typically work to pay rent or taxes on their lands, the Bakairí do not have these responsibilities, because they have perpetual usufruct. That is, they can use their lands indefinitely without paying for them, but they cannot buy, sell, or rent them. Resources, such as hardwoods and minerals found on indigenous lands, may be developed, depending upon the resource. However, laws restrict the extent to which Indians may enjoy the profits earned from such ventures.

What about the issues of restricted use of the means of production and of political subordination? In a general sense, Bakairí productive activities are constrained by their limited access to capital, technology, and know-how. And they are politically subordinate in a nation-state and region where they count as a disenfranchised minority. However, we know that their reality is more complex than this generalization implies. These Indians are plugged into the political system through the actions of certain government and nongovernment groups that represent their interests. They possess the ability to apply leverage and to get what they want. I would argue that the Bakairí are freer agents than are the peasants described by Wolf. Because of certain historical processes, they actually have more control over some of their means of production and are less rigidly subordinated in the state in which they live.

What role does intensive agriculture play in this? This is also a more complicated question in the case of the Bakairí because they utilize two different modes of production simultaneously. We know that the typical indigenous household uses traditional slash-and-burn methods to prepare about one-half of a hectare of land each year for their garden. The only technology they need for this is an ax, a machete, a digging stick, and seeds or tubers for planting. They use no fertilizers or pesticides. Nor do they claim ownership of, or repeatedly farm, the same piece of land. This is of course quite different from both peasants and small farmers.

We also know that the Indians use industrial technology to grow rice in the cerrado, but the extent to which they do so has fluctuated significantly over the past twenty years. Sometimes they plant no rice, and other times they cultivate up to 25 hectares. In addition, they have never depended upon the harvests from their agricultural fields in the same way that peasants or farmers rely on theirs.

The Bakairí's relationship to the market economy is another way in which they are different from small farmers. Although they have become increasingly sensitive to the market's prices, their horticultural plots buffer them from feeling the full effects of capitalism. If a man were sick and unable to work for wages, perhaps his family would miss coffee and sugar. And if no rice were planted in the cerrado for several years, the villages might miss the extra food and the cash that its sale brings them. However, they would not go hungry because their own garden harvests provide for their basic nutritional needs.

On the other hand, the Bakairí are similar to peasants in that they do not derive social status from maximizing profits. Unlike small farmers in the United States who constantly try to better their earnings and to increase the size of their establishment, they focus on other goals. Collective expectations and objectives grounded in kindred and community are critical to the choices they make and the gains they enjoy as a result.

The Bakairí are almost a hybrid in that they resemble peasants in some ways but small farmers in others. Michael Kearney (1996) speculates that perhaps the reality of peoples such as the Bakairí is not the problem; rather, it is the definition of peasant that is at fault. In his book, *Reconceptualizing the Peasantry*, he posits that this concept presupposes that the world is divided into two groups, one *developed* or industrialized, and the other *undeveloped* or unindustrialized. Those people such as peasants who fall into the undeveloped category are under some pressure to develop, or assume, the industrial way of life.

Kearney points out that this is, of course, ethnocentric because it makes two controversial assumptions: (1) that development and industrialization are the same things, when it is widely accepted today that the industrial way of life is highly problematic and that development might indeed involve other kinds of change; and (2) that the Western industrial way is inevitable, when evidence suggests that many nations are employing a variety of different economic strategies, rather than just the industrial method (Bodley 1996; Kearney 1996).

Although many introductory anthropology books continue to discuss peasant studies as a meaningful part of contemporary anthropology (Nanda 1994:171–184; Kottak 1999:100, 285), Kearney would prefer to abandon the concept and go on to devise a paradigm that would help us understand the complex nature of what he calls the "postpeasant subject" (Kearney 1996:8).

The Non-Indian View of Indian Identity

In Brazil it is not uncommon for groups of people to come forward and tell government officials that they are really Indians, claiming to be entitled to lands that are their ancestral territories. The government has had to develop some guidelines about how to differentiate genuine claims from bogus ones. The way in which the Bakairí meet these criteria is critical to outsiders' perception of them.

One of the most important ways to determine whether or not an individual is an Indian is to find out whether he or she speaks a language that is, or was, spoken by a community of people. Linguists are able to study languages and relate them to specific common ancestral languages. The Bakairí certainly inhabit a community, and it has been established that they speak a Carib language, one of the four major types of indigenous languages spoken in the lowlands of South America.

To be considered Indians, it is not necessary to speak an indigenous language exclusively. For example, some Bakairí also speak Portuguese. Teachers at the reservation school instruct the children in that language, and later on these young people have opportunities to practice speaking it with Brazilians in towns or on ranches. However, in the village, no Bakairí speaks Portuguese unless the presence of a non-Indian calls for it.

The people in question must also practice a set of cultural traditions that are shared among them and that are distinctive. Bakairí culture is made up of customs that readily contrast with Brazilian culture. Practices already discussed in detail in other chapters of the book include a characteristic social organization, which includes a kinship system and a set of marriage rules. They also have a religious system that is different from that of Brazilians. Customs such as ear-piercing ceremonies for adolescent boys, mask dancing during the dry season, and various other ceremonies distinguish the Bakairí from other peoples.

Bodley (1999) has attempted to develop a general definition of indigenous people that would apply globally. His definition includes two key characteristics. One pertains to the land. He states that indigenous peoples tend to hold land communally and to oppose technologies and development projects that might negatively affect the environment. They also see their societies as being egalitarian and classless, as opposed to highly stratified like most Western societies (Bodley 1999:146–147).

Bodley's definition provides us with some insights but it fits the Bakairí imperfectly. Although they use their lands communally and have a relatively unstratified society when compared to Western state societies, there are some obvious problems with the application of this definition to their case. I have argued that their communities are in transition between an egalitarian and a stratified type of society. As wealth differences emerge, they struggle with what this means to daily life in a small society. In addition, these Indians have not in the past rejected out of hand development projects that clearly have negative effects on their environment. The use of chemical fertilizers and pesticides on the cerrado fields was barely questioned despite warnings about runoff into the rivers.

The Bakairí are not the only indigenous peoples to embrace development projects that clearly threaten their environments. William Fisher (n.d.) has documented what he calls "the madness of the predatory mahogany trade" among the Xikrin Kayapó, Indians who live in the Brazilian state of Para (n.d.:introduction, p. 10). He shows how their near obsession with the acquisition of manufactured goods has led them to encourage miners and loggers to enter their reservation and exploit their resources. He then goes on to explain how and why this has happened, referring to specific historical processes that have caused the economic dependence of these Indians.

We know that the Bakairí, like most other indigenous peoples, have been profoundly changed by contact with non-Indians. For example, Bakairí material culture is very different than it was one hundred years ago. Not only do they use machetes and shotguns, but kerosene lanterns, trucks, tennis shoes, and medicine are now part of their lives. And although rice certainly has not replaced manioc's central place in their diet, it is an important everyday food.

Yet both Fisher (n.d.) and Jean Jackson (1991) argue that the transformation of indigenous culture over the past several generations is more far-reaching than just involving the adoption of technology. Groups like the Xikrin Kayapó and the Tukano Indians have experienced Western development in such a way that familiar indigenous institutions now function differently. Fisher calls this "the frontier within." His apt choice of metaphor focuses our attention on both the Brazilian frontier expansion into the west and the indigenous response to it.

Such observations about indigenous cultural responses to the non-Indian presence may indeed be valid. And if so, it is clear that reality is more complex than reflected in the simple statement that the Bakairí are Indians. Even if this point is technically accurate and if it legally allows them to occupy a demarcated reservation, it does not communicate fully who these people are.

The Bakairí as an Ethnic Minority

We need to place the Bakairí in a context that reflects not how exotic or different they are but how they, along with people like us, live together in an enormously complicated and intertwined world. In this section we will discuss these Indians as an emerging *ethnic group*.

What exactly is an ethnic group? Fredrik Barth's (1969) work in this area was pioneering. He defined ethnic groups as having members who identify themselves, and are identified by others, as being culturally distinct. Because the criteria for distinguishing ethnic groups change over time, Barth argued we should study the ethnic boundaries that distinguish groups, rather than the cultural content of ethnicity per se (1969:10–15). He opened a fertile research area, and since the 1970s anthropologists have gone on to investigate a wide range of topics.

Studies that might be particularly helpful for increasing our understanding of the Bakairí case concern the process of ethnic formation in Latin America (Hill 1988; Urban and Sherzer 1991; Chibnik 1991; Hendricks 1991; Jackson 1991, 1994; Reed 1995). Although this new body of work has clearly been influenced by Barth's seminal research, it strikes out in a new direction. Rather than emphasizing general culture contact as Barth does, it focuses instead on the relationship between nation-states and smaller internal minorities (Chibnik 1991; Jackson 1991; Reed 1995). It also emphasizes the emergence of ethnicity instead of starting with its existence as a given and draws on historical processes to shed light on how ethnic groups assume their identities (Hill 1988; Hendricks 1991; Jackson 1991, 1994). And it proposes the use of a continuum with "Indian" on one end and "ethnic group" on the other. Placement on the continuum is dependent upon such factors as history, demography, geography, and ecology (Urban and Sherzer 1991:7–13).

We can begin our examination of the Bakairí as an emerging ethnic group by trying to understand how they view their "Indianness" and what role they see themselves playing in the wider world. As Hill notes, it is essential to understand how individuals and groups interpret the objective conditions they experience, because it is from them that they create frameworks for understanding their social situations and for coping with a dominant society (1988:1–9).

The Bakairí's View of Their Identity

Edir Barros de Pina's (1977) research provides us with some clues. She attempted to untangle the various ethnic categories these Indians used at that time to organize their world. Using a schema constructed from a fundamental definition of culture that included language, technology, social behavior and ideology, she explained how the Bakairí contrasted themselves with others on the basis of a number of criteria.

During that period the Bakairí distinguished between people (*kura*) and nonhuman or animals (*kura ipa*). Within the kura category, they differentiated four major groups: (1) non-Indians (karaiwa), (2) other Indians whom they identified by tribal name, such as the Xavante, (3) Bakairí Indians who lived far away or in non-Indian settings (*xinale muka*), and (4) Bakairí Indians who lived either in the Santana Reservation or in the Bakairí reservation (*kurale kura*). Those who lived in the Bakairí reservation were divided into two sections based on where one's family came from. One's family either migrated from the Xingú culture area or came from the Paranatinga River region (Pina 1977:104–111).

My research notes confirm that the Bakairí continue to use at least some of the categories Pina defined in the mid-1970s. The Bakairí see themselves as different from, and even superior to, many other indigenous peoples. The Xavante Indians are an example of this. My research notes from the 1980s indicate that some of the Bakairí men reported participating in expeditions organized and led by the famous Indianist Francisco Meirelles in the 1950s. These expeditions resulted in the contact and temporary settlement of the Xavante Indians onto the Bakairí reservation, where they remained until they moved onto their own lands in 1974–1975.

While Pina reports that the Bakairí referred to these Indians as kura ipa (nonhuman) at one time (1977:104–105), they certainly consider them human now. And by 1999 a healthy competition had grown between the Bakairí and them. In my interview with Este, he criticized the Xavante, saying that although they have a lot of land, they want FUNAI to do everything for them. He contrasted the Bakairí's desire for autonomy with the Xavante approach, which he clearly saw as being less proactive.

The term *karaiwa* (non-Indian) is also frequently heard in the reservation, and the Bakairí persist in seeing themselves as being dissimilar from them. In 1999 interviews, they identified the caduete (the men's house where the masks are kept) as one of the key features that distinguished their culture from karaiwa society.

They also call attention to the Indian aspect of their identity. One way they do this is by emphasizing their Xinguano, rather than their Paranatinga, ancestry. Six of the key elders in the Pakuera report being descendents of families who migrated from Bakairí villages in the headwaters of the Xingú River at the beginning of the twentieth century. Although the specific names of the villages varied depending on the informant, at least one individual's family may have come from a village named *Kõrarieti*, which was located on the Batoví River, called the *Tamitotowalu* in Bakairí. Five others reported having families that moved from villages on the Kuliseu River. Two were from a village named *Mayeri*, two were from *Igueti*, and one was from *Iweti*.

It would be difficult to ascertain with any certainty the nineteenth- and early twentieth-century genealogy of any living Bakairí family, because the oldest Indian Protective Services records date back only to the 1940s, and these are quite incomplete. Oral histories are not a source of information, because they are shallow and do not stretch back beyond a generation or at most two. However, as Hill notes, history is not just "what really happened" (1988:2). Rather, it is the product of a dynamic process whereby groups interpret, and thereby personalize, events. The Xinguano link is clearly important to the Bakairí today whether or not they remember which villages their ancestors came from, or, indeed, whether any of their families even came from that area at all.

Why privilege that part of their identity? I believe it is because the headwaters of the Xingú River remained unaffected by European contact until relatively recently. Although visited by a few explorers in the late nineteenth century, this culture area did not confront continuous non-Indian presence until around World War II. Even in 1977 when I did fieldwork with the Nafuqua Indians, one of the ten Xinguano Indian groups that share cultural traditions, conditions were very different from those I found among the Bakairí. Despite the influx of Western goods such as guns and machetes and the presence of a

A Xinguano village with two Nafuquá men standing in front of a long house, holding a snake they just killed. This picture was taken by the author during a previous research project.

health clinic, a FUNAI administrator, and a grassy landing strip, few Nafuqua spoke Portuguese, wore clothing, or had the working knowledge of Western culture that the Bakairí possessed at that time.

A 1980s Brazilian miniseries celebrated the pristine conditions in which these Indians lived, and in many people's minds, the Xinguano became the symbol of "the real Indian," the Indian who lived a life unaffected by Western culture. This of course was untrue, but it was interesting for me to discover that the Bakairí romanticized their Xinguano cousins at least as much as urban Brazilians did.

We know from chapter 2 that the histories of the Bakairí from the Xingú and the Paranatinga areas are distinct. The Indians from the Paranatinga River were in permanent contact with non-Indians for a longer period of time. We have evidence that they met with Antonio Pires de Campos in the early 1700s and with Karl von den Steinen in the late nineteenth century when he wrote about their participation in the rural Mato Grosso economy. And we also believe that some of them were instrumental in leading the Bakairí from villages along the Batoví and Kuliseu Rivers to the Paranatinga area.

Length of contact history is not the only issue. Retention of culture is also important. Those objectives of the Kura–Bakairí Association that concern the protection and revival of their culture demonstrate their understanding of the importance of maintaining a traditional way of life. But the Bakairí themselves have told me that the Paranatinga Bakairí of seventy years ago, like the Santana Bakairí of today, have not retained their indigenous customs to any significant extent. Bakairí informants say these other Indians are "hardly Bakairí" at all.

That the Bakairí have chosen an historical construction that downplays their Paranatinga ancestry and emphasizes the Xinguano part of their past says something important about how they are positioning themselves in relation to the nation in which they live. As Jonathan Friedman says, "Making history is a way of producing identity . . ." (1992:837), and the Bakairí are working consciously to produce an indigenous rather than a Brazilian one. Instead of trying to blur the lines that distinguish the two groups, the Bakairí are actually underscoring the distinctions by evoking a time when there were few, if any, karaiwas around. By linking themselves to this era, they are establishing what Michael Dietler would call their "authenticity" (1994:595). All of this is in clear opposition to the Brazilian nation-state.

As the indigenous grassroots movement has grown in strength over the last thirty years, the term *Indian* has been transformed from a derogatory name used by non-Indians and Indians alike into a legitimizing expression. As Alcida Ramos puts it, "The appropriation of 'Indian' by the Indians has exorcised the heaviest spells of discrimination associated with the term" (1988:215). This comes during a time when both positive and negative attention is being focused upon the European political and economic domination of Brazil. On one hand, the new 1988 constitution abandoned the notion that the state of Indianness is a temporary one and that Indians must and will be assimilated by Western culture. On the other hand, in the year 2000, Brazil marks its five hundredth anniversary of the arrival of the Portuguese, and in every major city, huge machines count down the days until the celebration.

The Bakairí and a Deepening Sense of Ethnicity

Michael Kearney (1996) notes that a sense of ethnicity frequently strengthens among indigenous peoples when they more frequently interact with non-Indians and, concomitantly, begin to perceive themselves as being different from non-Indians on the basis of concrete, pragmatic issues. Human rights, and to a lesser extent, ecopolitics have effectively galvanized many Indian groups as they move between their home communities and other worlds. For example, incidents of abducting, torturing, and killing Mixtec Indians in Mexico have been noted by Amnesty International and Human Rights Watch, while concerns about deforestation, erosion, and the use of harmful pesticides in many parts of Latin America have resulted in the involvement of the Sierra Club, Greenpeace, and Earth First (Kearney 1996:182–184).

In the case of the Bakairí, the frequency with which they travel outside their lands has increased dramatically over the past twenty years. In the late 1970s it was unusual for people to visit the reservation or for Indians to leave it. Some Bakairí men, traveling and working in kin-based teams, might leave the reservation during the dry season for anywhere from a week to three months to earn wages. During this period, women traveled outside Bakairí territories even less frequently, and some had never left the reservation at all. In 1980 I was on a truck traveling to Cuiabá with some Indians from Pakuera. One of the women expressed amazement over the paved road and the speed with which the truck was moving. As we talked, I realized she had never been outside the reservation before.

In 1989, when I visited Pakuera to do some follow-up research, I sensed that things had changed. There seemed to be a lot of "coming and going." I decided to log anyone who entered or left the reservation and found, at the end of thirty days, an astonishing eighteen entries in my log book. Another change I noted was that there seemed to be an emerging vendor/service group. At that time, FUNAI had shops in many towns and cities, including Cuiabá, Brasilia, and Rio de Janeiro, where they sold cultural artifacts made by indigenous peoples. Bakairí men and women were making not only wood benches and masks that were part of their cultural tradition, but they were also manufacturing Brazilian crafts such as cotton placemats and doilies. They then sold these to FUNAI officials who sent them to the shops. A small number of Bakairí women attempted to travel to nearby ranches and to Paranatinga in search of domestic work, although FUNAI actively discouraged them from doing this.

By 1999, many families, like Yuka's, had at least one family member living outside the reservation. These individuals were either married to non-Indians or had jobs. Some commuted between the reservation and nearby towns, spending vacations with Bakairí relations or returning for key festivals. Others spent extended periods living in Brazilian towns, and equal amounts of time inside the reservation when they lost jobs, got divorced, or were sick.

At the time that I write this, there is a fairly large contingent of Bakairí living in Cuiabá. Many of them are living and working under the auspices of FUNAI. Some Indian women assume clerical roles, while men are drivers of the FUNAI vehicles that service indigenous reservations. We may lump these individuals in with the vending and services group that I described above.

A second kind of "city-reservation-commuting" Bakairí is now becoming visible. These are individuals, both males and females, who have completed high school and are even going on to take university classes. Some, who are older, own houses in Cuiabá; others have assumed jobs of a professional kind in FUNAI or at the Federal University of Mato Grosso.

A sense of Bakairí ethnicity is emerging most vigorously among the Bakairí who have spent long periods of time outside the reservation in schools or working. They are fluent Portuguese speakers, educated in a formal European sense, knowledgeable about Western culture, well-traveled in the sense that both Dora and Este have been outside of Brazil, and committed to furthering the cause of the Bakairí.

These tend to be individuals who have had what Paulo Freire (1970) would call a moment of *conscientização*, or consciousness-raising. This experience forces them to confront a reality they did not understand up to that point. It is an incident that underscores their indigenous identity in relation to non-Indians and that forces them to internalize what those differences mean in terms of social, political, and economic power.

You may recall the Paixola incident already described in chapter 7. This is when a group of Bakairí men arranged to have a part of the reservation that was occupied by Brazilians returned to them. In the end, the Indians burned out some of those farmers who refused to evacuate. Jere, a young Bakairí leader, played an important role in that incident. But perhaps even more important was how that event impacted on his life. Jere became enraged when an official from the Ministry of Interior, who had been sent to resolve the land dispute, returned secretly to Brasilia after agreeing to meet with the Bakairí representatives in Cuiabá. Jere described this as a watershed event that galvanized him and his friends. After that, he said there was no going back. He was quite determined to get the Paixola region of the reservation. It was then that they returned home and burned out those ranchers who did not flee when given the chance.

Another kind of politicizing experience for some of the Bakairí concerns ecopolitical issues that have become increasingly troublesome. Deforestation with population growth in a small reservation lie at the heart of the ecological problem. But the widespread use of chemical fertilizers as well as pesticides inside, but especially outside, the reservation have caused concern. During the rainy season the chemicals wash into the rivers, polluting it and killing fish. Reports of dead fish floating in the Paranatinga River are common. Indigenous leaders such as Dora have expressed anxiety about the impact of these toxic substances on their long-term fish supply and on other aspects of their environment. She, as well as others, have traveled to both the regional and national headquarters to report their findings.

The Bakairí are aware that their fears about the reservation environment are part of a more general, widespread movement that involves both Indians and non-Indians in North America, Latin America, and Europe. They are informed about the various meetings and summits that highlight environmental concerns, and some Bakairí are now in a position to travel to these conventions and voice the concerns of their people.

Dissonance and Identity

One of the more surreal experiences I had in Pakuera in 1999 was walking into the dirt plaza in front of the caduete and seeing a satellite dish. The Bakairí told me that the governor of Mato Grosso had committed himself to providing electric power that year to many of the more isolated towns and ranches in the area. Some of the Indians hoped to purchase televisions for watching the Soccer World Cup and other programs.

The effect of the image of the traditional and modern artifacts standing side-by-side was extraordinary. I had a sense that the intrusion of the satellite dish into the village, and in particular its placement next to the caduete, was somehow unreal. Such technology connotes national and global culture; it symbolizes the information age.

A satellite dish has been placed in the village in anticipation of the electrification of the community.

And the caduete, which is the home of the dancing masks and the site of ear piercing for men, represents the indigenous way of life.

Echoes of dissonance could be heard all over Pakuera. Clean, well-constructed outhouses are readily available near almost every house, but generally people do not use them. They go into the forest along the edge of the village. Spigots to deliver well water to the yards of the houses were put in place in the 1990s, but rather than use the water, people go down to the river to bathe and wash clothes. Tractors now open up the cerrado outside many of the villages, but the traditional slash-and-burn gardens continue to provide the mainstay of the diet.

Jackson (1991) reasoned that a key part of any definition of ethnicity is that the cultural traits of the ethnic group are significantly affected by interactions with the larger society. She added that specific traditions would be shed or retained in accordance with the ethnic group's strategy for survival. However, those customs the Indians kept would not be preserved intact. Rather, contact would transform them and their functions.

The Bakairí are in the middle of the process of self-consciously repackaging themselves. It goes without saying that their ultimate goal is survival on their own terms. But for now they seek an identity they can parlay into political and economic power. The creation of the Kura–Bakairí Association with its carefully articulated objectives and the rejuvenation of historical links to an authentic Indian past are evidence of attempts to establish legitimacy.

As Jackson predicted, the Bakairí appear to be sorting through cultural traits to maintain and even build upon, while discarding others. Those traditions they may abandon could include infanticide, which organizations like FUNAI actively discourage; the consumption of some kinds of game, such as anteater, that they believe marks them as "primitive"; and a reliance on curing rituals as modern medicine makes cognitive inroads. They will build upon those they have determined are attractive to non-Indians. These include their ritual dances that they performed on the UNESCO-sponsored tour through Europe, their masks and bench carvings, and the cerrado's burití palm, which they use in their homes.

Greg Urban and Joel Sherzer provide us with some insights into how the Bakairí may proceed from this point on with the nation-state context (1991:10–11). These researchers explain that nations are generally made up of many distinct ethnic groups. Two related processes take place as states evolve. The process of *folklorization*, or the placement of ethnic customs in a wider national urban context, is actually how nations unite and integrate themselves, while at the same time, differentiating themselves from other states. States signal control and ownership of ethnic groups by encouraging them to showcase their cultural traditions in the contained arenas they paternalistically provide.

At the same time, those cultural traditions that are celebrated become symbols that nations can use to distinguish themselves from others. A good example is the representation of the Indian that Brazil uses to off-set itself from European countries such as Portugal, its colonial parent.

A second process is that of *exoticization* in which the exotic image is emphasized either to individualize the state, as already mentioned, or to appeal to tourists and thus create or expand an industry (Urban and Sherzer 1991:11). I would add here that integration of nation-states also takes place through the tourist industry. The promotion of the Pantanal, both through the Brazilian television miniseries and the government support of ecotourism in the area, not only capitalizes on exotic pictures of unusual wildlife and rustic lodges that appeal to wealthy urban travelers, it also binds this border region more tightly to national Brazil.

Folklorization and exoticization are two processes the state employs to serve its own interests. Yet, they also tend to preserve aspects of indigenous culture. The Bakairí can exploit this knowledge for their own ends. By promoting their ritual dances and material culture, they are in fact ensuring themselves a place in the future of Brazil.

Appendix
LEARNING GUIDE

Chapter 1
Beginning Fieldwork

Concepts and Terms

1. FUNAI
2. fieldwork
3. culture
4. predilection
5. logistics
6. ethnocentrism
7. infanticide
8. "the Other"
9. quantitative methods
10. qualitative methods
11. "thick description"
12. a meaningful account

Discussion Questions

1. Have you traveled in another country? If so, in what ways were your experiences similar to and different from my first day in Pakuera?
2. Think about your own predilections. In which part of the world would you not want to study? Why? Which place would be your first choice for doing fieldwork? Why?
3. Ethnocentric reactions do not occur only when people are in foreign countries. In complex multicultural nations such as the United States, behaviors of people from different regions, classes, and ethnic/racial groups can surprise us because they are different (not better and not worse) than ours. Can you think of an ethnocentric reaction that you have had?

Suggested Readings

Chagnon, Napoleon. 1992. *Yanomamö: The Fierce People.* 4th ed. New York: Holt, Rinehart, and Winston. Although many are not convinced that the Yanomamö people are, in fact, as fierce as the title of the monograph suggests, most readers agree that Chagnon's description of this remarkable people is highly readable.

DeVita, Phillip, ed. 1992. *The Naked Anthropologist: Tales from Around the World.* Belmont, CA: Wadsworth. This is a collection of essays detailing many diverse experiences anthropologists have had in the field. Some are poignant, and some are funny. All are good reading.

Kensinger, Kenneth. 1995. *How Real People Ought to Live: The Cashinahua of Eastern Peru.* Prospect Heights, IL: Waveland Press. Kensinger's opening chapter on beginning fieldwork and subsequent chapters on sexuality have enthralled my students since I started assigning this book as one of their texts. Although the middle section on "real" and "unreal" categories can be daunting, this book, based on over twenty-five years of fieldwork and analysis, paints a holistic portrait of the Cashinahua.

Harner, Michael. 1972. *The Jivaro: People of the Sacred Waterfalls.* New York: Anchor Books, Doubleday. Harner's book is still one of the most vivid accounts of headhunting there is. Plus, he explains in "cook-book style" what to do with the head after it is cut off the body. The chapters on how the Jivaro see life after death are also excellent.

Theory and Methods Ideas

The first four works listed below are suggestions for those who would like to read more about theory. The first two are by Clifford Geertz. They describe *interpretive anthropology*. The third is a volume edited by Michael Painter and William Durham. The first and last chapters are excellent descriptions of *political ecology*. The last is the well-known essay written by Renato Rosaldo. In it he sets forth some of the basic tenets of *postmodern anthropology*.

Geertz, Clifford. 1973. "Thick Description: Toward an Interpretive Theory of Culture." In *The Interpretation of Cultures*, pp. 3–30. New York: Basic Books.

_____. 1983. "Interpretive Anthropology." *Local Knowledge, Further Essays in Interpretive Anthropology*, pp. 22–26. New York: Basic Books. A concise explanation of why it is important to study cultural symbols and the social context in which they occur. Geertz makes a strong case for anthropologists to "interpret" human action, rather than to seek causes for it.

Painter, Michael, and William Durham, eds. 1995. *The Social Causes of Environmental Destruction in Latin America*. Ann Arbor: University of Michigan Press. Painter's introduction and Durham's conclusion provide a good overview of political ecology. Beyond this, the book is one of the works in the series, *Linking Levels of Analysis*. As such, it seeks to achieve interlevel analysis—connecting what happens on a local level with what is going on in the larger, more inclusive system. While it focuses on such environmental problems as deforestation, it explains what role political and economic inequities play in causing such problems.

Renato, Rosaldo. 1984. "Grief and a Headhunter's Rage: On the Cultural Force of Emotions." In Edward Bruner, ed., *Text, Play, and Story: The Construction and Reconstruction of Self and Society*, pp. 178–195. Washington, D.C.: American Ethnological Society. This essay explains why postmodern anthropologists reject the distinction between the observed and the observer. Rosaldo uses his own life history to show how headhunting traditions made sense to him only after he himself had certain experiences.

The following works are for those who would like to further explore methodological issues.

Bernard, H. Russ. 1999. *Research Methods in Cultural Anthropology:*

Qualitative and Quantitative Approaches. 2nd ed. Walnut Creek, CA: Alta Mira Press. This book describes how to prepare for a field study and how to collect and analyze data. It discusses the relative merits of qualitative and quantitative data.

Kutsche, Paul. 1998. *Field Ethnography: A Manual for Doing Cultural Anthropology.* Upper Saddle River, NJ: Prentice Hall. This slim volume provides wonderful illustrations of the kinds of data that anthropologists can gather.

Chapter 2
The Changing World of the Bakairí Indians

Concepts and Terms

1. the "untouched primitive" myth
2. serendipity
3. the New World
4. rank
5. the Colonial Period
6. regional development
7. Polonoroeste Project
8. industrial agriculture
9. *posseiros*

Discussion Questions

1. The arrival of Europeans in North and South America led to the death and dislocation of many Native Americans. Drawing on your knowledge of American history, how did North America's Colonial Period differ from that of Brazil?
2. Rondonia, the northwestern Brazilian state targeted for development, has been called "The Wild West." Develop a list of five to seven characteristics of the United States's "Wild West" as it existed in the 1800s. Which of these do you view as negative? as positive?
3. If you were the Bakairí Indian agent, would you have proposed and supported the industrial agricultural project? Why or why not? What other projects could you have proposed?

Suggested Readings

Elias, Scott. 1997. "Bridge to the Past." *Earth* 6(2): 50–55. This fascinating article explains how campsites made by American ancestors dating back to twelve thousand years ago have been excavated in Siberia and in Alaska.

Hemming, John. 1987. *Amazon Frontier: The Defeat of the Brazilian Indians*. Cambridge, MA: Harvard University Press. Hemming's book describes how the Portuguese settled what is now called Brazil and how their presence affected the indigenous societies they displaced. Some of the story is painful reading, such as when Indians were encouraged to drink from wells poisoned by Europeans.

Stearman, Allyn MacLean. 1987. *No Longer Nomads: The Sirionó*. Lanham, MD: Hamilton Press. Stearman provides us with a restudy of a people made famous by Allan Holmberg in his book, *Nomads of the Long Bow*. She also explains the process whereby a culture changes under contact conditions.

Theory Ideas

Those who are interested in exploring theories about culture change may want to look at the following sources.

Wallerstein, Immanuel. 1988. "Development: Lodestar or Illusion." *Economic and Political Weekly* 23(39): 2017–2023. Wallerstein's works espouse the position that early theories such as those of modernization and dependency did not take into consideration global political and economic forces that were affecting the world. He emphasizes the importance of analyzing the exploitative relations between rich and poor blocks of nations and showing how the richer countries actually prevent the poorer from developing.

Wolf, Eric. 1982. *Europe and the People Without History*. Berkeley: University of California Press. This book can be read along with Wallerstein's works. Wolf develops a dimension that Wallerstein omits, showing that as the more powerful block of Western nation-states expanded and established exploitative relations with the less powerful, the latter responded in their own ways. He shows how cultures such as those indigenous ones in the New World responded actively to the West's penetration.

Acheson, James. 1994. *Anthropology and Institutional Economics*. New York: University Press of America. Acheson's work introduces a new micro-level perspective into the theoretical problem of change. He urges us to examine how internal bureaucratic institutions function to effect either negative or positive politico-economic changes in communities.

Chapter 3
Bakairí Demography: Households, Fertility, and Mortality

Concepts and Terms

1. anthropological demography
2. fertility-inhibiting practices
3. median
4. mean
5. crude birth rate
6. age-specific fertility rate
7. total fertility rate (TFR)
8. lifetime fertility rate
9. sex taboo
10. lactational anovulation
11. indirect infanticide
12. anthropomorphize
13. crude death rate
14. rate of natural increase
15. population doubling time

Discussion Questions

1. Bakairí housing is very different from what the average American is used to. Think about the place you grew up in and compare it to the typical Bakairí home. List some advantages and disadvantages to growing up in a Bakairí-style house.
2. The average age of marriage for Bakairí men and women is about fifteen or sixteen years of age. Think back to yourself at that age. What qualities would have made you a good spouse? Which might have detracted from your performance?
3. A recent newspaper article in my hometown described how a single mother of six children set fire to her house one night. Her eight-year-old boy was killed and her new infant barely escaped death when a neighbor rescued her from her crib. The mother and the other children made it safely out of the house. Could this be considered indirect infanticide? Why or why not?
4. Compare causes of death among the Bakairí with major causes of death for Americans. How are they different and how are they similar?

Suggested Readings

Crocker, William, and Jean Crocker. 1994. *The Canela: Bonding Through Kinship, Ritual, and Sex.* Ft. Worth, TX: Harcourt Brace College Publishers. A fascinating account of the sexual behaviors of the Canelas Indians of Brazil. Although very different from what we find in our own society, the Crockers treat some controversial issues with sensitivity. Materials from this book would be excellent to discuss in small groups.

Hill, Kim, and A. Magdalena Hurtado. 1996. *Ache Life History: The Ecology and Demography of a Foraging People.* Hawthorne, NY: Aldine de Gruyter. A real *tour de force* about the demographic characteristics of a Paraguayan foraging group with whom Hill and Hurtado have worked for fourteen years. Although the text treats complex issues and becomes somewhat mathematical in the final theory section, the first part of the book explains in a clear and coherent fashion why we should be interested in demography.

Howell, Nancy. 1979. *Demography of the Dobe !Kung.* New York: Academic Press. Howell's early, and very fine, work on the !Kung of southern Africa, provides readers with demographic information about another group that they can compare with the Bakairí data.

Theory Ideas

There is a lot of disagreement about the relative importance of the respective roles played by population increase and mode of food production in culture change and culture evolution. One group of thinkers who deal with the theoretical implication of this question is listed below.

Boserup, Ester. 1967. *The Condition of Agricultural Growth: The Economics of Agrarian Change Under Population Pressure.* Chicago: Aldine. Boserup led a generation of researchers to study the cultural evolutionary implications of population pressure on the intensification of food production.

Johnson, Allen, and Timothy Earle. 1987. *The Evolution of Human Societies from Foraging Groups to Agrarian States.* Stanford, CA: Stanford University Press. While Johnson and Earle are in agreement that population pressure can lead to the emergence of new ways to produce food, they add that food supplies set limits to population growth over the short run.

Murphy, Martin, and Maxine Margolis, eds. 1995. *Science, Materialism, and the Study of Culture.* Gainesville: University Press of Florida. The introduction of the volume and the essays in it show how the infrastructure of a culture, which includes productive and reproductive institutions, provides both the "opportunities and constraints for the development of its social and political formations and their attendant ideologies" (p. 1).

Chapter 4
Making a Living, Bakairí Style

Concepts and Terms

1. sustainable agriculture
2. hybrid technologies
3. *cerrado*
4. gallery forest
5. simple random sample
6. slash-and-burn horticulture
7. agriculture
8. time allocation study
9. "tragedy of the commoners"

Discussion Questions

1. Describe two possible positive and two negative consequences of FUNAI's development project.
2. Because only 4 percent of Americans are involved in agricultural production, the Bakairí project would be as foreign to most of us as it was to the Indians. If you were to help the Indians to implement the technology and methods, where do you think you could make the greatest contribution?
3. The Indians depend on protein from vegetable, fish, and meat sources. What kinds of protein do you consume? On which do you depend the most? The least? What are some of the health advantages of consuming high percentages of vegetable and fish protein?
4. In your opinion, is emergence of the concept of private ownership in the reservation a good thing, or a bad one?

Suggested Readings

Clay, Jason. 1988. *Indigenous Peoples and Tropical Forests: Models of Land Use and Management from Latin America.* Cambridge, MA:

Cultural Survival Inc. In this book Clay looks at how indigenous economic activities, such a fishing and slash-and-burn horticulture, have been affected by pressures placed on them by non-Indians.

Le Breton, Binka. 1993. *Voices from the Amazon*. West Hartford, CT: Kumarian Press. This is an interesting introduction to the various kinds of people who live in the Amazon today. Written in journalistic style for the layperson, it discusses such groups as Indians, loggers, miners, settlers, ranchers, and rubber tappers.

Sponsel, Leslie, ed. 1995. *Indigenous Peoples and the Future of Amazonia: An Ecological Anthropology of an Endangered World*. Tucson, AR: University of Arizona Press. A more technical book than Le Breton's, this volume examines issues concerning the Amazon, such as environmental conservation, economic development, and indigenous societies. Sponsel's final essay makes a strong statement.

Werner, Dennis. 1990. *Amazon Journey: An Anthropologist's Year Among Brazil's Mekranoti Indians*. Englewood Cliffs, NJ: Prentice Hall Publishing Co. An ethnography about a group of Indians who are quite different from the Bakairí although they live near them. Some of Werner's adventures make great reading—such as his scorpion bite and the times he spent "trekking" with the Mekranoti.

Theory Ideas

One theme that runs through many of the chapters of this book concerns the theoretical question—what role will smallholder households, whose labor is organized by marriage and family relationships, play in feeding the people of our planet during the twenty-first century? Many people from North American and European countries assume that small households such as those described in this chapter will play only a minor role. They believe that industrial technology and large-scale production will dominate the agricultural scene. However, others disagree. They point to smallholders as the only producers who possess the flexibility and adaptability needed to experiment with new ways of producing food, especially if food production is to occur in marginal ecosystems.

The special issue of *Human Ecology* cited below is dedicated to the memory of Robert Netting, whose research in Africa and Europe addressed some of these ideas. In addition to his commitment to the collection of empirical data, his work is notable for its contributions to the fields of ecology, agriculture, and demography. Those essays included in this issue lay out some of the work being done by those he influenced. Of particular value for those interested in a theoretical overview are the introduction by Richard Wilk and Priscilla Stone and the final essay by David Cleveland.

Wilk, Richard, and Priscilla Stone. 1998. "Special Issue: A Very Human Ecology Celebrating the Work of Robert McC. Netting." *Human Ecology* 26 (2).

Chapter 5
Living and Working In Groups

Concepts and Terms

1. productive labor
2. reproductive labor
3. polygyny
4. sororate
5. monogamy
6. village endogamous
7. extended family
8. nuclear family
9. cross cousins
10. parallel cousins
11. bride service
12. matrilocal residence
13. Iroquois kinship system

Discussion Questions

1. In what general ways are Bakairí routines different from and similar to our own? Would you conclude that Bakairí child-rearing practices stress skill development more than U.S. child-rearing practices do?
2. Look closely at Bakairí time allocation. Many students have commented that their time, as students, is structured much like Bakairí time is. Would you agree with this? What percentage of your time is spent in productive labor, as defined by Reed?
3. Give examples of "public" versus "backyard" spaces for men and women in our society. What are the penalties for inappropriately using them?
4. Research findings in the 1990s show that the number of extended families in the United States is growing in many different ethnic groups. What advantages do such families offer their members? What disadvantages?

5. Although Gregor's quasi-psychological theory may account for certain aspects of all-male associations, there are other sociopolitical ways to explain these groups. Can you think of any?

Suggested Readings

Chernela, Janet. 1993. *The Wanano Indians of the Brazilian Amazon: A Sense of Space*. Austin: University of Texas Press. This book discusses the ranked society of the Wanano Indians of the northwest Amazon. While neither strictly stratified nor egalitarian, these Indians are somewhere in between. Chernela shows how their descent groups, which are related to ranked ancestors, affect many other aspects of culture, including resource utilization. Although somewhat technical to read, this volume gives another perspective on South American Indians.

Murphy, Yolanda, and Robert Murphy. 1974. *Women of the Forest*. New York: Columbia University Press. An elegant and intelligent book that stands the test of time, the Murphys describe how the Mundurucú Indians of central Brazil live in divided communities. The men occupy the men's house, where they sleep and live for all practical purposes, while the women and children live in houses that form a perimeter around this house. Although somewhat focused on women and their role in this society, the book informs us about Mundurucú men and culture in general.

Wagley, Charles. 1977. *Welcome of Tears: The Tapirapé Indians of Central Brazil*. New York: Oxford University Press. Another classic, this book builds on research begun in the late 1930s. Not only does Wagley describe how the Tapirapé have changed over that time, but how Brazil has been transformed. Of particular interest is the chapter on social organization that explains how these Indians live in villages that are connected by formal associations affecting rituals and marriage.

Theory Ideas

This chapter broaches the topic of gender and power. Power frequently derives from social or public statuses, and in many cultures, such as the Bakairí's, women are denied access to such standings. In the 1970s, researchers documented the cross-cultural range of this asymmetry and went on to develop models to account for it. But the question of how changing modes of production affect notions of gender and power continues to be a significant theoretical problem.

Silverblatt, Irene. 1987. *Moon, Sun, and Witches: Gender Ideologies and Class in Inca and Colonial Peru.* Princeton, NJ: Princeton University Press.

_____. 1988. "Women in States." *Annual Reviews* 17:427–460. Palo Alto, CA: Annual Reviews, Inc. Silverblatt uses a refined historical perspective to illustrate how concepts of gender and power change over time. In the first cited work, her richly detailed study about Inca women reveals how Spanish patriarchal models negatively affected women's lives as well as how these women were able to mobilize their own cultural traditions to resist total domination. In the second work, Silverblatt sketches with broader strokes how women fare in general in state societies. Relatively egalitarian gender systems may be transformed into hierarchical systems in which men have more control over production and more access to key political positions. One consequence is that women may become increasingly subservient and marginalized.

Rosenbaum, Brenda. 1993. *With Our Head Bowed: The Dynamics of Gender in a Mayan Community.* Albany, NY: Institute for Mesoamerican Studies.

Tice, Karin. 1995. *Kuna Crafts, Gender, and Global Economy.* Austin: University of Texas Press. Although women may end up working harder and having less power in state societies, these two authors stress the fact that the issues are complex and cannot be reduced to a simple cause-and-effect statement. Human agency, or the involvement of individuals in the construction of their own social history, plays a role. Tice in particular presents interesting cases showing how this works among the Kuna.

Chapter 6
The Bakairí and Their Dancing Masks

Concepts and Terms

1. ritual power
2. *kwamba*
3. *yakwigado*
4. example of typical *kwamba* behavior
5. example of ritual sexual antagonism
6. example of ritual age reliance
7. sacred

8. profane
9. animism
10. shaman

Discussion Questions

1. Masks are found in many societies. When do we use masks in the U.S.? How are our mask traditions different than those of the Bakairí?
2. Halloween was at one time connected to Celtic myths about nature as well as life and death. In your opinion, do any of these beliefs still persist in the Halloween tradition?
3. Can you think of any American rituals that contribute to the redistribution of wealth in society?
4. Antagonism between the genders exists in many societies, including our own. Are there any U.S. rituals you can think of that exacerbate these tensions?

Suggested Readings

Descola, Philippe. 1993. *The Spears of Twilight: Life and Death in the Amazon Jungle.* New York: The New Press. A fascinating book about the Achuar who live on the border between Ecuador and Peru. Of special interest are the descriptions of their songs, rituals, and encounters with their spirits. Descola's epilogue is also of interest. In it he explains how fieldwork transformed him.

Graham, Laura. 1995. *Performing Dreams: Discourses of Immortality among the Xavante of Central Brazil.* Austin: University of Texas Press. This book describes how a Xavante leader involves his entire community in the preparations, rehearsals, and performance of a myth-related dream he had. Through this expressive performance, Warodi, the headman, works to ensure the continuity and integrity of his people's customs.

Gregor, Thomas. 1985. *Anxious Pleasures: The Sexual Lives of an Amazonian People.* Chicago: University of Chicago Press. In this monograph, Gregor describes the myths and dreams of the Mehinaku who live in the headwaters of the Xingú River, where the Bakairí lived during the last century. The author's theoretical orientation is decidedly Freudian. In keeping with this model, one of the goals of the book is to show how "sex is an organizing metaphor for the villagers that structures their understanding of the cosmos and the world of men and spirits" (p. 3).

Theory Ideas

The masks and the rituals associated with them are both religious and artistic in nature and may be studied as such by anthropologists. A theoretical school that spans these two areas is symbolic anthropology. It analyzes art and religion in three important ways: (1) as forms of symbolic communication in society, (2) as culturally defined sources of emotion and value, and (3) as reflections and supporters of social structural features.

Turner, Victor. 1977. "Symbols in African Ritual." In Janet Dolgan, et al., eds., *Symbolic Anthropology*, pp. 183–194. New York: Columbia University Press. In this solid and valuable article, Turner describes kinds of symbolic anthropological research and explains why this approach is valuable.

If compared to symbolic anthropology, discourse studies are a relatively new area of research. They examine a range of expressive acts, which I would argue could include mask dancing. Focusing not on content but on form, they provide us with a fresh perspective on culture.

Basso, Ellen. 1995. *The Last Cannibals: A South American Oral History*. Austin: University of Texas Press.

Urban, Greg. 1991. *A Discourse-Centered Approach to Culture: Native American Myths and Rituals*. Austin: University of Texas Press.
These researchers distinguish between what is being communicated and what they call "discourse practice," how a message is transmitted. In doing so, they call our attention to shared interpretive frameworks within societies. Basso's work emphasizes narratives. She analyzes nine stories told to her by Kalapalo storytellers. Urban describes how Xokleng Indians present their myths and then goes on to make more general observations about South American societies.

Chapter 7
Leading the Bakairí into the Twenty-First Century

Concepts And Terms

1. headman
2. anchoring effect
3. middle ground
4. redistribution
5. double marriage

6. silence
7. oration
8. consensual leadership
9. authoritarian leadership

Discussion Questions

1. The way in which headmen come to power has changed. They used to inherit their positions, but now they compete for them. Describe two positive and two negative aspects of this change.
2. Think of an organization or a club to which you belong. Which of the headman techniques discussed in this chapter have you used or seen others use?
3. Americans, like the Bakairí, tolerate both authoritarian and consensus-forming leaders. With your knowledge of current events, give examples of how the current president of the United States exhibits both authoritarian and consensual leadership styles.

Suggested Readings

Kracke, Waud. 1978. *Force and Persuasion: Leadership in an Amazonian Society.* Chicago: University of Chicago Press. Kracke's work shows how indigenous headmen must sensitively balance between pressuring and persuading their constituents into doing what must be done.

Maybury-Lewis, David. 1965. *The Savage and The Innocent.* Boston: Beacon Press. Maybury-Lewis's well-known and highly readable work describes his and his wife Pia's journey to central Brazil where they studied the Sherente and Shavante Indians. Questions raised by their interactions with leaders of these groups lead to some important theoretical suggestions.

Theory Ideas

One fascinating type of research looks at the shape of indigenous communities and their kind of political leaders as responses to regional and global forces that have been in operation for centuries. Defining and tracing the links between the macrolevel and the microlevel become intriguing challenges for researchers interested in this kind of work.

Brown, Michael, and Eduardo Fernandez. 1991. *War of Shadows: The Struggle for Utopia in the Peruvian Amazon.* Berkeley: University of California Press. This study provides the reader with an account of how the Asháninka of eastern Peru tried to maintain political and cultural autonomy in the face of the encroaching frontier. Their reliance on resistance, flight, warfare, and banditry as ways of adapting to the non-Indian presence makes an interesting contrast to the Bakairí case.

Ehrenreich, Jeffrey, ed. 1985. *Political Anthropology in Ecuador: Perspectives from Indigenous Cultures.* Albany, NY: The Society for Latin American Anthropology and The Center for the Caribbean and Latin America—SUNY at Albany. These essays draw on research done in both the highlands and lowlands of South America. What they have in common is a commitment to understanding political process in indigenous communities. The themes of "resistance and persistance" (p. xv) in the face of culture change run through each of the works.

Ferguson, R. Brian, and Neil Whitehead, eds. 1992. *War in the Tribal Zone: Expanding States and Indigenous Warfare.* Santa Fe, NM: School of American Research Press. The essays in this volume illustrate how contact with Europeans put in place a complex set of factors that resulted in conflict and warfare both between Europeans and indigenous peoples and between indigenous villages.

Chapter 8
The Bakairí: Indians, Ethnic Minority, or Both?

Concepts and Terms

1. the Pantanal
2. the Hidrovia
3. the *Kura–Bakairí* Association
4. sustainable social forestry
5. Grassroots Support Organization
6. praxis
7. peasant
8. small farmer
9. Indian
10. developed/undeveloped
11. ethnic group
12. *kura/kura ipa*
13. *karaiwa*
14. *conscientização*
15. folklorization
16. exoticization

Discussion Questions

1. The indigenous self-determination movement, whether it is in Brazil, Canada, or the United States, is controversial. Discuss ways in
   which it is a positive development, and ways in which it is not, for
   both indigenous peoples and non-Indians.
2. FUNAI constantly struggles with securing an adequate budget.
   What are some ways you would attempt to secure funds if you were
   a FUNAI administrator?
3. Indians like Este live in two worlds. Do you believe that such people will be able to continue to do this? Or will they need to make a
   choice?

Suggested Readings

Bodley, John. 1999. *Victims of Progress*. 4th ed. Mountain View, CA:
Mayfield Publishing Company. This book examines the efforts of what
Bodley calls "small-scale cultures" to retain their cultural integrity in
the face of efforts by state societies to assimilate them. The viewpoint of
the author is unabashedly proindigenous, and since some of his points
are controversial, the reading can be quite stimulating. It includes helpful appendices with lists of resources.

Peters, John. 1998. *Life among the Yanomami: The Story of Change
Among the Xilixana on the Mucajai River in Brazil*. Peterborough,
Ontario, Canada: Broadview Press. In Peters's preface to this book, he
explains that he first started working with the Yanomami in 1958 in
the capacity of a missionary. Later he left his calling and pursued
degrees in anthropology and sociology. His book includes a lengthy
section about the impact of missionaries on Indians.

Reed, Richard. 1995. *Prophets of Agroforestry: Guarani Communities and Commercial Gathering*. Austin: University of Texas Press. In
this readable ethnography, Reed provides us with an example of an
indigenous group who are surviving as a distinct society and culture.
He explains that their successful adaptation to Paraguayan society is
based on the way they harvest and sell forest products without
destroying the forests. Those who are interested in sustainable forest
management will be particularly interested in this book.

Theory Ideas

The future of indigenous peoples like the Bakairí is a key concern of
this book. How they will fare in the nation-states they occupy is an

important question. If we consider a variety of scenarios based on what has happened to other groups or in other times, then some possibilities present themselves. Certainly one possibility is that there will be gross violations of their human rights, such as illegal entries into their reservation, killing or imprisoning them, and so forth. More subtle, but also dangerous, is withholding health care, education, and infrastructural support that may be more important to their survival than such programs are to others who have a different biological and cultural heritage. Another option is ignoring them as they are forced to eke out a meager existence on an inadequate reservation (while the size of their population grows steadily). This may destine them to a bleak future. A final possibility is that the Bakairí may become part of a transnational class of people who are able to compete politically for what resources they need to survive through the twenty-first century. The following books examine the theoretical and policy implications of the existence of ethnic minorities such as the Bakairí in nation-states.

Kearney, Michael. 1996. *Reconceptualizing the Peasantry: Anthropology in Global Perspective.* Boulder, CO: Westview Press. Kearney envisions a future where people like the Bakairí will share multiple identities, which will emerge from the process of moving between cultural worlds. He sees their ethnic identity being linked to their concerns about human rights and environmental issues.

Maybury-Lewis, David. 1997. *Indigenous Peoples, Ethnic Groups, and the State.* Boston: Allyn and Bacon. In this book Maybury-Lewis looks at the implications of questions about ethnicity for indigenous peoples living in nation-states. He argues that Indians are a special case of ethnic minority because they are small in number and "alien to the mainstream of the states in which they live" (p. x).

Sponsel, Leslie. 1995. "Relationships among the World System, Indigenous Peoples, and Ecological Anthropology in the Endangered Amazon." *Indigenous Peoples and the Future of Amazonia,* pp. 263–293. Tucson: University of Arizona Press. Sponsel stresses the importance of indigenous societies to the survival of such ecosystems as Amazonia and makes a strong case that anthropologists should be more active in ensuring that there is a future for both.

REFERENCES

Agar, Michael. 1980. *The Professional Stranger: An Informal Introduction to Ethnography.* New York: Academic Press.

Anderson, Anthony, Peer May, and Michael Balick. 1992. *The Subsidy From Nature: Palm Forests, Peasantry, and Development in the Amazon Frontier.* New York: Columbia University Press.

Arvelo-Jimenez and Horacio Biord. 1994. "The Impact of Conquest on Contemporary Peoples of the Guiana Shield: The System of Orinoco Regional Interdependence." In Anna Roosevelt, ed., *Amazonian Indians from Prehistory to the Present*, pp. 55–78. Tucson: University of Arizona Press.

Atanes, Alessandro, and Cristina de Lamonica. 1998. A base fica forte: o estado investe em infra-estrutura para desenvolver-se nos próximas anos. *Anual Balanço* 2(2): 8–10.

Bari-Kolata, Gina. 1974. "!Kung Hunter-Gatherers: Feminism, Diet, and Birth Control." *Science* 185:932–934.

Barth, Fredrik. 1969. "Introduction." In Fredrik Barth, ed., *Ethnic Groups and Boundaries*, pp. 9–38. Boston: Little and Brown Publishing Co. Reissued, Prospect Heights, IL: Waveland Press, 1998.

Beckerman, Stephen. 1996. "Partible Paternity Among the Bari." Presented at the 20th South American Indian Conference, Bennington College, Bennington, Vermont.

Berkes, F. 1985. "Fishermen and 'The Tragedy of the Commons.'" *Environmental Conservation* 12(3):): 199–209.

Bloom, Pamela. 1997. *Brazil Up Close.* Edison, NJ: Hunter Publishing Co.

Bodley, John. 1994. *Cultural Anthropology: Tribes, States, and the Global System.* Mountain View, CA: Mayfield Publishing Co.

————. 1996. *Anthropology and Contemporary Human Problems*. 3rd ed. Mountain View, CA: Mayfield Pubishing Co.

————. 1999. *Victims of Progress*. 4th ed. Mountain View, CA: Mayfield Publishing Co.

Bowen, Elenore. 1954. *Return to Laughter*. New York: Harper and Brothers.

Brown, Michael. 1993. "Facing the State, Facing the World: Amazonia's Native Leaders and the New Politics of Identity." *L'Homme* 33(2–4): 307–326.

Caldwell, J. C., and P. Caldwell. 1983. "The Demographic Evidence for the Incidence and Cause of Abnormally Low Fertility in Tropical Africa." *World Health Statistics Quarterly* 36:2–34.

Campbell, K. L., and J. W. Wood. 1988. "Fertility in Traditional Societies." In P. Diggory, M. Potts, and S. Teper, eds., *Natural Human Fertility: Social and Biological Determinants*, pp. 39–69. London: MacMillan.

Campos, Antonio Pires de. 1862. "Breve Notícias que dá o capitão Antonio Pires de Campos do gentio bárbaro que há na derrota da viagem das minas do Cuyabá o seu reconcavo etc. . . ." *R. Trimensal do Instituto Histórico, Geográfico, e Etnográfico do Brasil*, Rio de Janeiro 25:437–449.

Carneiro, Robert. 1979. Personal communication.

————. 1995. "History of Ecological Interpretations of Amazonia." In Leslie Sponsel, ed., *Indigenous Peoples and the Future of Amazonia: An Ecological Anthropology of an Endangered World*, pp. 45–70. Tucson: University of Arizona Press.

Chagnon, Napoleon. 1968. *Yanomamö: The Fierce People*. New York: Holt, Rinehart, and Winston.

————. 1977. *Yanomamö: The Fierce People*. 2nd ed. New York: Holt, Rinehart, and Winston.

————. 1983. *Yanomamö: The Fierce People*. 3rd ed. New York: Holt, Rinehart, and Winston.

————. 1992. *Yanomamö: The Fierce People*. 4th ed. New York: Holt, Rinehart, and Winston.

Chagnon, Napoleon, and Thomas Melancon. 1983. "Epidemics in a Tribal Population." In Jason Clay, ed., *The Impact of Contact: Two Yanomamö Case Studies*, pp. 55–78. Cambridge, MA: Cultural Survival and Bennington College.

Chibnik, Michael. 1991. "Quasi-ethnic Groups in Amazonia." *Ethnology* 30:167–182.

Cleveland, David. 1998. "Balancing on a Planet: Toward an Agricultural Anthropology for the Twenty-first Century." *Human Ecology* 26(2): 323–340.

Cleveland, David, F. J. Bowannie, D. Eriacho, A. Laahty, and E. P. Perramond. 1995. "Zuni Farming and United States Government Policy: The Politics of Cultural and Biological Diversity." *Agriculture and Human Values* 12:2–18.

Coale, Ansley. 1986. "The Decline of Fertility in Europe Since the Eighteenth Century as a Chapter in Demographic History." In A. Coale and S. Cotts Watkins, eds., *The Decline of Fertility in Europe*, pp. 1–30. Princeton, NJ: Princeton University Press.

Conklin, Beth. 1993. "Hunting the Ancestors: Death and Alliance in Warí Cannibalism." *The Latin American Anthropology Review* 5(2): 65–70.

Conklin, Beth, and Laura Graham. 1995. "The Shifting Middle Ground: Amazonian Indians and Eco-Politics." *American Anthropologist* 97(4): 695–710.

Crocker, William, and Jean Crocker. 1994. *The Canela: Bonding Through Kinship, Ritual, and Sex*. Orlando, FL: Harcourt, Brace College Publishers.

Cuiabá Gazete. 1999. Crise prejudica aguda aos índios. *Cuiabá Gazete*, 6 de janeiro, 1999:1C.

Cultural Survival. 1981. "In the Path of Polonoroeste: Endangered Peoples of Western Brazil." *Occasional Papers #6*. Peterborough, NH: Transcript Printing Company.

Dalton, George. 1972. "Peasants in Anthropology and History." *Current Anthropology* 13:385–416.

Da Matta, Roberto. 1976. "Quanto custa ser índio no Brasil?: Considerações sobre o problema de identidade e étnica. " *Dados* (Publ. semestral do Instituto Universitário de Pesquisas do Rio de Janeiro) 13:33–54.

Descola, Philippe. 1993. (Trans. 1996.) *The Spears of Twilight: Life and Death in the Amazon Jungle*. New York: New York Press.

DeVita, Phillip, ed. 1992. *The Naked Anthropologist: Tales from Around the World*. Belmont, CA: Wadsworth.

Dickeman, Mildred. 1975. "Demographic Consequences of Infanticide in Man." In R. E. Johnston, P. W. Frank, and C. D. Michener, eds., *Annual Review of Ecology and Systematics*, Vol. 6, pp. 107–137. Palo Alto, CA: Annual Reviews Inc.

Dietler, Michael. 1994. "'Our Ancestors the Gauls:' Archaeology, Ethnic Nationalism, and the Manipulation of Celtic Identity in Modern Europe." *American Anthropologist* 96(3): 584–605.

Diggory, Peter, Malcom Potts, and Sue Teper, eds. 1988. *Natural Human Fertility: Social and Biological Determinants*. London: MacMillan.

Eckstrom, Christine. 1996. "A Wilderness of Water: Pantanal." *Audubon* 98(2): 54–67.

Ehrenreich, Jeffrey. 1997. "Forward." In Ann Miles and Hans Buechler, eds., *Women and Economic Change: Andean Perspectives*, pp. vii–viii. Society for Latin American Publication Series 14.

Ehrenreich, Paul. 1929. "A segunda expedição alemã ao Rio Xingú." *Revista do Museu Paulista* XII, São Paulo:247–275.

Embratur. 1997. (Internet address) www.embratur.gov.br.

Ferguson, R. Brian. 1992. "A Savage Encounter: Western Contact and the Yanomami Tribal Zone." In R. B. Ferguson and N. Whitehead, eds., *War in the Tribal Zone*, pp. 199–227. Santa Fe, NM: School of American Research.

Ferguson, R. B., and N. L. Whitehead, eds. 1992. *War in the Tribal Zone: Expanding States and Indigenous Warfare*. Santa Fe, NM: School of American Research Press.

Fisher, William. n.d. *The Frontier Within*. Manuscript. Williamsburg, VA: College of William and Mary.

Flanagan, James. 1989. "Hierarchy in Simple 'Egalitarian' Societies." *Annual Review of Anthropology* 18:245–266.

Flowers, Nancy. 1994. "Demographic Crisis and Recovery: A Case Study of the Xavante of Pimentel Barbosa." In K. Adams and D. Price, eds., *South American Indians Studies*, Special Issue, *The Demography of Small-Scale Societies: Case Studies from Low South America:*18–36.

Freidl, Ernestine. 1975. *Women and Men: An Anthropologist's View*. New York: Holt, Rinehart, Winston.

Freire, Paulo. 1970. *Pedagogy of the Oppressed*. New York: Seabing.

Friedman, Jonathan. 1992. "The Past in the Future: History and the Politics of Identity." *American Anthropologist* 94(4): 837–859.

Frisch, R. 1984. "Body Fat, Puberty, and Fertility." *Science* 199:22–30.

FUNAI. 1977. "Ante projeto de subsistência para o P.I. Bakairí." 5a D.R. Ministério do Interior, FUNAI:1–11.

———. 1980. *Projeto de Desenvolvimento Agropecuário de P.I. Bakairí*. Ministério do Interior. Brasilia, Brazil: FUNAI.

———. 1988. "Políticas e Programas de Ação da FUNAI." Brasilia, Ministério do Interior: Coronario Editora, Ltda.

Garrison, John. 1993. "UNCED and the Greening of Brazilian NGOs." *Grassroots Development* 17(1): 2–11.

Geertz, Clifford.1973. *The Intrepretation of Cultures*. New York: Basic Books, Inc.

Golde, Peggy, ed.1986. *Women in the Field: Anthropological Experiences*. 2nd ed. Los Angeles: University of California Press.

Graham, Laura. 1995. *Performing Dreams: Discourses of Immortality Among the Xavante of Central Brazil*. Austin: University of Texas Press.

Greene, Margaret, and William Crocker. 1994. "Some Demographic Aspects of the Canela Indians of Brazil." In K. Adams and D. Price, eds., *South American Indians Studies*, Special Issue, *The Demography of Small-Scale Societies: Case Studies from Lowland South America*: 47–62.

Gregor, Thomas. 1977. *Mehinaku: The Drama of Daily Life in a Brazilian Indian Village*. Chicago: University of Chicago Press.

———. 1979. "Secrets, Exclusion, and the Dramatization of Men's Roles." In M. Margolis and W. Carter, eds., *Brazil: Anthropological Perspectives*, pp. 250–269. New York: Columbia University Press.

———. 1985. *Anxious Pleasures: The Sexual Lives of an Amazonian People*. Chicago: University of Chicago Press.

———. 1988. "Infants are Not Precious to Us: The Psychological Impact of Infanticide Among the Mehinaku Indians." The 1988 Stirling Prize Paper Recipient, Presented at the Annual Meeeting of the American Anthropological Association, Phoenix Arizona.

Gross, D. 1979. Personal communication.

Gross, D., G. Eiten, N. Flowers, F. Leoi, M. Lattman Ritter, and D. Werner. 1979. "Ecology and Acculturation Among Native Peoples of Central Brazil." *Science* 206:1043–1050.

Gudeman, Stephen. 1978. *The Demise of the Rural Economy: From Subsistence to Capitalism in a Latin American Village*. London: Routledge Kegan Paul.

Hardin, G. 1968. "The Tragedy of the Commons." *Science* 162:1243–1248.

Harner, Michael. 1972. *The Jívaro: People of the Sacred Waterfalls*. Reissued UC Press.

Harpending, H. 1994. "Infertility and Forager Demography." *American Journal of Physical Anthropology* 93:385–390.

Headland, Thomas. 1997. "Revisionism in Ecology." *Current Anthropology* 38(4): 605–630.

Helm, C. M. Vieira, and J. M. M. Carneiro. 1978. *O projeto Kaingang*. Estudos Brasileiros. Curitiba, Paraná: Univer. Federal do Paraná, Setor de Ciências Humanas.

Hendricks, Janet. 1991. "Symbolic Counter-hegemony among the Ecuadorian Shuar." In Greg Urban and Joel Sherzer, eds., *Nation-States and Indians in Latin America*, pp. 53–71. Austin: University of Texas Press.

Herdt, Gerald. 1981. *Guardians of the Flutes: Idioms of Masculinity*. New York: Columbia University Press.

Hill, Jonathan. 1984. "Social Equality and Ritual Hierarchy: The Arawakan Wakuenai of Venezuela. *American Ethnologist* 11(3): 528–544.

———. 1988. *Rethinking History and Myth: Indigenous South American Perspectives on the Past*. Chicago: University of Illinois Press.

———. 1993. *Keepers of the Sacred Chant: The Poetics of Ritual Power in Amazonian Society*. Tucson: University of Arizona Press.

Hill, Kim, and A. Magdalena Hurtado. 1996. *Ache Life History: The Ecology and Demography of a Foraging People*. Hawthorne, NY: Aldine de Gruyter.

Hopkins, Nicholas. 1987. "Mechanized Irrigation in Upper Egypt: The Role of Technology and the State of Agriculture." In B. Turner II and Stephen Brush, eds., *Comparative Farming Systems*, pp. 223–247. New York: Guilford Press.

Hopwood, Nancy, Robert Kelch, Paula Hale, Tarina Mendes, Carol Foster, and Inese Beitins. 1990. "The Onset of Human Puberty: Biological and Environmental Factors." In John Bancroft and June Reinisch, eds., *Adolescence and Puberty*, pp. 29–49. Oxford: Oxford University Press.

Howell, Nancy. 1979. *Demography of the Dobe !Kung*. New York: Academic Press.

Hull, Cindy. 1992. "Lessons from the Field: Gullibility and the Hazards of Money Lending." In Phil DeVita, ed., *The Naked Anthropologist: Tales from Around the World*, pp. 130–136. Belmont, CA: Wadsworth.

ISER (Instituto de Estudos da Religião). 1992. *As ONG nos Anos 90: A Visão de Suas Liberanças*. Rio de Janeiro, Brazil: ISER.

Jackson, Jean. 1991. "Being and Becoming an Indian in the Vaupés." In Greg Urban and Joel Sherzer, eds., *Nation-States and Indians in Latin America*, pp. 131–155. Austin: University of Texas Press.

———. 1994. "Becoming Indians: The Politics of Tukanoan Ethnicity." In Anna Roosevelt, ed., *Amazonian Indians from Prehistory to the Present*, pp. 383–406. Tucson: University of Arizona Press.

Johnson, A. 1975. "Time Allocation in a Machiguenga Community." *Ethnology* 14(3): 301–310.

Johnson, Patricia. 1990. "Changing Household Composition, Labor Patterns, and Fertility in a Highland New Guinea Population." *Human Ecology* 18(4): 403–416.

Kearney, Michael. 1996. *Reconceptualizing the Peasantry: Anthropology in Global Perspective*. Boulder, CO: Westview Press.

Kottak, Conrad. 1999. *Mirror for Humanity: A Concise Introduction to Cultural Anthropology*. 2nd ed. Boston: McGraw-Hill College Publishers.

Kracke, Waud. 1978. *Force and Persuasion: Leadership in an Amazonian Society*. Chicago: University of Chicago Press.

———. 1987. "Encounter with Other Cultures." *Ethos* 15(1): 58–81

Krause, Fritz. 1960. "Máscaras grandes do Alto-Xingú." *Revista do Museu Paulista*, n.s. XII, São Paulo:87–124.

Kurin, Richard. 1980. "Doctor, Lawyer, Indian Chief." *Natural History* 89(11): 6–24.

Levi-Strauss, Claude. 1948. "The Tribes of the Upper Xingú River." In Julian Steward, ed., *Handbook of South American Indians VIII: The Tropical Forest Tribes*, pp. 321–348. New York: Cooper Square Publishers.

Llewelyn-Davies, Melissa. 1996. "Women, Warriors, and Patriarchs." In R. Jon McGee and R. Warms, eds., *Anthropological Theory: An Introductory History*, pp. 414–429. Mountain View, CA: Mayfield Publishing.

Manganaro, Marc, ed. 1990. *Modernist Anthropology: From Fieldwork to Text*. Princeton, NJ: Princeton University Press.

McCay, B. 1984. "Capturing the Commons: A Foray into the Field." Paper Presented at the Annual Meetings of the Society for Applied Anthropology, Toronto.

McGee, R. Jon, and R. Warms, eds. 2000. *Anthropological Theory: An Introductory History*. 2nd ed. Mountain View, CA: Mayfield Publishing Co.

———. 2000. "Post-Modernism and Its Critics." In R. Jon McGee and R. L. Warms, eds., *Anthropological Theory: An Introductory History*, 2nd ed., pp. 517–520. Mountain View, CA: Mayfield Publishing Co.

McKee, Lauris. 1997. "Women's Work in Rural Ecuador: Multiple Resource Strategies and the Gendered Division of Labor." In A. Miles and H. Buechler, eds., *Women and Economic Change: Andean Perspective*, pp. 13–30. Society for Latin American Publication Series, Vol. 14. Washington, DC: Soc. For Latin American Studies/American Anthropological Association.

McNeilly, A. S. 1993. "Breastfeeding and Fertility." In R. H. Gray, H. Levidon, and A. Spira, eds., *Biomedical and Demographic Determinants of Reproduction*, pp. 391–412. Oxford, UK: Clarendon Press.

Mead, Margaret. 1972. *Blackberry Winter: My Earlier Years*. New York: Pocket Books.

Mead, Margaret, and Gregory Bateson.1962. *Balinese Character: A Photographic Analysis*. New York: New York Academy of Sciences.

Meggers, Betty. 1971. *Amazonia: Man, Culture in a Counterfeit Society*. Chicago: Aldine.

Melancon, T. 1982. *Marriage and Reproduction Among the Yanomamö Indians of Venezuela*. Doctoral Dissertation. Department of Anthropology, Pennsylvania State University.

Menezes, C. 1982. "Os Xavantes e o Movimento de Fronteira No Leste Mato Grossense." *Revista de Antropologia*. São Paulo: Universidade de São Paulo, Dep. de Ciéncias Sociais.

Minge-Klevana, Wanda. 1980. "Does Labor Time Increase with Industrialization? A Survey of Time Allocation Studies." *Current Anthropology* 21(3): 279–298.

Morgen, Sandra. 1989. "Gender and Anthropology: Introductory Essay." In S. Morgen, ed., *Gender and Anthropology—Critical Reviews for Research and Teaching*, pp. 1–20. Washington, DC: American Anthropological Association.

Murphy, Robert. 1978. "Comments on Berreman." *Current Anthropology* 19:239–40.

Murphy, Yolanda, and Robert Murphy. 1974. *Women of the Forest.* New York: Columbia University Press.

Nanda, Serena. 1994. *Cultural Anthropology.* 5th ed. Belmont, CA: Wadsworth Publishing Co.

Neel, J. V., and K. M. Weiss. 1975. "The Genetic Structure of a Tribal Population, The Yanomamö Indians." *Biomedical Studies XII, American Journal of Physical Anthropology* 42:25–51.

Netting, R. McC. 1974. "Agrarian Ecology." *Annual Review of Anthropology* 3:21–56.

————. 1993. *Smallholders, Householders: Farm Families and the Ecology of Intensive, Sustainable Agriculture.* Stanford, CA: Stanford University Press.

Nimuendajú, Curt. 1963. "Tribes of the Lower and Middle Xingú River." In Julian Steward, ed., *Handbook of South American Indians III: the Tropical Forest Tribes,* rev. ed., pp. 213–243. New York: Cooper Square Publishers.

Oliveira, J. 1979. *O projeto Tukuna: uma experiençia de ação indigenista.* Rio de Janeiro: Universidade de Brasil.

Petrullo, Vincent. 1932. "Primitive Peoples of Matto Grosso, Brazil." *The Museum Journal,* Philadelphia, University Museum, 23(2): 83–173.

Picchi, Debra. 1982. *Energetics Modeling in Development Evaluation: The Case of the Bakairí Indians of Central Brazil.* Ann Arbor, MI: University Microfilms.

————. 1991. "The Impact of an Industrial Agricultural Project on the Bakairí Indians of Central Brazil." *Human Organization* 50(1): 26–38.

————. 1995. "Village Division in Lowland South America: The Case of the Bakairí Indians of Central Brazil." *Human Ecology* 23(4): 477–498.

Pina, Edir Barros de. 1977. *Kura Bakairí/Kura Karaíwa: dois mundos em confronto.* Master's Thesis. Brasilia, Brazil: University of Brasilia Anthropology Department.

Por, F. D. 1995. *The Pantanal of Mato Grosso (Brazil): World's Largest Wetlands.* Monographiae Biologicae, 73. Dordrecht, Netherlands: Kluwer Academic Publishing Co.

Powdermaker, Hortense. 1966. *Stranger and Friend: The Way of an Anthropologist.* New York: W. W. Norton and Company.

Poyer, Lin. 1993. "Egalitarianism in the Face of Hierarchy." *Journal of Anthropological Research* 49:111–133.

Price, David. 1981 "Nambiquara Leadership." *American Ethnologist* 8:686–708.

Ramos, Alcida. 1988. "Indian Voices: Contact Experienced and Expressed." In Jonathan Hill, ed., *Rethinking History and Myth: Indigenous South American Perspectives on the Past,* pp. 214–234. Urbana and Chicago: University of Illinois Press.

Reed, Richard. 1995. *Prophets of Agroforestry: Guaraní Communities and Commercial Gathering.* Austin: University of Texas Press.

Romaniuk, A. 1981. "Increase in Natural Fertility during the Early Stages of Modernization: Canadian Indian Case Study." *Demography* 18:157–172.

Roosevelt, Anna, ed. 1994. *Amazonian Indians: From Prehistory to the Present.* Tucson: University of Arizona Press.

Rosaldo, Michelle. 1980. *Knowledge and Passion: Notions of Self and Social Life*. Stanford, CA: Stanford University Press.

Santos, Ricardo Ventura, Nancy Flowers, Carlos Everaldo Coimbra, and Silvia Angela Gugelmin. 1997. "Tapirs, Tractors, and Tapes: The Changing Economy and Ecology of the Xavante Indians of Central Brazil." *Human Ecology* 25(4): 545–566.

Scheper-Hughes, Nancy. 1992. *Death Without Weeping: The Violence of Everyday Life in Brazil*. Los Angeles: University of California Press.

Schmidt, Max. 1947. "Os Bakairí." *Revista do Museu Paulista*, n.s. 1:11–58.

Schmink, Marianne. 1986. "The Rationality of Tropical Forest Destruction." Paper presented at Conference on the Management of the Forests of Tropical America, San Juan, Puerto Rico.

Scrimshaw, Susan. 1978. "Infant Mortality and Behavior in the Regulation of Family Size." *Population and Development Review* 4(3): 383–403.

———. 1983. "Infanticide as Deliberate Fertility Regulation." In R. Bulato and R. Lee, eds., *Determinants of Fertility in Developing Nations: Supply and Demand of Children*, pp. 245–266. New York: Academic Press.

Seeger, Anthony. 1981. *Nature and Society in Central Brazil: The Suya Indians of Mato Grosso*. Cambridge, MA: Harvard University Press.

Shenon, Philip. 1994. "Last Rain Forest." *New York Times*, June 5.

Silverblatt, Irene. 1987. *Moon, Sun, and Witches: Gender Ideologies and Class in Inca and Colonial Peru*. Princeton, NJ: Princeton University Press.

———. 1988. "Women in States." In *Annual Reviews*, pp. 427–460. Palo Alto, CA: Annual Reviews, Inc.

Smith, Richard. 1988. "Natural Fertility in Pre-industrial Europe." In P. Diggory, M. Potts, and S. Teper, eds., *Natural Human Fertility*, pp. 70–88. London: MacMillan.

Smith, S., and Philip Young. 1998. *Cultural Anthropology: Understanding a World in Transition*. Boston: Allyn and Bacon.

Souza, Carlos Frederic Mares de. 1994. "On Brazil and Its Indians." In Donna Lee Van Cott, ed., *Indigenous Peoples and Democracy in Latin America*, pp. 213–233. NY: St. Martins Press.

Spindler, George, ed. 1970. *Being an Anthropologist: Fieldwork in Eleven Cultures*. New York: Holt, Rinehart, Winston.

Sponsel, L., ed. 1995. *Indigenous Peoples and the Future of Amazonia: An Ecological Anthropology of an Endangered World*. Tucson: University of Arizona Press.

Stanley, Denise. 1990. *Environmental Technology Adoption and Sustainability: An Analysis of Inter-American Foundation Projects*. Project Review. University of Wisconsin-Madison.

Stearman, Allyn MacLean. 1997. "Reply." *Current Anthropology* 38(4): 622–623.

Stonich, Susan. 1995. "The Environmental Quality and Social Justice Implications of Shrimp Mariculture Development in Honduras." *Human Ecology* 23(2): 143–168.

Tax, Sol. 1953. *Penny Capitalism: A Guatemalan Indian Economy*. Washington, DC: Smithsonian Institution.

Torres, Manoel Rodrigues. 1738. "Intendente e provendor do fazenda real de Cuiabá, a sua majestade D. João V. Cuiabá, 30/06/1738." *Arquivo Históri-*

co Ultramarino de Lisboa. Papeis Avulsos de Mato Grosso, Caixa 2, Documentos 83–84.

Turnbull, Colin. 1961. *The Forest People.* New York: Simon and Schuster.

———. 1972. *The Mountain People.* New York: Simon and Schuster.

Tylor, Edward. 1920 (orig. 1873). *Primitive Cultures.* New York: G. P. Putnam's Sons.

Urban, Greg, and Joel Sherzer, eds. 1991. "Introduction." In Greg Urban and Joel Sherzer, eds., *Nation-States and Indians in Latin America,* pp. 1–18. Austin: University of Texas Press.

Vayda, Andrew, and Bradley Walters. 1999. "Against Political Ecology." *Human Ecology* 27(1): 167–179.

Vieira Filho, J. 1981. "Problemas da aculturação alimenta dos Xavantes e Bororo." *Revista de Antropologia* 24:34–40.

Von den Steinen, Karl. 1940. *Entre os aborígenese do Brasil central.* São Paulo: Departamento de Cultura.

Wagley, Charles. 1977. *Welcome of Tears: The Tapirape Indians of Central Brazil.* New York: Oxford University.

Wagner, Roy. 1975. *The Invention of Culture.* Englewood Cliffs, NJ: Prentice Hall.

Weismantel, Mary. 1997. "Time, Work-Discipline, and Beans: Indigenous Self-Determination in the Northern Andes." In Ann Miles and Hans Buechler, eds., *Women and Economic Change: Andean Perspectives,* pp. 31–54. Society for Latin American Publication Series 14.

Werner, Dennis. 1982. "Leadership Inheritance and Acculturation Among the Mekranotí of Central Brazil." *Human Organization* 41:342–345.

———. 1990. *Amazon Journey: An Anthropologist's Year Among Brazil's Mekranoti Indians.* Englewood Cliffs, NJ: Prentice Hall.

Wheatley, James. 1966. "Revivescência de uma dança Bakairí." *Revista de Antropologia* XIV, São Paulo:73–80.

White, Richard. 1991. *The Middle Ground: Indians, Empires, and Republics in the Great Lakes Region, 1650–1815.* New York: Cambridge University Press.

Whitehead, Neil. 1994. "The Ancient Amerindian Polities of the Amazon, the Orinoco, and the Atlantic Coast: A Preliminary Analysis of Their Passage from Antiquity to Extinction." In Anna Roosevelt, ed., *Amazonian Indians from Prehistory to the Present,* pp. 33–54. Tucson: University of Arizona Press.

Whiting, J., R. Kluckhohn, and A. Anthony. 1958. "The Function of Male Initiation Ceremonies at Puberty." In E. MacCoby, ed., *Readings in Social Psychology,* pp. 359–370. New York: Holt.

Wilk, R. R. 1996. "Sustainable Development: Practical, Ethical, and Social Issues in Technology Transfer." In K. Ishizuka and S. Hasajima, eds., *Traditional Technology for Environmental Conservation and Sustainable Development in the Asian-Pacific Region,* pp. 206–218. Tsukaba, Japan: University of Tsukaba.

Winther, Paul. 1992. "The 'Killing' of Weni Bai." In Phil DeVita, ed., *The Naked Anthropologist: Tales from Around the World,* pp. 100–106. Belmont, CA: Wadsworth.

Wolf, Eric. 1966. *Peasants.* Englewood Cliffs, NJ: Prentice-Hall.

————. 1969. *Peasant Wars of the Twentieth Century.* New York: Harper and Row.

Wood, J., and P. Smouse. 1982. "A Method of Analyzing Density-Dependent Vital Rates With an Application to the Gainj of Papua New Guinea." *American Journal of Physical Anthropology* 58:403–411.

INDEX

Abortion, 23, 62, 63–64
Ache Indians, 59, 62–63, 70–71
Adolescence, 100–101
Age-specific fertility, 60–62
Agriculture, 82. *See also* Gardening,
   Horticulture
   Bakairí manipulation of, 45
   FUNAI project, 20, 41, 73–74,
     86–89
Anchoring effects, 139
Animism, 134
Anthropological demography, 47. *See*
   also Demography
Anthropomorphize, 65
Aturua, 2, 43
   cattle, 93, 94, 145
   rice cultivation, 89

Bandeirante paulista, 30
Bateson, Gregory, 9
Barth, Fredrik, 174
Beckerman, Stephen, 60
Bicycles, 79
Birth rate, 60, 69
Bodley, John, 109, 173

Breast-feeding. *See* Nursing
Bride service, 110
Brown, Michael, 149

Cadueti, 117, 181. *See also* Men's house
Canoes, 81
Carib language, 172
Cash, 38, 95–97
Cattle, 93–94
   diet, 90
   time allocation, 103
Canela Indians, 55, 59, 107
Cerrado, 41, 76–78
Chagnon, Napoleon, 5, 21–22, 26
Child-rearing practices, 99–100
   adoption, 60
   deaths, 61, 65
   labor, 84
   nursing, 63
   sleeping with parents, 118
CIMI (Conselho Indigenista Mission-
   ario), 163
Climate, 1, 5
Colonial period, 30–32. *See also*
   History

Conklin, Beth, 27, 141–142
Conscientização, 180
Crocker, William, 55, 107
Crops, 73
    area cultivated, 85, 89
    harvests, 85, 88–89
    planting, 83
Cross cousins, 109, 112
Cuiabá, 30
    flights from, 1, 157–158
    FUNAI offices, 142, 158
    history, 30–31
    jump-off town, 11
    Indian jobs, 179
Cultural anthropology, 7
Culture, 7

Daily life, 99–102
Death, 65–67
Death rate, 65, 69
Demography, 57
Dentistry, 67
Diamantina, 32
Diet, 57, 89–91. *See also* Food, Cattle
Dietler, Michael, 178
Disease, 65–67
Division of labor, 84
    by age, 100, 132–133
    by sex, 84, 100, 118, 130, 179. *See
        also* Gender roles
Divorce, 110
Double marriage, 148

Ear piercing, 115–117, 173
Ecology, 76, 97–98
    development, 76
    leadership, 138
    problems, 8, 180
    technology, 139
Ecotourism, 160, 162, 183
Economic development, 39–41, 73–74
Ehrenreich, Paul, 124
Electricity, 54, 97, 181
Ethnic categories, 175
Ethnic minority, 174, 178
    Indian, 175, 178
    process of emergence, 175,
        178–179
Ethnocentrism, 13

Europeans
    arrival in New World, 28, 30
    colonial period, 30–32
Exoticization, 183
Eyeglasses, 67, 158

Families
    extended, 108
    nuclear, 108–109
Fauna, 79,80, 81–82, 94
Ferguson, R. Brian, 139, 143,
    145–146
Fertility, 48, 60–63
    data collection methods, 49
Fertility-inhibiting practices, 48, 71
Fieldwork, 2, 24
    beginning, 5
    leaving the field, 14
    predilections, 9
    preparing for, 6, 9–10
    role negotiations, 15–18
    routines, 13
Fisher, William, 174
Fishing, 89, 91–92
    diet, 90
    time allocation, 103
Folklorization, 182–183
Food. *See also* Crops, Diet
    cattle as, 92
    crop types, 73
    food groups, 90
    harvest estimates, 85
    sharing, 95
    taboos, 61
    turtle eggs, 92
Freidl, Ernestine, 106
Freire, Paulo, 180
Friedman, Jonathan, 178
FUNAI (Fundaçao Nacional do Índio)
    agriculture project, 41, 73, 74
    budget problems, 165
    change, 162
    facilities, 13, 50
    formation, 38
    headmen, 147
    health programs, 66, 67, 165
    jobs for Indians, 96, 144
    middle-ground concept, 141–143
    research permits, 10

research library, 24, 28
reservation administration, 2, 41, 44
FUNRURAL, 96

Gallery forest, 78
    amount of, 76
    gardening, 79
    rice cultivation, 88
    traditional economy, 84
Gardening, 73, 83. *See also* Horticulture, Crops
    Bakairí history and, 34, 35
    diet, 90
    distance from village, 79–80
    gallery forest, cerrado, and, 78–79
    harvests, 85
    shortage of land, 8
    size, 85
    time allocation, 103
    tropical rainforest, 29
Geertz, Clifford, 20
Gender roles, 16–17, 115–119. *See also* Division of labor by sex, Masks gender
    labor, 130, 179
    space usage, 104–106
Goffman, Erving, 10
Graham, Laura, 9, 10, 27, 141–14
Grassroots Support Organization (GSO), 163–16
Gregor, Thomas, 55, 64, 104–105, 108–110
Gross, Daniel, 90

Hardin, Garrett, 93
Headman, 137
    demographic effects, 138
    economics, 144
    kinship, 146–148
    techniques, 149–154
    technology, 139–141
Herdt, Gerald, 20–21, 22
Hidrovia, 160
Hill, Jonathan, 123, 153, 176
Hill, Kim, 59, 62–63, 70
History
    colonial, 30–32
    early 20th century, 36–38

ethnicity, 174–175
    masks, 124
    19th century, 32–35
    Xinguano era, 34–36, 176–178
Horticulture, 82–85. *See also* Gardening
Household composition, 53
Housing, 51–53
Hunting, 91, 94–95
    time allocation, 103
Hurtado, A. Magdalena, 59, 62–63, 70

Infanticide, 14, 23, 63–64
    indirect, 64
Iroquois kinship terminology, 111

Jackson, Jean, 174, 182
Johnson, Allen, 90

Kaiahoualo, 42, 43, 146
Karaiwa, 15, 176
Kayapó Indians, 142, 143, 149. *See also* Xikrin Kayapó Indians
Kearney, Michael, 172, 178
Kin relations, 111–113
    between cousins, 112
    between headman, 146, 148
Kinship terminology, 113
Kracke, Waud, 153
Kura-Bakairí Association, 162–163, 178
Kwamba, 122, 126, 133

Landsat Images, 76, 81
Leadership techniques, 149–154
    authoritarian, 153
    consensual, 153
Life-time fertility, 60
Logistics, 11

Marriage, 106–108, 119
    ceremony, 109
    double marriage, 148
    fertility, 57–59
    non-Indian, 107
    residence after, 110
Masks
    age, 132–133
    economy, 128–130

future, 136, 182
gender, 125, 130–131
history, 124
names, 124–125
ownership, 125
rituals, 123, 129
spirits, 122, 126
taboos, 125, 127
values, 135
Mato Grosso
economy, 158–160
economic development, 39–40,
181
history, 30–32, 36
soybean production, 159
tourism, 160
Matrilocal residence, 110
McCay, Bonnie, 94
Mead, Margaret, 9, 15
Meaningful account, 21
Mehinaku Indians, 55, 118
Men's house, 117–118, 167. *See also*
Cadueti
Menstruation, 56–57
Ear piercing and, 115
Middle-ground concept, 141–142
Missionaries, 16, 146
Monogamy, 107
Murphy, Robert, 119, 137

Nafuquá Indians, 35, 177
Navajo Indians, 162, 165
Netting, Robert, 74
Nimuendajú, Curt, 34
Nursing, 14, 48, 63, 71

Oration, 153
Orthography, 1113
The Other, 18
Outposts, villages, 42–43
Outposts, Western, 146

Paikum, 43, 146
Paixola, 42, 43
dispute over, 44, 45, 153, 180
akuera, 1–2, 43, 49–50
cattle, 93, 145
gardens, 139
mask dances, 121

Paleo-Indians, 29
Pantanal, 160, 183
Parallel cousins, 109, 112
Participant-observation, 16
Peasants, 167–168
Bakairí as, 170–171
small farmers compared to,
171–172
Pina, Edir Barros de, 175
Political ecology, 8–9, 45, 97–98
Polygyny, 107
Polonoroeste project, 39
Population doubling time, 67–70, 71
Posseiros, 42, 150. *See also* Squatters
Postmodernism, 18–19
Powdermaker, Hortense, 5
Predilections, 9
Productive labor, 103. *See also*
Reproductive labor
Profane domain, 133
Price, David, 153

Qualitative methods, 20–21
Quantitative methods, 20–21

Ramos, Alcida, 164, 178
Random sample, 79
Redistribution, 144
Reed, Richard, 103, 104
Reproductive labor, 103. *See also*
Productive labor
Rituals
ear piercing. 115–116
marriage, 109
mask dancing, 133, 182
power of, 123
Rivers, 81
Rondonia, 39
Rosaldo, Michelle, 105

Sacred domain, 133
Sardinha, Idevar José, 39–41
Satellite dish, 54, 181
Scheper-Hughes, Nancy, 22, 65
Schmidt, Max, 36
Secondary fathers, 60
Sex taboos, 60–61, 71
Sexual antagonism, 131
Sexually transmitted diseases, 48

Sexual relations, 55–56
Shamans, 134
Sherzer, Joel, 182
Soil samples, 77
Sororate, 107
Sowapo, 43, 146, 152
SPI (Serviço Proteção Índigeno), 36–38, 50
Spirits, 122, 126, 134–135, 170. *See also* Animism
Sponsel, Leslie, 74–75
Squatters, 150. *See also* posseiros
Sustainable agriculture, 74
Sustainable social forestry, 163

Taboos. *See* Sex taboos, Food taboos, Mask taboos
Technology
cash, 97
change, 139–140, 146, 180
fishing, 91
hunting, 94
hybrid, 75
mechanized, 86–87
traditional, 83
Theory, 7–8
Thick description, 20
Time allocation method, 90, 102–104
Total fertility rate (TFR), 60–63, 71
Tragedy of the commoners, 93

Tragedy of the commons, 93
Tukano Indians, 174
Turnbull, Colin, 19

UNESCO tour, 182
Urban, Greg, 182

Von den Steinen, Karl, 32, 35, 124, 177

Wakuénai Indians, 123
Water, 4, 54–55
Werner, Dennis, 13, 149
White, Richard, 141
Witchcraft, 14
Wolf, Eric, 167

Xavante Indians, 142, 175
agriculture project, 41, 74, 141
Xikrin Kayapó, 173–174

Yakwigado, 126, 132–133
Yanomamö, 26
birth intervals, 63
contact experiences, 26, 143
fertility rate, 71
fieldwork experiences, 5, 22
myths, 134
sex ratio imbalances, 58